Ian Allan's
50 YEARS OF RAILWAYS
1942-1992

Two 'powerhouses' climb away from Gasworks Tunnel on the exit from King's Cross on 1 May 1968 in the year that steam operation ended on BR's standard gauge railways. LNER 'A3' Pacific No 4472 *Flying Scotsman*, a favourite amongst railway enthusiasts, was withdrawn from BR service in 1963 but was purchased for preservation by Alan Pegler in the same year. Although he no longer owns this locomotive, Alan Pegler will always be admired for saving this fine LNER Pacific. The 'A3s' together with the 'A4' Pacifics were the pride of the ECML but the 'Deltics' took over this title from the early 1960s. This occasion commemorated the 40th anniversary of the 'Flying Scotsman's first non-stop run from King's Cross-Edinburgh. The steam train is being rapidly overhauled by Class 55 'Deltic' No D9021 *Argyll & Sutherland Highlander* on the regular 10.10 from King's Cross. *Patrick Russell*

Facing page, bottom:
The 'Night Ferry' service from London to Paris commenced operation on 4 October 1936. After abandonment of the service during the war, Bulleid Light Pacifics took over postwar duties on the 'Night Ferry'. In prewar years the duties had been the province of double-headed 4-4-0s. This dramatic scene shows 'Battle of Britain' Pacific No 21C156 *Croydon* double-headed with a Class L1 4-4-0, No 1757, preparing to depart with this Continental express. The final 'Night Ferry' ran on 31 October 1980. *C. J. Marsden Collection*

Ian Allan's
50 YEARS OF RAILWAYS
1942-1992

Rex Kennedy

BCA

LONDON   NEW YORK   SYDNEY   TORONTO

Contents

This edition published 1992 by BCA by arrangement with IAN ALLAN LTD.

CN 8964

DEDICATION

This book is dedicated to all who have kept Britain's railways running over the years, in all weathers, and to those volunteers who have given up countless hours of their time to preserve Britain's heritage — the preservation societies.

Bibliography

Trains Illustrated (Various issues)
Railway Magazine (Various issues)
Railway World (Various issues)
Modern Railways (Various issues)
The Railway Observer (Various issues)
BR Diary 1948-1957 by S. Creer (Ian Allan)
BR Diary 1958-1967 by J. Glover (Ian Allan)
BR Diary 1968-1977 by C. Heaps (Ian Allan)
BR Diary 1978-1985 by J. Glover (Ian Allan)

Foreword

'A week', said Harold Wilson, 'is a long time in politics'; 50 years in railways does not seem such a vast span. That is until one sits down and thinks about it and casts one's mind back to 1942 when four highly individualistic railway companies were each doing their own respective thing and were managed by their own highly individualistic officers, of whom the General Manager was supreme.

The wartime theme was 'Make way for the guns' and freight and troop trains took priority, the locomotives were all in uniformly drab unlined black and most goods vehicles were unfitted four-wheelers which clanked and banged as their buffers buffed. Peace saw the return of colour to locomotives, Pullman cars and restaurant cars reappeared and the coaches regained their respective green, maroon, chocolate & cream and varnished teak liveries, albeit a bit long in the tooth and capable of not much more than 60mph at a pinch; but then, of course, the clapped-out locomotives couldn't have done much more anyway. Then came Nationalisation, the Locomotive Exchanges and all sorts of excitements as to what the new national railway would look like, run by the British Transport Commission, headed in quick succession by civil servants, soldiers and railwaymen, none of whom seemed to satisfy either the people or the government of the day.

Steam locomotives were standardised in an efficient manner and diesels made their sporadic and very unstandardised advent. Dr Beeching came and much of our railway system went as a result. Steam went too, but too soon, for the new diesels all proved incompatible with each other and a deal of chaos ensued.

There were regions, divisions and areas: then there were sectors, and divisions went, regions went and General Managers disappeared into near oblivion. InterCity and Network SouthEast began to emerge and Chris Green painted every lamp post in the south, red. Locomotives almost disappeared, multiple units took over almost everywhere and HSTs became IC125s. Coaches developed from Mk 1 to Mk 4 and every main line except the Great Western was electrified.

So what we see in 1992 really is, after all, a vastly different scene from what we saw 50 years earlier. In fact, the metamorphosis is such that a returning wanderer would hardly recognise the system — from Waterloo's internationalised grandeur to the tramwayed Bury and Altrincham lines, the change has been enormous and, to my mind, (ignoring the loss of the ethos of steam) the modern railway, with all its warts, is a superb and wonderful industry and a jewel in the nation's crown.

In this book, Rex Kennedy encapsulates the half-century in word and pictures, and for some it will be pure nostalgia — for others, progress.

Ian Allan

Below:
On 1 September 1949 an Ian Allan 'Locospotters Club Special' arrives at Swindon hauled by Great Western 'King' No 6021 *King Richard II*. Can you recognise yourself, or maybe a friend, in this early photograph? *C. C. B Herbert*

Introduction

During the second half of 1942, Ian Allan, who at the time was employed at Waterloo by the Southern Railway, was constantly being asked for information by fellow railway enthusiasts which was not readily available to the general 'trainspotter/enthusiast'. As a keen enthusiast himself, he requested permission from his superiors to publish a list of Southern locomotives to which locomotive enthusiasts could relate their sightings. The Southern was soon followed by the GWR, LMS and LNER. This was the start of trainspotting as we know it today and from those little acorns grew a mighty oak — Ian Allan Ltd. Ian Allan had become the 'Godfather of trainspotting'. This was followed in 1946 by the introduction of the 'Ian Allan Locospotters Club' offering trips to a variety of locations — an organisation of which many a railway enthusiast, including myself, who also purchased the first spotting book in 1942, became a member.

To commemorate these 50 years of railway publishing, I have gathered a collection of some of the finest railway photographs taken over the same period — mid-1942 to mid-1992 — to pay a tribute to the progress of Britain's railways over 50 years. This book includes a great deal of unpublished material together with some photographs which have not been seen in print for some considerable time, but it is not necessarily intended to depict, photographically, particular events of the years covered, but to create the atmosphere in the best way possible, of the railway scene of that particular year, by the use of some fine and interesting photography. However, the text covering each year does relate important events of the year — and some of the less important and often amusing ones, together with some of the tradgedies.

For myself, having been an ardent railway enthusiast for the entire period of this book, the research, picture selection and scenes have brought back countless memories from my youth as a nine-year-old standing on Worcester Shrub Hill station to the present day modern scene of fast electrics and steam preservation.

So much has happened on Britain's railways over the past 50 years from the ex-pre-Grouping company locomotives passing into Nationalisation in 1948, the early prototype diesels, the Beeching closures and the introduction of production diesels, through to mammoth electrification schemes and the progress involving the forthcoming opening of Britain's rail link to Europe — the Channel Tunnel!

We have seen the demise of steam on BR in 1968 through to the return of steam on the BR main line — a sight to please all railway enthusiasts. We have seen steam preservation with a vengeance as derelict locomotives were dragged from scrapyards to emerge eventually, thanks to years of hard work and fund-raising by keen volunteers, to look even better than they did when in service on British Railways. No praise can be high enough for these men (and women) who have restored a major part of Britain's heritage. Closed lines have been privately purchased, creating one of the greatest tourist attractions in Britain — the preserved steam railway.

We have seen diesels come and go — far more short-lived than their steam counterparts, the demise of diesel-hydraulic transmission and various generations of diesel and electric multiple-units.

This book attempts to capture in facts and figures, and in interesting photographs from all over Britain, the history of Britain's railways of the past 50 years. To me it has been a nostalgic trip through time — one I shall not forget. I hope that this book will bring back memories for you also and give you countless hours of pleasure.

Selection of the photographs has not been easy due to having been presented with such a fine selection of often amazing pictures so, if your particular area or your favourite class of locomotive has been sparsely covered, or even omitted, I apologise, but hope that it will not detract from your enjoyment of the book.

Finally, this mammoth task would not have been possible without the help of many railway photographers and close friends whose contributions have been invaluable in compiling this 50-year story. My sincere thanks go firstly to a very special friend, Brian Morrison, who has helped considerably, especially as a modern scene contributor and provider of information, and to Jane Viggers who has sat for endless nights typing over 80,000 words from my hand-written scroll. I am deeply indebted to these two 'special' people. My grateful thanks also go to the extremely helpful Brian Stephenson, and to Les Nixon, Mike Esau, Lewis Coles, Colin Marsden, Peter J. Robinson, Gavin Morrison and John Whiteley and to many more for the use of their photographic material. I have also been extremely fortunate to have had the opportunity to use material from such fine photographers as Dick Riley, Eric Bruton, J. Russell-Smith, J. D. Mills, B. A. Butt,

M. Pope, J. H. Cooper-Smith, Ben Ashworth, Jim Carter, David Fish, Mike Mensing, P. H. Wells, and S. Rickard, and from some sadly no longer with us such as Bishop Eric Treacy, Bill Anderson, The Revd 'Bill' Cawston, Maurice Earley, David Hepburne-Scott, Tom Williams, Derek Cross, Ivo Peters, Roy Vincent, T. G. Hephurn and Ernest Wethersett — a veritable 'hall of fame'. These, and many more, have helped enhance this tribute to 50 years of Britain's railways with their exceptional photography.

Who knows what the next 50 years will bring — fast trains direct to Europe for certain. Perhaps even electrification to South Wales and the West Country and definitely more 'Light Rail' schemes in Britain's crowded cities. Probably the few remaining branch lines will disappear. Or will we turn full circle and return to a larger railway network once again, taking more traffic off the roads — who knows — even full privatisation?

Despite this, let us hope that railway preservation goes on from strength to strength well into the next century ... and beyond.

In the meantime let us look back in time through the pages of this book and view the changing scenes on the railways of Britain from mid-1942 to mid-1992 — 50 glorious years — and look at locomotives at work, built over a period of more than 100 years.

Rex Kennedy

Facing page, top:
The 'Ian Allan Locospotters Club' Special to Exeter of 12 April 1953 was so popular that it had to be run in two parts. The first 'special' was hauled by 'Merchant Navy' Pacific No 35013 *Blue Funnel* and the 'relief', pictured here, by 'West Country' Light Pacific No 34010 *Sidmouth*. A good time was had by one and all. *Brian Morrison*

Facing page, bottom:
On 25 September 1955, an Ian Allan party travelled to the Hopton Incline in Derbyshire, on the Cromford & High Peak line where they were conveyed in goods wagons and hauled by two ex-North London Railway 0-6-0s Nos 58860 and 58850. *W. Dixon*

The Blitz

By mid-1942, we were deep into the war with regular air-raids, sirens and the blackout. The war brought locomotive casualties at York when the station was bombed and the locomotive shed demolished in a 'Baedeker Raid'. LNER 'A4' Pacific No 4469 *Sir Ralph Wedgwood* was damaged beyond repair but its nameplate survived to be transferred to another locomotive of the same class, No 4466, previously named *Herring Gull*. Another locomotive damaged beyond repair during this raid was LNER 'B16' 4-6-0 No 925. Other railway stations in Britain bombed during 1942 included Middlesbrough, Eastbourne, Bath, Canterbury, Exeter and Norwich, the non-industrial cities and towns in retaliation for the bombing of Lubeck in Germany.

In November, the LMS ran its 50,000th special train for the fighting services during World War 2 but the war caused withdrawal of certain services and facilities. All buffet cars between King's Cross and Edinburgh and restaurant cars between Euston and Glasgow, and in the Midlands on the LMS, were withdrawn, although restaurant car services on routes from London to Liverpool, Manchester, Blackpool, Morecambe and Holyhead remained. Restaurant car services were also withdrawn from certain GWR routes and sleeping car services between England and Scotland were halved. The Southern Railway withdrew its Pullman services in June and, in December, the LNER withdrew four East Coast main line trains, leaving only the 'Flying Scotsman'

and its relief train in each direction the only ECML day services between London and Edinburgh.

Black livery appeared on Southern Railway locomotives in 1942 and all GWR locomotives, except 'Castles' and 'Kings', were also painted black (unlined), similar to those on the LNER.

Owing to the demand for shunting engines, 25 ex-Great Central 'Q4' 0-8-0 tender-engines were converted to 0-8-0 side tanks. Their tenders were allocated to the new 'O2' class — No 5058 being the first in service.

The LMS owned the distinction in 1942 of holding the record for the world's longest daily non-stop run worked by either a steam or diesel locomotive, in addition to holding the British record for the number of daily runs of over 100 miles, totalling 53 — with 61 on Fridays — between Euston, Crewe, Carlisle and Glasgow. The longest daily non-stop run was the 9.15pm Euston-Glasgow and the 9.30pm Glasgow-Euston, which ran non-stop from Crewe to Glasgow — a distance of 243¼ miles.

Amongst the many railwaymen who retired in 1942 was Mr A. J. Taylor of King's Cross shed, who at that time was the only man in Great Britain to have ever driven a locomotive for 25 miles continuously at a speed of 100-112½ mph — a remarkable accomplishment. This feat was achieved on the trial trip of the LNER's 'Silver Jubilee' on 27 September 1935 with 'A4' Pacific No 2509 *Silver Link*.

New locomotive building in 1942 saw construction of the GWR '38xx' 2-8-0s and '46xx' pannier tanks at Swindon and the final GWR streamlined diesel railcars were introduced — Nos 37 and 38. These were twin-coach units with buffet and lavatory facilities, similar to Nos 35 and 36, built the previous year. When new, these two-car units worked as three-car sets by the addition of a 70ft corridor coach.

From Brighton Works came the first 'Q1' 0-6-0 Austerities (Nos C1-C3). Nos C17-C20 were completed at Ashford. The first 'USA' 2-8-0 heavy freight locomotive, No 1604, was handed over to the Minister of War Transport at Paddington station in December. The SR-allocated 'USA' 0-6-0T engines were also introduced.

On the LMS, rebuilding commenced on 4-6-0 'Jubilees' Nos 5735 *Comet* and 5736 *Phoenix*, uprating them to 7P classification, and fitting them with a larger boiler and double chimney. New 'V2s' on the LNER also continued to appear.

Below:
The war years brought bomb damage to many of Britain's main-line stations. This view shows St Pancras station, on 26 August 1942, after LMS engineers had put platforms back into operation. Thankfully, the overall roof structure was almost undamaged, except for the glass. This interesting scene shows an ex-MR 0-4-4T, having worked into the station with empty coaching stock, and a 'classic' line-up of London taxis of the period.
Keystone Collection

The dispersal of Southern locomotives around the country was now reaching mammoth proportions with ex-LB&SCR 'Remembrance' class 4-6-0s, Urie 'H15s' and Marsh 'I3s' on the GWR, 'Z' class 0-8-0s in Scotland (at Stranraer) and, in the northeast, Stroudley 'D1s' at Peterborough and ex-LB&SCR 'B4s' in Yorkshire.

A 'sticky' situation occurred on 13 November when a derailment at Appleford level crossing, involving GWR 'Saint' No 2975 *Lord Palmer*, resulted in a goods van, in the train it was hauling, spilling golden syrup, marmalade and corned beef along a roadside — all available without a ration book! This accident also involved a passing express from Paddington.

Above:
Pictures taken by railway enthusiasts were few and far between during World War II owing to the lack of availability of film and the fact that, for security reasons, railway photography was frowned upon. However, we are fortunate to obtain this view of ex-NER 'J24' class 0-6-0 No 1892 piloting Class J27 0-6-0 No 2384 on a wartime petrol train during the early summer of 1942. The train is seen approaching Harrogate from Leeds, and the container wagon behind the second locomotive is being used as a block vehicle. *M. N. Clay/Copyright Rail Archive Stephenson*

Left:
On 6 July 1942, Southern Railway 'H15' class 4-6-0 No 491 passes through Virginia Water, in Surrey, with a mixed freight train. No 491 was the one member of the class which was a Urie locomotive rebuilt with a later 'N15'-type boiler, with a smaller firebox. *Southern Railway*

Crewe Centenary

September 1943 saw the centenary of the Crewe Locomotive Works, originally built for the construction of Grand Junction Railway (later L&NWR) locomotives in 1843. This was the largest locomotive-building establishment in the world. The first engine to be built at Crewe was *Columbine*, followed by many fine locomotives such as the 'Precedents' (1874-1901), the 'Precursors' (1904-1907), the 'Prince of Wales' 4-6-0s (1911-1921), 'Claughtons' (1913-1921), the 'Royal Scots' (1927-1930), the 'Jubilees' (1934-1936) and the Stanier Pacifics which were built from 1933 until Nationalisation in 1948.

The LMS 'Royal Scot' rebuilding programme was carried out in 1943. These were Stanier rebuilds of Fowler locomotives and incorporated superheated taper boilers, double blast-pipes, new cylinders and double chimneys.

Also on the LMS scene, on 20 July, Streamlined Pacific No 6245 was named *City of London* at a ceremony at Euston. The locomotive was painted black, unlined, with lettering and its number in red-shaded yellow.

In May, through locomotive workings over the 401½ miles between Euston and Glasgow recommenced. One outcome was that the wartime version of the up 'Royal Scot' was running non-stop over the 299.1 miles from Carlisle (Citadel) to Euston, no longer calling at Crewe and Rugby.

Also in May, an enemy air attack destroyed arches of the famous Brighton railway viaduct leaving rails and sleepers suspended. Brighton station was also damaged in the same air attack. With Britain's railways constantly under attack, a notice was posted on Liverpool Street station, on an occasion during the year, advising passengers of delays on main line services to Colchester, due to a 'failure' at Ingatestone. In fact, the 'delay' was caused by a locomotive of a Liverpool Street-Harwich train falling into a large 'bomb crater', where the track had been bombed. Sadly both driver and fireman were killed in this incident. However, there was one very unusual wartime incident during the year when an enemy aircraft was 'destroyed' by a locomotive! As a passenger train in the southeast was being attacked from the air, the locomotive's boiler exploded sending fragments of metal into the air with such force that the enemy aircraft was hit and brought down. The train was not even derailed, no passengers were hurt, the fireman was scalded and the driver thrown clear.

During 1943 the first LNER 'A2/2' class Pacifics appeared. These locomotives were original Thompson rebuilds of Gresley 'P2' class 2-8-2s, originally introduced in 1934. Eventually, they totalled six, *Cock o' the North*, *Earl Marischal*, *Lord President*, *Mons Meg*, *Thane of Fife* and *Wolf of Badenoch*. On 1 March, for the first time since war broke out, a non-stop passenger service through York, over the 126.8 miles between Grantham and Darlington, became the longest regular non-stop run on the LNER. This was the 9.50am King's Cross to Edinburgh, calling at Grantham, Darlington and Newcastle.

The mighty Ministry of Supply 2-8-0s and 2-10-0s appeared on Britain's railways in 1943. These 70 ton plus and 78 ton plus locomotives carried out sterling work throughout the entire railway system in Britain until the end of steam, the remaining examples ending their days in the Wakefield area of West Yorkshire.

Weatherwise, the heavens opened in the northwest in July 1943 creating severe flooding on the Liverpool-Southport line, resulting in water lying four-feet deep in places.

Below left:
A 1943 scene showing LNER Gresley 'Sandringham' class 4-6-0 No 2854 *Sunderland* on a down train at Whittlesford, near Cambridge. No 2854 was classified B17/4 and was introduced in 1943 with a B1-type boiler.
Real Photographs

Right:
On 9 September 1943, the 3.40pm Bartlow-Saffron Walden train was worked by ex-GNR Class C12 4-4-2T No 4520. These Ivatt-designed Great Northern locomotives were introduced in 1898 and prior to the introduction of the 'N2' class 0-6-2Ts, the 'C12's were fitted with condensing apparatus for working through the Metropolitan tunnels. This apparatus was later removed. *E. R. Wethersett*

Below:
Double-headed 4-4-0s, as ex-SE&CR Class D1 No 1487 pilots 'L1' No 1758 with a mixed train on 6 June 1943. The 'D1s' were rebuilds of Wainwright locomotives, the rebuilding incorporating superheated Belpaire boilers.
Rev. A. C. Cawston

Above:
American Transportation Corps locomotives graced our lines during World War 2. These impressive 'beasts' hauled wartime freight trains throughout the country and No 2339 is seen at Reading West Junction during 1943.
M. W. Earley

Below:
LNER Class E4 0-6-0 No 7477 hauls an interesting collection of vehicles on 9 September 1943 whilst working a Cambridge-Haverhill train. The train comprises an LNER horse box, an LMS full-brake parcels van, an NER gaslit clerestory brake third, a GER composite, an

LNER Gresley composite and another GER composite coach. *E. R. Wethersett*

Norton Fitzwarren

The year 1944 saw more than its share of railway accidents. The worst occurred on 4 November at Norton Fitzwarren (GWR) where 27 were killed and 75 injured. This was the second accident at this location, the first one being during the same month in 1890. In the 1944 incident, the Paddington-Penzance sleeper, hauled by No 6028 *King George VI*, ploughed into the ground at open trap points following the misreading of signals set for a 'King'-hauled newspaper train. Six coaches of the sleeper telescoped and were spread across all four tracks. Other accidents during this year included a collision at Ilford (LNER) on 16 January when nine people lost their lives, and two accidents on 21 August. One involved LNER 'A4' Pacific No 2512 *Silver Fox* hauling the down Leeds express at Wood Green where she left the track at the crossover at the south end of the station followed by 11 coaches of the train. The second incident on that day occurred on the Southern where two 'H 'class 0-4-4 tanks (running light) collided with a train from Hastings hauled by 'Schools' class 4-4-0 No 903 *Charterhouse*. In fact there was another accident at Wood Green (LNER) during August 1944, the second occurring only eight days after the first. On this occasion, No 2675 left the rails at the foot of the flyover north of the station. Fortunately no one was hurt in either of the Wood Green incidents.

On the Great Western, two coaches of the 'Cornish Riviera' became derailed as the train left Paddington station. Thankfully no injuries occurred on this occasion either, but it was a sad year for railway disasters.

The war continued and, due to their light axle-loading, LNER 'B12/3' 4-6-0s were selected to work ambulance trains throughout Britain — and not just over LNER metals. On 'foreign' territory they were frequently piloted by 'home' line locomotives. Another class of locomotive which drifted away from home during 1944 was the 'King Arthur' 4-6-0. For the first time they worked over Great Western metals from Southampton and over the LNER to Woodford Halse on Newcastle trains.

On the Southern, a 'Merchant Navy' Pacific worked the Eastern Division for the first time, on 13 October, when No 21C7 *Aberdeen Commonwealth* worked a Victoria-Dover train which included four Pullman cars. The Southern Railway's involvement was also apparent in the final days of operation for Scotland's Wick-Lybster Light Railway as a Stroudley 0-4-2T locomotive borrowed from the SR was used during the line's final days of operation. The line closed on 1 April 1944.

February 1944 saw the withdrawal of the Southern's last surviving 'A12' class 0-4-2 of the earlier batch, No 555. In fact, this locomotive had been the only survivor for the past 12 years. These earlier 'A12's were fitted with screw reverse gear and valves below the cylinders. During the same month the 'first' ex-LB&SCR 'H1' Atlantics to be withdrawn — Nos 2040 *St*

Catherine's Point and 2041 *Peveril Point* — ended their days.

On the Great Western scene, construction of the 'Modified Halls' commenced and, in April, GWR streamlined diesel rail-cars Nos 6 and 19 were loaned to the LNER for working the Newcastle-North Wylam services. Later in the year they returned to the GWR to be allocated to Worcester shed.

Development of the 'A2/1' LNER Pacific incorporating the 'V2'-type boiler proceeded with Nos 3696-3699 being converted.

On the diesel front, new 0-6-0 350hp diesel shunters emerged from Doncaster Works, in July, in the form of Nos 8000 and 8001 (later renumbered 15000 and 15001) both originally being allocated to Stratford. During August 1944 Canterbury became home for a number of 0-6-0 LMS diesel-electric shunters — some painted in brown and black (camouflage colours).

But the war continued and, in April, all remaining restaurant car services were withdrawn in Britain and an LNER bridge at Grove Road, Bow, was destroyed by a flying bomb on 13 June.

Below:
SR 'Lord Nelson' No 857 *Lord Howe*, with large diameter chimney, hauls a down Bournemouth express in 1944 and is seen passing Byfleet Junction. *Rev. A. C. Cawston/John S. Whiteley Collection*

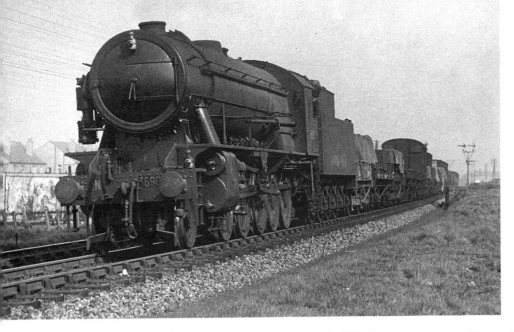

Left:
Ministry of Supply 2-8-0 and 2-10-0 locomotives were introduced in 1943 and worked all over Britain. No 3690 is pictured working a freight train during April 1944 over an LNER Scottish route. This locomotive was later renumbered 73690 and was transferred to Dutch Railways (NS) in 1946. Renumbered 5019 in the Netherlands, the locomotive was finally withdrawn in February 1950. *W. J. Reynolds*

Above:
One the best kept secrets of the war had just been released. This was that 44,000 LMS workers had been building tanks, guns, aeroplanes, assault craft, bridges and armoured trains, etc – for the last five years. Two-thirds of this work had been carried out in the seven LMS workshops and these 12in rail-mounted howitzers, pictured leaving an LMS works on 12 December 1944, were a part of the LMS workers' contribution to the war effort. *Keystone Collection*

Left:
During 1944, Great Western railcars were tried out in the northeast to test their capabilities on branch lines in the area, creating unusual scenes in this part of the country. On 25 April 1944, GWR railcar No 19, resplendent in its chocolate and cream livery, stops at Blackhill (NER) still proudly sporting its 'GWR' and Great Western crest. *A. W. Croughton/Copyright Lens of Sutton*

Solution or Pollution?

In an endeavour to find a solution to the fuel crisis, the comparatively short-lived idea that oil would prove to be more economical than coal resulted in the commencement of locomotive conversions in 1945. First to be converted to oil burning were 10 '28xx' class 2-8-0s and eight '42xx' 2-8-0Ts of the Great Western. The converted engines were intended for use in South Wales on coal and freight traffic, two refuelling depots being set up — one at Llanelly and the other at Severn Tunnel Junction. Converted GWR 2-8-0s were renumbered in the '48xx' series and, eventually, converted Great Western 'Halls', *Garth Hall* being the first, were renumbered in the '39xx' series. The oil-burning conversion programme comprised 110 SR locomotives of the 'West Country', 'N15', 'H15,' 'N', 'U', 'D15', 'L11' and 'T9' classes, and was expected to save 70,000 tons of coal as against 60,000 tons of oil. LMS locomotives scheduled for conversion totalled 485, including Beyer-Garretts, '8Fs', 'Black 5s', Class 4s and Class 7s — 290,000 tons of oil replacing 380,000 tons of coal — or so it was intended.

Other locomotive news included the introduction of Churchward's 4-6-0 'Counties' for the Great Western. Of the first produced, No 1000 was allocated to Old Oak Common, No 1001 to Newton Abbot and No 1002 to Bristol Bath Road.

On the Southern, the first of the 'West Country' class Light Pacifics, No 21C101

was completed and painted in Malachite Green at Brighton on 7 May carrying out its first trial run three days later, and in June, the last SR-built 'Merchant Navy' Pacific No 21C20 was completed.

On the LNER, Thompson rebuilt the original GNR Pacific, No 4470 *Great Northern* and the rebuilding of the 2-8-2 'P2' locomotives into 'A2/2' Pacifics was completed. Also during 1945, Thompson rebuilt the Gresley 'K4' *MacCailin Mor* reclassifying the locomotive 'K1/1'. The first British locomotive of a new design, to be built since the war ended, emerged — No 9000, the LNER 2-6-4T Class 'L1' locomotive, the first of an LNER-announced five-year plan to construct 1,000 locomotives.

The last of the Great Northern 'Klondykes' was withdrawn in July 1945. These small Ivatt Atlantics, known as 'Klondykes' due to their appearance following the famous 'Gold Rush', were built between 1898 and 1903, the last survivor being No 3252.

At the beginning of 1945, there were around 800 locomotives still in service on the LNER which were built in 1895 or before — over 50 years of age. In the LNER's locomotive programme they announced their intention to withdraw 1,000 engines over the next five years, involving the elimination of 49 classes, and all to be replaced by new locomotives.

On the LMS, H. G. Ivatt was appointed

Chief Mechanical Engineer. It was Ivatt who eventually (in 1947) introduced the first diesel-electric main line express locomotives, Nos 10000 and 10001. This year also saw the introduction on the LMS of the Fairburn 2-6-4T locomotives and Derby Works produced diesel shunters numbered 12033-12138.

On 1 October, the reinstatement of travelling post offices from Euston to Aberdeen and from Paddington to Penzance took place. For the record, the 'Aberdeen Postal' was maintained throughout World War 2 as a train of stowage vans.

An accident at Miles Platting, on the ex-L&YR in January, resulted in three fatal injuries when a locomotive's boiler burst and during the following month, at King's Cross, the 6pm King's Cross-Leeds express stalled at Gasworks Tunnel and ran backwards into the 7pm 'Aberdonian' which was standing in Platform 10.

On the night of 6 September, the Shropshire Union Canal burst its banks between Llangollen and Ruabon washing away the earthworks of the railway which passed immediately below the canal, leaving the track suspended in the air. Unfortunately, GWR Mogul No 6315 hauling a goods and mail train arrived at this point before the situation was detected and as the locomotive was impossible to lift, after its derailment, it was cut up on site.

With the war now over, restaurant and buffet services were reinstated on the LNER, LMS and the Southern (but not on the GWR) in October, and a 58min scheduled time for the London (Victoria)-Brighton 11am departure came into force.

August saw passenger services withdrawn from the Talyllyn Railway and the Wantage Tramway finally closed to traffic on 21 December.

Left:
Ex-L&YR 2-4-2T, No 10798 awaits departure from Wakefield Kirkgate station on 3 September 1945. These locomotives were introduced in 1889 and certain members of the class were rebuilt with larger bunkers doubling the coal capacity. *E. R. Wethersett*

15

Above:
Luddendenfoot on 7 September 1945, and LMS Fowler 0-8-0 No 9634 hauls a down coal train over the water troughs. These locomotives were introduced in 1929 and were a development of the L&NWR 'G2' class engines.
E. R. Wethersett

Left:
A 1945 scene showing an LNER locomotive hauling LMS stock through Micklefield. Class D49/1 Atlantic No 236 (later 2707) *Lancashire* is seen with a Hull – Liverpool working and fitted with a ex-Great Central boiler. *Real Photographs*

Below:
On 21 May 1945, Great Western 'Saint' No 2921 *Saint Dunstan* arrives at Oxford on a semi-fast Banbury service. Sadly none of this class have been preserved, No 2920 *Saint David*, the last to go, lying in hope at Swindon for quite a while in 1953. *R. H. G. Simpson*

Above:
A double-headed goods train, hauled by LNER Class D20 4-4-0 No 1260 and 'K3' Mogul No 2763, passes through Cross Gates, in 1945, working a Starbeck-Leeds train, via Wetherby. In the 1946 LNER renumbering scheme, these locomotives became Nos 2395 and 1892 respectively. *Real Photographs*

Right:
LNER 'D17/2' class 4-4-0, No 1902, leads a Brough-Hull train during 1945. This 7ft 1¼in 1897-built locomotive, together with No 1873, were the only survivors of the class at this time. *E. R. Wethersett*

Below:
A class which had reduced to six members only by the time of the 1946 LNER renumbering scheme was the 'B15' 4-6-0. No 819 (later 1695) powers a down coal train through Ferriby in 1945. This class became extinct prior to Nationalisation. *Real Photographs*

LNER Renumbering

Although the Government had announced its intention to nationalise the railways of Britain, which would eventually result in a wholesale renumbering scheme, the LNER entered into its own renumbering scheme on 13 January 1946, postponed from 1943 due to the war. Under this scheme locomotives of each class were arranged in order of construction and classes were grouped together. In each group the earlier numbers were left blank for those of new construction. These were followed by the oldest locomotives in the group making their numbers available for further newly-constructed engines. Confusion reigned amongst enthusiasts as renumbering was carried out over a long period of time; a certain amount of thought being required to ascertain which locomotive was which, as some existing numbers were used by renumbered locomotives.

The year got off to a bad start, as on New Year's Day, at Lichfield (Trent Valley) station, a Fleetwood-London (Broad Street) fish train, hauled by a 4-6-0, No 5495, collided with a stationary passenger train headed by 'Prince of Wales' class 4-6-0 No 25802. Sadly, 20 lives were lost. This unfortunate incident was followed in the February by the collapse of part of the Shepton Mallet viaduct on the Somerset & Dorset line. On 27 June, the 11.50pm goods train from Paddington to Carmarthen was wrecked at Wootton Bassett completely blocking the GWR main lines to Bristol and South Wales for 24 hours. These were just some of the 1946 calamities.

On the locomotive scene, in 1946, Doncaster Works proudly turned out 'A2/3' Pacific No 500 (later named *Edward Thompson*), its 2,000th locomotive, 79 years after producing its first product — 'Stirling' 0-4-2, GNR No 18. Also during this year the first LNER oil-burning conversion appeared — Class O7 2-8-0 No 3152, a Ministry of Supply Austerity type. The LNER also announced that their entire fleet of 6,400 locomotives were to be painted in either green or blue – 'streamlined' Pacifics would be painted 'Garter Blue', everything else green!

The Southern Railway purchased 15 'USA' 0-6-0 tank locomotives in 1946 to work Southampton Docks, replacing the 'B4' 0-4-0Ts and they also withdrew 'X6' class 4-4-0 locomotive No 658, bringing to an end this famous L&SWR class. But to commemorate the Battle of Britain, the Southern Railway introduced more Bulleid Light Pacifics and named them after RAF squadrons, airfields and personalities in the new 'Battle of Britain' class.

The Great Western's first 7000 'Castle' appeared – No 7000 *Viscount Portal* (fitted with mechanical lubricators) and the 5000 'Castles' were completed with the introduction of Nos 5098 *Clifford Castle* and 5099 *Compton Castle*. The GWR also ordered their first gas turbine locomotive during this year. At this time the GWR stocklist totalled nearly 4,000 locomotives, allocated over nine divisions, the largest being Newport Division with over 700 engines allocated to its nine depots. The largest depot allocations were to be found at Old Oak Common (over 200 locomotives), Bristol St Philips Marsh and Ebbw Junction (160+ each) and Cardiff Canton (over 130) — even Worcester had a locomotive allocation of 98.

On the LMS, the last 'River' class 4-6-0 was scrapped — No 14760. These locomotives were F. G. Smith's only engines during his 3½ year term of office as Locomotive Superintendent with the Highland Railway and only two of the class were delivered to the Highland as they were too heavy for certain 'Highland' bridges — they were passed to the 'Caley' prior to the Grouping. In addition to 1946 commemorating the centenary of the L&NWR, new classes of locomotives were also introduced by H. G. Ivatt, Chief Mechanical Engineer of the LMSR since 1945. These were the '2P' 2-6-2Ts ('12xx' class), the '2F' 2-6-0 tender locomotives ('64xx' class) and the Ivatt rebuilds of the Fowler 'Patriots' — rebuilt with taper boilers and reclassified from '5XP' to '6P' (examples being Nos 5512 *Bunsen*, 5521 *Rhyl* and 5530 *Sir Frank Ree*).

The war being now over certain 'Pullmans' returned to service. The London-Paris 'Golden Arrow' was reinstated on 15 October having been withdrawn in 1939 (first introduced 1929) and the 'Yorkshire Pullman' (King's Cross-Hull-Harrogate-Bradford Exchange) returned on 4 November. The summer 1946 timetable included no less that 46 non-stop runs of over 100 miles — 31 on the LMS, 10 on the GWR and 5 on the LNER – the longest being Euston-Carlisle representing 301.1 miles in 389 minutes. Prior to the war the only Southern non-stop run exceeding 100 miles was between Waterloo and Bournemouth which by 1946 had not been revived.

As 1946 drew to a close, LMS 'Patriots' were again in the news, with No 5525 *Colwyn Bay* being involved in a collision on 22 November and No 5500 *Patriot* was involved in another on 7 December.

Two fascinating Scottish lines closed in 1946. In February, the ex-Highland Railway Dingwall-Strathpeffer branch closed to passengers and, at the end of the year, the ex-NBR line from Spean Bridge-Fort Augustus eventually closed completely with the loss of 23¼ miles of track, alongside the Caledonian Canal. It originally closed to passengers in 1933 and was only kept open for the last 13 years for the weekly 'household' coal train of around six wagons!

But the most significant news of the year came on 28 November when the Government announced its intention to nationalise Britain's railways, which would end the life of the 'Big Four' on 31 December 1947, after a lifespan of 25 years.

Facing page, top:
A powerful 'on shed' scene at King's Cross motive power depot on 11 May 1946 with Sir Nigel Gresley's first Pacific locomotive, No 4470 *Great Northern*, beside 'A2' Pacific No 3697 (later renumbered 508 and named *Duke of Rothesay* in 1947). The Gresley Pacifics were introduced in 1922, the prototype, No 1470 becoming No 4470 in LNER days. It is seen in its 1945 rebuilt state, incorporating full-length cab and apple green livery. *Great Northern* became the forerunner of the Thompson 'A1' Pacifics.
E. R. Wethersett

Facing page, bottom:
LNER 'A2/3' Pacific No 500 was the Thompson 1946-rebuild of the 'A2/2' Pacific which was introduced in 1943. With nameplate affixed but covered No 500 *Edward Thompson* prepares to leave Nottingham Victoria for Marylebone on 29 May 1946 for the naming ceremony.
John P. Wilson

Left:
Great Western 'King' No 6011 *King James I* heads a Paddington-Birkenhead express through Gerrards Cross in 1946. The locomotive was a regular performer over this route. *Lewis Coles*

Below:
On 26 August 1946, 'mixed' motive power, comprising Great Western Mogul No 6387 piloting a Southern 'T9' class 4-4-0, approaches Cowley Bridge Junction, near Exeter, on a southern passenger working. *B. A. Butt*

Facing page, top:
A Corris Railway train crosses the River Dovey near Machynlleth, headed by locomotive No 4 in July 1946. The 1921-built Kerr Stuart engine hauls end-door iron-bodied 1-ton open wagons, slab trestle wagons and a Corris Railway brake van. *Lens of Sutton*

Facing page, bottom:
A 1946 scene at Swansea Victoria shed showing ex-L&NWR Beames 0-8-4T No 7941 being prepared for her next duty. Introduced in 1923, the first 15 locomotives in the class carried L&NWR numbers, but the letters LMS appeared on their tank-side, No 7941 being L&NWR No 792. A 'Cauliflower Goods' 0-6-0T is seen alongside in this view.
H. C. Prudden

Above:
On 27 July 1946, LNER 'C4' class Atlantic No 6089 (later 2913) passes Firsby South Junction with a Lincoln-Skegness train. *T. G. Hepburn/Copyright Rail Archive Stephenson*

Left:
A permanent way train, hauled by LNER 'J39' 0-6-0 No 1974, and incorporating the Great Northern Engineer's Department van, scampers along through Pecscliffe on 15 July 1946. *E. R. Wethersett*

Right:
Fowler 2-6-4T No 2421 prepares to depart from Glasgow Central on 13 April 1946 with a Clyde Coast train. These Fowler tanks were fitted with cabside windows. *H. C. Casserley*

Right:
A push-pull train running on the 'Ally-Pally' line.
LNER 'F2' 2-4-2T No 7107, seen prior to the
1946 renumbering, is seen at Crouch End on
30 March 1946 with a two-coach train.
E. R. Wethersett

Below:
The first 'Merchant Navy' Bulleid Pacific
appeared in 1941 creating a unique streamlined
locomotive design incorporating a 'troublesome'
chain-driven gear. All members of the class were
named after shipping companies and the
centrepiece of the nameplate was finished in
vitreous enamel displaying the house flag of the
shipping line with the flag flying towards the rear
of the locomotive. The first member of the class,
No 21C1 *Channel Packet*, is pictured at Bargrove
on 22 April 1946 on the down 'Golden Arrow'.
Rev. A. C. Cawston/John S. Whiteley Collection

Main Line Diesels

The big attraction of the year was the introduction of Britain's first main line diesels, Nos 10000 and 10001. The designer, H. G. Ivatt personally drove No 10000 out of Derby Works on 8 December. These powerful English Electric locomotives, each weighing over 121 tons, paved the way for the future in locomotive-hauled travel for years to come, although the LMS had possessed English Electric shunting locomotives since 1936. Other new diesel shunters appeared in 1947, like DS1173, the Drewry 0-6-0 shunter, the forerunner of the later-classified 'O2' BR shunters, DS1173 starting its days at Gorton and ending up on the Southern after a period in East Anglia.

During 1947, Ivatt continued his rebuilding programme on the 'Patriots', continued building his '2P' 2-6-2Ts and '2MT' 2-6-0s, and created yet another 2-6-0 class, the '4F' 3000 series, again fitted with Walschaerts valve gear, superheated, and with taper boiler, as on his '64xx' '2MT' 2-6-0s. In contrast, during 1947, the Great Western introduced their '94xx' class 0-6-0PT locomotives which were initially to be found working predominantly on the London Division. These newly-designed pannier tanks were constructed at Swindon Works and were a more powerful version of the '8750' class. A 1947 conversion to oil burning on the GWR was the popular 'Castle' 'A1' *Lloyds*, an unusual locomotive in that its numberplate carried a second plate 'A1' below it and the nameplate just carried the word *Lloyds*. Previously this locomotive was 4-6-0 'Star', No 4009 *Shooting Star*.

Ashford Works (ex-SE&CR) celebrated its centenary in 1947 and the new 'Battle of Britain' Bulleid Light Pacifics started to enter service. Brighton Works completed construction of its 1,000th locomotive — Bulleid 'West Country' Pacific No 21C164 — on 9 June and on the Isle of Wight an ex-LB&SCR 'E4' 0-6-2T arrived — No 2510. It was only on the island for trials and did not stay long.

At Exmouth Junction a new vacuum-operated turntable was installed to enable the large 'Merchant Navy' Pacifics to be turned there. This was also the case at Padstow where it was necessary to turn 'West Country' Pacifics on the 'Atlantic Coast Express' arriving from Okehampton. In July, the first oil-burning 'West Country' Pacific, No 21C119 *Bideford* left Eastleigh Works and also during the year, further progress was made on the Southern when electro-pneumatic braking was adopted on

9 December after trials.

Arctic conditions paralysed Britain's railways during the first three months of 1947, with blizzards and frost being followed by a rapid thaw, gales and heavy rain — and the inevitable flooding. Even in early March, deep snowdrifts created havoc in South Wales at Craig-y-Nos.

On the Settle & Carlisle line, during February and March, cuttings were filled with snow to the height of the overbridges. Locomotives fitted with snowploughs the previous autumn, in preparation for a hard winter, were unable to cope as the weather worsened. Both soldiers and prisoners of war were brought in to clear tracks at Dent Head, but high winds created drifting. Was this to be another 1942?

By 1947, well over 1,400 locomotives had been built at Doncaster Works and the 1,434th, the 'A2' Peppercorn Pacific, No 525 *A. H. Peppercorn* was the last to be built by the LNER. In fact, the original nameplates carried the name *Arthur H. Peppercorn* but this name proved to be too long for the smoke deflectors and therefore had to be shortened. In 1947, two LNER classes became extinct. These were the 'M1s', when 0-6-4T No 9082 (built for the LD&ECR) was withdrawn, and the 'G10s', on the scrapping of ex-GNSR 0-4-0T No 7505. In September 1947 the pioneer electric locomotive constructed for working the Manchester-Sheffield trains over the Woodhead electrified route, No 26000 was sent to Holland. Built in 1941 as No 6701 by the LNER this was the only one of its type built at the time as electrification work on this route was suspended until the 1950s. Later numbered 6000 the Dutch named the locomotive *Tommy*. On final withdrawal in Britain the later Class 77 electrics, which used to haul passenger trains over this route, eventually ended their days working on the Dutch railways.

The year 1947 gave us a Royal Wedding with Princess Elizabeth (now Queen Elizabeth II) marrying Prince Philip. Their wedding train, which conveyed them from Waterloo to Winchester, comprised two Pullman cars, *Rosemary* and *Rosamund*, plus three SR coaches, all hauled by SR 'Lord Nelson' class 4-6-0 No 857 *Lord Howe*, carrying a plaque on its smokebox door depicting the Coat of Arms of the Princess Elizabeth on a bed of roses, thistles, leeks and shamrocks.

On 20 June the 'Devon Belle' was inaugurated with an observation car at the rear

of the train. This train departed from Waterloo at noon on Mondays to Fridays, stopping at Sidmouth Junction and Exeter, changing engines at Wilton. At Exeter the train divided, with sections for Plymouth and Ilfracombe. Also in 1947 the 'Master Cutler' was inaugurated. This Marylebone-Sheffield (Victoria) train was routed via Rugby, Leicester and Nottingham,. On the Southern the Dover to Dunkerque Train Ferry resumed services from 15 December.

On 21 July 1947 a Euston-Liverpool express, comprising 16 screw-coupled bogie vehicles hauled by LMS 'Coronation' Pacific No 6244 *King George VI*, became derailed at Polesworth and the locomotive overturned. This followed a previous incident on the LMS in May when 'Princess Royal' Pacific No 6211 *Queen Maud*, hauling the up Postal, made a sudden stop on the junction with the Morecambe line resulting in the motion seizing up. Oxy-acetylene had to be used to cut the motion so that the engine could be moved.

In August, the 1.25pm King's Cross to Leeds express comprising LNER 'V2' No 936 and 12 coaches collided at 40 mph between Bridge Junction and Balby Junction signalboxes — 18 passengers lost their lives.

October and November brought an amazing flood of accidents, it is sad to report. On 24 October, during fog at South Croydon, 32 people were killed as a Tattenham Corner-London Bridge electric collided violently with a Haywards Heath-London Bridge train. No less than two days later, on the East Coast main line, the 11.15am Edinburgh-King's Cross express, made up of 'A3' Pacific No 66 *Merry Hampton* and 15 coaches, became derailed whilst traversing the up main at Goswick at high speed on the Berwick-on-Tweed to Newcastle-on-Tyne section. The train was packed with 420 passengers, of whom 27 lost their lives. Within two weeks, on 6 November, the 4.15pm Ramsgate-Victoria steam-hauled express collided on a diamond crossing in dense fog at Herne Hill with the 6.58pm electric train from Holborn to West Croydon as it passed the up main home signals at 'danger'.

On 26 November 1947, the 3.05pm Bournemouth West-Waterloo train, with 'Lord Nelson' No 860 *Lord Hawke* and 10 coaches, ran into the 12.15pm Ilfracombe-Waterloo train ('King Arthur' No 453 *King Arthur* with 11 coaches) as it approached west of Farnborough under incorrect

instructions. This was a critical period on Britain's railways.

The picturesque Great Western branch line to Yealmpton in Devon closed on 4 October, and the Elham Valley branch on the Southern, closed to passengers on 14 June. Also on that date the Southern's oldest depot, New Cross Gate, (ex-LB&SCR) finally closed.

Above:
No 4028 was one of the 0-6-0 locomotives built by the LMS and developed from the Midland Railway design with reduced boiler mountings. The locomotive is seen at Upminster on the LT&S line with a stopping train on 24 September 1947. *E. R. Wethersett*

Right:
Two Bowen-Cooke ex-L&NWR Class G1 '6F' 0-8-0s which did not survive into Nationalisation were Nos 9206 and 9299, pictured here passing at Northchurch, near Berkhamsted, at the north end of the tunnel on 17 June 1947. In fact the first engines of this class were withdrawn in 1947. *E. R. Wethersett*

Left:
Belle Isle on 7 June 1947 and LNER 'A3' Pacific No 51 *Blink Bonny* prepares to enter Copenhagen Tunnel with a down train for Newcastle. *E. R. Wethersett*

Bottom left:
Cowlairs Bank, Glasgow, on the North British line coming out of Queen Street station, regularly saw Class N14 0-6-2Ts working empty coaching stock. On this occasion, on 22 August 1947, No 9124 slowly works its way up the incline with empty coaches. *E. R. Wethersett*

Right:
On ex-L&YR metals, Sowerby Bridge-allocated LMS 0-6-0 No 12574, an Aspinall rebuild of a Hughes Class F22, is pictured at Luddendenfoot in Yorkshire, just west of Halifax with a stopping train on 18 August 1947. *E. R. Wethersett*

Below:
Following the introduction of the Thompson 4-6-0s — classified 'B1' — the ex-Great Central 4-6-0s (formerly 'B1') were reclassified 'B18'. Only two of these Robinson-designed locomotives were built and both were withdrawn in 1947 after 44 years in service. This fine study of No 1479 in action was captured on 10 August 1947 as she headed the 6.16pm Nottingham Victoria-Marylebone relief.
T. G. Hepburn/Rail Archive Stephenson

Left:
The last LMS 'Coronation' Pacific to be de-streamlined was No 6243 *City of Lancaster*. In June 1947 this locomotive was seen in its streamlined state approaching Leighton Buzzard Tunnel on a Perth-Euston express. *W. S Garth*

Bottom left:
Great Western 'Castle', No 100 A1 *Lloyds*, having been converted to oil burning, partners No 6937 *Conyngham Hall* through Stockley on 31 May 1947 on a down express. A1 *Lloyds* was officially named at a ceremony at Paddington station on 17 February 1936. This locomotive was originally 'Star' class 4-6-0 No 4009 *Shooting Star* but was rebuilt as a 'Castle' in 1925 retaining the name *Shooting Star* until the 1936 naming. Commonly known as *A1 Lloyds*, the 'A1' was, in fact part of the number as can be seen on the cabside and buffer beam. *E. R. Wethersett*

Above:
Cowlairs Junction on 22 August 1947 and LNER 'B1' class 4-6-0 No 1217 passes through the station with the 11.15am ex-Glasgow Queen Street. These Thompson-designed stalwarts were introduced in 1942. There is so much of interest to see in this pre-Nationalisation station view. *E. R. Wethersett*

Centre right:
Ex-Caledonian Railway Pickersgill '3F' 0-6-0 No 17668 (with its shedplate high on the smokebox door) is pictured at Uddington, near where the CR line passes beneath NBR metals, on 23 August 1947, with a down goods train. *E. R. Wethersett*

Right:
On 20 August 1947, a six-car Tyneside electric train, carrying the LNER 'Totem' and blue and off-white livery, forms a Newcastle-Manors service. Trains were formed of two-car articulated units and operated on a 600V dc system which was inaugurated in 1904. The Tyneside stock seen in this view was built in 1937 by Metro-Cammell. *E. R. Wethersett*

29

Nationalisation

This was one of the most important years in railway history as, on 1 January, Britain's railways were Nationalised bringing to an end the era of the 'Big Four'. The new Nationalised British Railways was split into six regions — the London Midland (4,993 route miles), Eastern Region (2,836 route miles), North Eastern Region (1,823 route miles), Scottish Region (3,730 route miles), Southern Region (2,250 route miles) and Western Region (3,782 route miles).

The first GWR locomotive to display the title BRITISH RAILWAYS on its tender was No 4946 *Moseley Hall*; the first LNER was 'A3' Pacific No 112 *St Simon*, and the first Southern engine, 'Battle of Britain' Pacific No 21C158 *Sir Frederick Pile* whose number was then prefixed by a letter 'S'.

In April 1948, the Locomotive Exchanges commenced a programme of trials using locomotives previously unfamiliar to certain routes. These locomotives worked with dynamometer cars to record speeds and other data. Locomotive classes used on passenger routes were LMS 'Duchess', LNER 'A4', SR 'Merchant Navy' and LMS 'Royal Scot' and routes involved were Euston-Carlisle, King's Cross-Leeds, Paddington-Plymouth, and Waterloo-Exeter, and a GWR 'King' also ran between King's Cross and Leeds. There were also 'mixed traffic' exchanges when LMS 'Class 5', LNER 'B1' and SR 'West Country' classes were used over routes Perth-Inverness, St Pancras-Manchester, Bristol-Plymouth and Marylebone-Manchester — a route operated by a GWR 'Hall'. Freight locomotive exchanges also took place using LMS '8F', LNER 'O1' and War Department 2-8-0 and 2-10-0 locomotives. These operated between Toton and Brent, London and Peterborough, London and South Wales and Bristol and Southampton. A GWR '38xx' 2-8-0 was scheduled to cover all these routes except Toton-Brent. All locomotives during the locomotive exchanges used the same grade of coal and were manned by enginemen who normally worked them. The tests covered a period of four months.

During the year, the oil conversion programme for 1,229 locomotives set up in 1945 was abandoned after only 100 conversions, and by the end of the year all GWR oil-burners were again burning coal. It was also the end for certain pre-Grouping classes. No 16095, the last survivor of the G&SWR locomotives taken over by the LMS in 1923 was withdrawn in April, as was the last McIntosh ex-'Caley' 'Dunalastair II' No 14333. The last 'Dunalastair III',

No 14432, and the last 'King George V' class ex-L&NWR locomotive No 25350 were also withdrawn. There were a couple of firsts too! The first Midland 'Compound' was withdrawn as was the first Whitelegg ex-LT&SR 4-4-2 tank, No 2105.

The new main-line diesel, No 10000, completed its first trial runs on 14/15 January hauling a 12-coach train of 393 tons over the St Pancras-Manchester route. Almost at the same time emerged two Stanier Pacifics Nos 6256 *Sir William Stanier FRS* and 6257 *City of Salford*. Each worked the Euston-Glasgow route competing with main line diesel No 10000 working in tandem with No 10001. On the London Midland Region, a new blue livery appeared on LMS Stanier Pacifics. The first to be so treated were Nos 46224/27/30/31/32/41. To enable LMS Pacifics to be turned at Crewe South depot a new 70ft turntable was installed replacing the existing 60ft one.

The first train to appear in the 'Plum & Spilt Milk' experimental livery was the Southern Region's 3.30pm Waterloo-Bournemouth, hauled by 'Lord Nelson' No 30861 *Lord Anson*. In fact, Waterloo station celebrated 100 years of service in 1948. Also on the Southern, Co-Co Electric locomotive No 20003 entered service, a locomotive which was eventually generally used on Newhaven boat trains along with the two others of the class.

'Pullmans' which were introduced in 1948 included the 'Thanet Belle' (Victoria-Kent Coast) on 31 May, and the 'Tees-Tyne Pullman' (King's Cross-Darlington-Newcastle). On 5 July the 'Queen of Scots' weekday 'Pullman' from King's Cross to Glasgow was operated for the first time since 2 September 1939, the first reinstated trains being hauled by LNER 'A3' Pacifics Nos 60107 and 60109. This 'Pullman' train departed from King's Cross at 11.30am arriving at Glasgow Queen St at 9.22pm and the return working departed Glasgow Queen St at 10.15am arriving at King's Cross at 8.10pm. The train comprised 10 Pullman cars (8 in the Glasgow portion, 2 in the Leeds portion). Stops were made at Leeds Central, Harrogate, Darlington, Newcastle Central and Edinburgh Waverley. The London-Leeds section was, in fact, 10min faster than the Leeds Pullman. On 16 February, the 'Royal Scot' name was reinstated as the 10am Euston-Glasgow express, and also during 1948 the 'Norfolkman' (Liverpool St-Norwich) was introduced. On 31 May, the non-stop King's Cross-Edinburgh Waverley service

was restored.

On the locomotive scene, the first of the new 'A1' class 6ft 8in Pacifics, No 60114, was completed in July and commemorative plaques were affixed to the side sheeting of LNER 'A4' Pacific *Mallard*, reading 'World Speed Record run of 126mph on 12-7-38'. The LNER's only Beyer-Garrett locomotive, No 69999, was transferred from duty on Worsborough Bank, near Barnsley, to work the Lickey Incline at Bromsgrove in Worcestershire on the Midland line.

More Ivatt Moguls in the 43000 class emerged from Horwich Works during the year and the GWR 'Modified Halls' started to appear. The Wantage Tramway locomotive *Shannon* was mounted on a pedestal at Wantage Road Station. Diesel shunters emerged from Swindon Works for the Western Region numbered 15101-06.

Line closures in 1948 saw the last train on the Corris Railway on 20 August, seven days after the Jedburgh-Roxburgh line closed to passengers. In November the Easingwold Light Railway in the North Riding of Yorkshire and the East Kent Light Railway (Shepherds Well-Wingham) closed to passengers.

The worst floods for years hit Northumberland and southeast Scotland. These were caused by torrential rain on 11/12 August and the East Coast main line was blocked in 11 places between Newcastle and Edinburgh. Between Reston and Grantshouse seven bridges were washed away together with track and ballast and the 'Flying Scotsman' was diverted over the Settle & Carlisle route via Carlisle and Carstairs and was hauled by two LMS locomotives.

Serious accidents continued to occur due to the run-down state of the railways. Examples were on 17 April (Glasgow-Euston express), 18 May (11.45 Bradford-St Pancras train), 17 July (Aberdeen-Glasgow train), and also on 17 July a serious derailment of the up Edinburgh-King's Cross express at the south end of Oakleigh Park Tunnel involved LNER Pacific No 508 *Duke of Rothesay*. An accident on 9 August, resulting in the loss of 18 lives, occurred at Bridge Junction (LNER) when two express passenger trains from Leeds to King's Cross collided and on 30 November a double-headed express ran into the back of a local train at Stockport.

Above:
A Great Western 'oil burner' 2-8-0 No 4808, works a down freight and passes through Norton Fitzwarren in May 1948. Prior to conversion to oil burning, a venture which proved to be unsuccessful, this locomotive was numbered 2834. *E. C. Griffith*

Left:
Ex-Powlesland & Mason 0-4-0 outside cylinder saddle-tank No 935 carries out shunting duties at Swansea on 27 August 1948. Just nine P&M locomotives were absorbed into the GWR on 1 January 1924 and only four reached Nationalisation. All were 0-4-0 saddle-tanks. No 935 eventually became No 1152. *R. M. Casserley*

Above:
During the 1948 locomotive exchanges enthusiasts were keen to see 'foreign' motive power entering their stations. On 22 April 1948, LNER 'A4' Pacific No 60033 *Seagull* worked out of Paddington creating tremendous interest. The dynamometer car, which recorded route information and performance, can be seen directly behind the locomotive. *C. C. B. Herbert*

Left:
At St Pancras, on 14 June 1948, Bulleid 'West Country' Pacific No 34005 *Barnstaple* turned up for duty and is seen preparing to depart with an evening express. Note the LMS tender but the absence of a dynamometer car. For the locomotive exchanges new British Railways numbers had to be applied to all engines taking part. *C. C. B. Herbert*

Above right:
The newly-formed British Railways Western Region provided No 6018 *King Henry VI* for locomotive exchange duties and here the 'King' is seen on LNER metals leaving Hadley Wood Tunnel on 19 May 1948 having worked the 7.50am from Leeds. *M. W. Earley*

Right:
Another locomotive which worked into King's Cross was LMS 'Royal Scot' No 46162 *Royal Westminster Rifleman* which, on 30 April 1948, also worked a train from Leeds. This is much to the interest of the crew of LNER 'A3' Pacific No 59 *Tracery*, preparing to depart from King's Cross with the 12.20pm Newcastle express. *C. C. B. Herbert*

Above:
The rural branch lines of Britain always produced a perfect setting for railway photography. On 27 March 1948, LNER 'E4' class 2-4-0 No 2783 (a class introduced in 1891) is seen at Audley End, tender-first, with an up Saffron Walden two-coach train. Certain members of this class were fitted with cabside windows. *E. R. Wethersett*

Left:
Another rural scene, this time on the Southern as ex-LB&SCR Class C2x 0-6-0 No 32535 hauls a short up goods train into Oxted on 13 September 1948. These locomotives were Marsh rebuilds of R. J. Billinton 'C2' engines, conversion incorporating the larger 'C3'-type boiler and extended smokebox. *E. R. Wethersett*

Above right:
On 25 June 1948, the down Newhaven boat train departs from Lewes with ex-LB&SCR 'H2' class Marsh Atlantic No 2425 *Trevose Head* in charge. The last member of this class to survive was No 32424 *Beachy Head*, withdrawn in 1958, and it was also the last Atlantic locomotive to run in service on Britain's railways. *C. C. B. Herbert*

Right:
Commencing their journey down the Settle & Carlisle route, LMS Compound No 1141 and a 4-6-0 'Jubilee' leave Carlisle Citadel station on an up express for Leeds in 1948. A fine combination of motive power. *H. Gordon Tidey*

Name that Train!

This was the year that was flooded with the introduction and reinstatement of named trains on Britain's railways.

Newcomers on the Eastern Region came in the form of the 'Capitals Ltd' (King's Cross-Edinburgh), the 'White Rose' and 'West Riding' (King's Cross-Leeds/Bradford) and 'The Fenman' (Liverpool St-King's Lynn). On the Scottish Region came the introduction of the 'Bon Accord', 'St Mungo' and 'Granite City' (all Glasgow-Aberdeen), the 'Fife Coast Express' (Glasgow-St Andrews) and 'The Irishman' (Glasgow-Stranraer Harbour). When the winter timetable came into force the 'Northumbrian' (King's Cross-Newcastle) and the 'North Briton' (Leeds City-Glasgow Queen St) were introduced.

Reinstated named trains included, on the London Midland Region, 'The Mid-day Scot' (Euston-Glasgow), the 'Ulster Express' (Euston-Heysham), the 'Thames-Clyde Express' (St Pancras-Glasgow), 'The Comet' (Euston-Manchester), the 'Mancunian' (Manchester-Euston) and the 'Merseyside Express' (Liverpool-Euston). Also reinstated were the 'Pines Express' and the 'Devonian'.

New liveries were also announced during 1949. These were as follows: blue, with black and white lining (heavy duty express passenger locomotives); dark green, with black and orange lining (selected passenger locomotives); black with red, cream and grey lining (other passenger and mixed traffic locomotives); black, unlined (freight locomotives); crimson lake, with cream panels (passenger coaches — main line); crimson lake (other coaching stock — including vans); and, green (electric multiple-units).

On 21 June, the first of Bulleid's controversial 'Leader' locomotives underwent steaming trials outside Brighton Works. Externally similar to locomotive No 20003, the entire boiler and bunker were enclosed in a superstructure with a cab at both ends. With the driver being able to work from either end, the fireman had a compartment of his own near the centre of the locomotive, connected to the driver's cab by a corridor. During its steaming trials the 'unnumbered' 'Leader' was painted grey, with black bogies. It was later numbered 36001. Its early workings mainly entailed test runs from Brighton to Crowhurst. Work continued at Brighton on the only other two 'Leaders', Nos 36002 and 36003. O. V. S. Bulleid, in fact, retired as Chief Mechanical Engineer of the Southern Region during this year.

Another Southern Region 'newcomer' from O. V. S. Bulleid was the four-car double-deck electric unit No 4001, built at Lancing Works for the London-Dartford services. Trials took place between Brighton and Haywards Heath in September and sets Nos 4001 and 4002 entered regular service on 2 November.

Also on the electric scene Newhaven boat trains became electric-locomotive hauled and the replacement of steam by a full electrified service took place on 7 November on the Liverpool St-Shenfield line. The last steam train over this route was hauled by Class 'L1' No 67718 which was decorated with a Union Jack and a laurel wreath. However, on 7 November, some overhead wires at Seven Kings came down causing utter chaos during the rush hour — so 'steam trains' from Southend picked up all stranded passengers!

At the Derby Carriage & Wagon Works, an all-steel 60ft prototype composite coach was constructed. Also built were catering vehicles, sleeping cars and postal sorting vans.

On the Western Region the new Hawksworth short-wheelbase heavy shunting '15xx' class 0-6-0PTs, built at Swindon Works, were introduced. These locomotives were fitted with Walschaerts valve-gear.

From Ashford Works emerged diesel shunters Nos 15211-15236 and from Doncaster Works came No 15004. Motor-fitted 'H' class 0-4-4 tanks started to appear on the Southern converted for push-pull workings and the first of Earle Marsh's 4-4-2s, No 2423 *The Needles* was withdrawn.

By mid-1949, all but one of the oil burners were finally converted back to coal-burning; the last survivor being SR 'West Country' Pacific No 34046 *Braunton*.

It was withdrawal time for three veterans of the track during this year — 'Claughton' No 6004, 'Prince of Wales' No 25752 and 'Precursor' No 25297 *Sirocco* — and on the Western Region the only steam locomotive ever to run on the GWR with poppet-valves (in place of slide-valves or piston-valves), No 2935 *Caynham Court*, was also withdrawn. The Western Region also lost its last 'Aberdare' 2-6-0 — No 2667. The Eastern Region withdrew the final 'J75' 0-6-0, No 8365 (ex Hull & Barnsley Railway). Finally on the locomotive front, the last streamlined LMS Pacific, *City of Lancaster*, was 'defrocked' in May 1949. Pacific locomotives also returned to the Great Central.

On 23 June the first of a remarkable series of fires on express passenger trains occurred at Penmanshiel Tunnel when fire broke out in the corridor of the 10th coach of a train, resulting in this coach being gutted by flames. Remarkably, only one person, a lady, was seriously injured, as many passengers jumped through broken windows on to the track.

On 19 August, an ex-Somerset & Dorset Joint 0-6-0 Class 3 locomotive, No 3260, collided with a diesel tractor near Ascott and dived into the dyke alongside the track.

On the permanent way scene the Railway Executive adopted flat-bottom rail as 'standard' replacing bull-head rail and chairs and, although Nationalisation only came into being on 1 January 1948, boundary changes were already taking place as the London Midland Region lost the London, Tilbury & Southend line to the Eastern Region, and certain Central and South Wales lines to the Western.

Top right:
With a train of potatoes from Bodmin Moor, Ministry of Supply 2-8-0 No 77388 passes along the sea wall between Teignmouth and Parson's Tunnel, on 2 June 1949 bound for London and destinations beyond. Although introduced in 1943, these 'Austerity' locomotives were only 'on loan' to British Railways at this time. *E. D. Bruton*

Bottom right:
On the ex-L&SWR main line between Brookwood and Farnborough, Southern 'U' class Mogul No 1621 hauls a down freight on 9 July 1949. Over 18 months after Nationalisation, many locomotives were still awaiting their new five-digit British Railways numbers. *R. W. Beaton*

Top left:
An interesting variety of Class R1 motive power graces Folkestone Junction shed on 30 June 1949. On the left is seen Stirling-designed SER 'R1' 0-6-0T No 1128 (rebuilt with domed boiler) and in the centre of the line-up is No 1339, used on the Canterbury & Whitstable line, another 'R1' 0-6-0T, but with cut-down boiler mountings to meet the C&W branch loading gauge. The short chimney was Urie-designed and was introduced in 1938. The third 'R1' 0-6-0T on the right, No 31340, is of a similar design to No 1128, but carries the new BR number. *E. R. Wethersett*

Bottom left:
A Torquay train, hauled by '51xx' class 2-6-2T No 5132, leaves Exeter St Davids station on 5 June 1949. The second coach in the train is one of the GWR 'Dreadnoughts'. *John P. Wilson*

Top:
In 1949, Bulleid introduced his short-lived 0-6-6-0T 'Leader' locomotive. Three members of the class were built, but only one reached trials stage. The firebox was situated in the centre of the locomotive creating for the fireman an area of unbearable heat in which to work, a factor in the abandonment of the project. No 36001 is pictured running trials on 22 November 1949. *BR (Southern Region)*

Right:
Another Bulleid design, introduced on the Charing Cross-Dartford services to overcome overcrowding, was the 4DD double-deck four-car electric multiple-unit. Similar in design to the SUB units, the 4DD set had seating on two levels. Pressure ventilation was fitted as there were no opening windows on the upper floor. The 4DD units remained in service until 1971. No 4001 is pictured on a trail run on 14 September 1949. *BR (Southern Region)*

Left:
Forty-three ex-L&NWR Webb-designed Class 1P 2-4-2Ts reached nationalisation. These locomotives were introduced in 1890 and, on 20 April 1949, No 46620, having completed station shunting duties at Swansea Victoria, pauses a while prior to taking out the next Swansea to Pontardulais local train. *H. Daniel*

Above:
An unusual combination of LMS motive power is seen on 7 May 1949 just south of Ayres End Lane Bridge, near Harpenden. Horwich 'Crab' No 42763 is seen piloting ex-LMS Fowler/Beyer-Peacock 2-6-6-2T Beyer-Garratt No 47987 with down empty mineral wagons. *E. D. Bruton*

Left:
On 23 April 1949, 'G2A' class 7F 0-8-0 No 49180 is pictured on the West Coast main line near Carpenders Park with an up freight working. *E. R. Wethersett*

Right:
The Seaton-Stamford (Lincs) push-pull services were normally operated during the summer of 1949 by Rugby-allocated ex-Midland Railway 0-4-4T locomotives Nos 1420 and 1421. In this view No 1420 approaches Stamford with a midday arrival on 23 July 1949. *P. H. Wells*

Above:
An extremely interesting collection of rolling stock is seen on 6 August 1949 being hauled by LNER 'J37' 0-6-0 No 64636 at Inverkeithing. The nine coaches in the train, from front to back are a GNoSR six-wheel brake, a GER semi-corridor composite, an NER third, a GER composite, another NER third, an NBR third, another GER semi-corridor composite, an LNER brake third and an LNER four-wheel brake — some train! *E. R. Wethersett*

Right:
The 'East Anglian', hauled by 'B1' 4-6-0 No 61041, passes Trowse Yard on 6 September 1949. The 'East Anglian', a Liverpool Street-Norwich express, was introduced in 1937 — Coronation year. When introduced, 'B1' locomotives Nos 2859 and 2870 were specially streamlined to work the new service and were named *East Anglian* and *City of London* respectively. *E. Tuddenham*

The Gas Turbine

A new form of power for Britain's railways entered the country in 1950 as the Western Region's gas turbine locomotive, No 18000, arrived at Harwich from Switzerland on 14 January, having been ordered some four years earlier. It was hauled by LNER 'B1' No 61003 from Temple Mills to the Western Region where 'Modified Hall' No 7901 *Dodington Hall* took over for the remainder of the journey to Swindon. Trial runs with the locomotive were carried out in February and regular services were undertaken by No 18000 to the West of England in May. Also introduced was North British Bo-Bo diesel-electric No 10800 and Ashford-built 0-6-0 diesel-mechanical shunter No 11001.

Plans were announced by British Railways to build a vast number of locomotives and rolling stock by the end of 1951. Locomotives included 35 Pacifics, 50 x 4-6-0s, 54 x 2-6-4Ts, 20 x 2-6-2Ts (Class 3), 113 Moguls, 40 x 2-6-2Ts (Class 2), 20 x '16xx' class pannier tanks for the Western Region, eight 'J72' 0-6-0Ts for the Eastern and North Eastern regions, five 0-4-0STs (Class 1F Nos 47005-9), 51 diesel-electric 0-6-0 350hp shunters and four diesel-mechanical 0-6-0 200hp shunters for the Eastern Region. This list of 400 locomotives excluded previously ordered stock such as the 200 x '94xx' 0-6-0Ts for the Western Region, Brush diesels (400hp) and 36 electric engines and Class 4 Moguls already under construction. Included in the plans were also 2,386 carriages, 369 brake and luggage vans and 34,938 miscellaneous vans and wagons.

Locomotive withdrawals included the last 'Clan', No 54767 *Clan Mackinnon* on 30 January, an ex-Highland 4-6-0 which had put in 29 years' service. The last veteran double-framed Kirtley 0-6-0 goods engine No 22853, built by the Midland Railway in 1873, was also withdrawn, as was the last ex-Great Central 'B5' 'Fish' class locomotive, No 1686, withdrawn on 12 June. The first Great Western 'Castle' to go, No 100 A1 *Lloyds* was withdrawn in 1950 and the last member of the 'Castle' class, No 7037 was named *Swindon* by HRH Princess Elizabeth at Swindon Works on 15 November where, in December, the last 'Manors' were completed.

During 1950, Crewe Locomotive Works built its 7,000th locomotive since it came into existence. This was Ivatt 2-6-2T No 41272, these locomotives also appearing for the first time on the Somerset & Dorset line. Ex LMS 'Royal Scot' No 46100 *Royal Scot* was also rebuilt and deprived of its

'bell'. The last four 'Jersey Lilies', as the ex-GCR Atlantics were affectionately known, completed their final journeys in 1950. Nos 62908 and 62919 were withdrawn on 22 November and, only six days later, No 62901 met a similar fate followed on 2 December by No 62918.

The introduction of more named trains continued into 1950 with the 'Inter City' (Paddington-Wolverhampton via Birmingham) on 25 September, the 'Easterling' (Liverpool St-Yarmouth South Town, via Lowestoft), 'The Red Dragon' (Carmarthen-Paddington), 'The Broadsman' (Liverpool St-Sheringham via Ipswich and Norwich Thorpe), 'The Tynesider' (King's Cross-Newcastle) and the 'Capitals United' (Paddington-Cardiff). New cross-country services were also introduced between Newcastle and Lowestoft and between Bournemouth West and Sheffield. All former SR lines west of Exeter came under the control of the Western Region and the Didcot, Newbury & Southampton line, and the Reading-Basingstoke line moved from Western Region to Southern Region control.

On the Southern Region at Southampton the new Ocean Liner Terminal was opened and, on 5 June, Bo Peep Tunnel, at St Leonards, was reopened after more than six months of closure due to subsidence and cracks found in November 1949.

On 27 August, there was a serious accident at Penmaenmawr in North Wales when a collision between the 'Irish Mail' hauled by 'Royal Scot' No 46119 *Lancashire Fusilier* and a light engine, No 42885, resulted in the loss of six lives.

Following the fire on a train at Penmanshiel in 1949, another fire broke out on a Glasgow to Euston express on Beattock Summit on 8 June, this time spreading to two coaches. This followed a rather alarming accident, also on the Scottish Region, on 20 January, at Beith, when the only through service of the day from Glasgow St Enoch overran the station, crashed through the buffers, and crossed the main road before coming to rest.

On 7 October the Talyllyn Railway closed, to be followed just three days later by the formation of the now highly-successful Talyllyn Railway Preservation Society. Later in the year, on 2 December, the ex-SE&CR Sheppey Light Railway, in Kent, closed to all traffic.

The last train comprised a two-coach articulated set and an eight-wheel utility van hauled by 'R1' class 0-4-4T No 31705

carrying a wreath. The train carried a coffin bedecked in a signalman's cap, a wooden model locomotive, a bunch of tulips and a wreath of cabbage-leaves decorated with potatoes, beetroot and onions.

From the Great Eastern Section of the Eastern Region, Woodhead electrics Nos 26001-3 were moved to Ilford on 3 November for trials over the Ilford-Shenfield route.

On the preservation scene ex-Shropshire & Montgomery Railway 0-4-2WT *Gazelle* was saved and sent to the Royal Engineers' Longmoor Museum of Transportation. This locomotive was constructed in 1893.

On 5 June British Railways introduced new standard headlight codes throughout Britain (except on the Southern Region). This resulted in 10 differing lamp combination positions for various types of traffic.

Top right:
The 4.20pm Carlisle-Manchester Victoria stopping train, hauled by LMS '5XP' unrebuilt 4-6-0 'Patriot' No 45537 *Private E. Sykes VC*, approaches Clifton, south of Penrith, on 11 June 1950. The locomotive is in dark green livery and bears the 'lion' totem on the tender. *E. D. Bruton*

Bottom right:
In North Wales, LMS 'Royal Scot' No 46127 *Old Contemptibles* is seen near Bethesda Junction during the summer of 1950. The 'Royal Scots', introduced in 1943, were Stanier rebuilds of 1927 Fowler locomotives. *J. D. Mills*

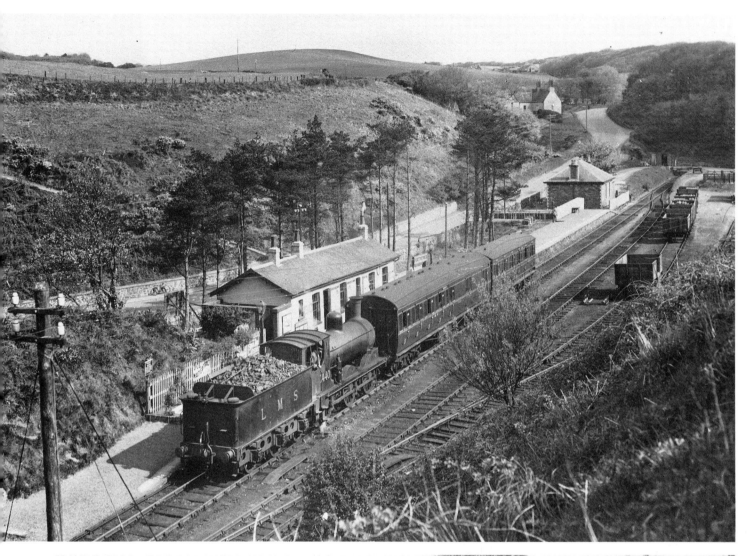

Top left:
A perfect 'modellers' location — Portpatrick, in southwest Scotland. The branch from Stranraer to this coastal location closed to passengers on 6 May 1950 and, just prior to closure, ex-Caley Drummond 0-6-0 'Jumbo' No 17440 prepares to leave for Stranraer with a two-coach train. No 17440 was withdrawn on closure of the line to passengers. *BR (Scottish Region)*

Bottom left:
Shunting duties at Aylesbury on 22 August 1950 are carried out by ex-LNER Thompson-designed Class L1 2-6-4T No 67714. This was a Neasden-based locomotive which, at the time, had an allocation of well over 30 members of this particular class.
E. C. Griffith

Above:
Ex-GCR Robinson Pacific tanks were the mainstay of Marylebone Chiltern line services for many years before being replaced by Thompson 'L1' 2-6-4Ts — these eventually succumbed to the diesel multiple-unit. Classified 'A5' by the LNER, 21 of the 4-6-2Ts were originally built by the GCR although a further 23 were constructed between 1923 and 1926 after the Grouping. No 69821 is seen here with a up local train, on 20 February 1950, at Harefield.
E. R. Wethersett

Right:
In May 1950, Great Western '42xx' class 2-8-0T No 4298 pulls away from the wharves at Fowey in Cornwall with empty china clay wagons for St Blazey. *B. A. Butt*

Left:
An interesting view showing the Ilkley branch from Skipton crossing the ex-Midland Leeds-Carlisle main line just east of Skipton. Two LNER Class J39 0-6-0s are seen double-heading a goods train from Skipton on 23 June 1950 whilst a cattle train is seen on the Midland line below. *H. Weston*

Below:
On 10 October 1950, 'Dean Goods' No 2401 heads a northbound train over the Mid-Wales line, and is pictured near Erwood. At the end of August 1950, 48 of these Wolverhampton-built 67-year old locomotives were still in service, 20 of these on the Cambrian. *J. F. Russell-Smith*

Top right:
Two Southern 'Paddleboxes', Nos 444 and 447 accompany the now-preserved 'West Country' Pacific No 34023 *Blackmore Vale* at Nine Elms shed early in 1950. The 'T14' class 4-6-0 'Paddleboxes' were rebuilt from Drummond locomotives introduced in 1911. They ended their days at Nine Elms. *Lewis Coles*

Centre right:
A Southampton-Fawley goods train passes through Southampton Central on 14 October 1950 with Class E4 0-6-2T No 32491 in command. *Pursey C. Short*

Bottom right:
Displaying its number on the back of the bunker, 'J1' Pacific tank locomotive No 32325 leaves Tunbridge Wells West, on 1 June 1950 with the 1.57pm train for Lewes. The ex-LB&SCR Marsh 4-6-2T was formerly named *Abergavenny* and was built in 1910. *E. R. Wethersett*

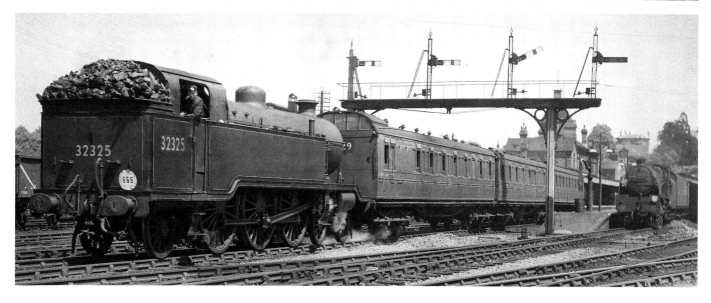

Building Standards

The first British Railways Standard steam locomotive was completed at Crewe Works on 2 January 1951. This was Pacific locomotive No 70000 *Britannia* and its naming took place at Marylebone station. During May, the first of the Standard '73xxx' class 4-6-0s emerged from Derby Works and was allocated to Derby and during the same month Class 4 Standard No 75000 was out-shopped from Swindon Works. By July, Brighton Works were turning out the Standard '80xxx' 2-6-4 tanks, some of the early ones being allocated to Tunbridge Wells. The early 'Britannias' were allocated to the Eastern Region (Stratford and Norwich in particular) and these were followed by a Western Region-allocated batch which were almost instantly loaned to the London Midland Region — the Standards had arrived with a vengeance!

On the non-steam front, the second gas turbine locomotive, built by Metro-Vickers for the Western Region, No 18100, was hauled from Trafford Park to Swindon on 15/16 December and of the three new 1Co-Co1 diesel locomotives, No 10201 left Ashford Works — built for main line expresses on the Southern Region. Also on the Southern Region, the 'USA' 0-6-0Ts used at Southampton Docks were experiencing firebox problems — the steel boxes wearing out quickly. To overcome temporarily the shortage of motive power, 'E1' 0-6-0Ts Nos 32138 and 32689 were imported. A 'Terrier' from Fratton was even tried on the docks but proved unsuccessful due to inadequate braking power and weight.

November 1951 saw the extinction of the GWR's 'Bulldog' class — a class of locomotive introduced in 1898. The last to go was No 3454 *Skylark*, allocated to Reading, along with No 3453 *Seagull* which was withdrawn earlier the same month.

Sadly, during 1951, the death was announced of one of the famous Chief Mechanical Engineers — A. H. Peppercorn — who held the post for the LNER and British Railways Eastern and North Eastern regions from 1946 until the post was abolished in 1949. He designed fine locomotives such as the 'A1' and 'A2' Pacifics — powerhouses of their time.

New coaching stock started to appear on the scene in March. The 1951 building programme announced 12 types of standard corridor coaches with the widest possible route availability, all with automatic couplers and double-bolster bogies. On 15 March five examples were put on display at Marylebone, each coming from a different workshop — Derby, Doncaster, York, Eastleigh and Wolverton.

On the preservation scene it was announced that GWR 4-6-0 No 4003 *Lode Star* (built Swindon, 1907) and Kirtley 2-4-0 No 20002 (built Derby, 1866) should be preserved and as 1951 was 'Festival of Britain' year, BR Standard Pacific No 70004 *William Shakespeare* arrived at the South Bank site on 2 April for display in the exhibition.

Owing to non-viability, 1951 saw 133 branch lines earmarked for closure and some that met this fate during the year included the North Sunderland Railway

(LNER), Llantrisant-Cowbridge (ex-GWR), Bangor-Bethesda (ex-L&NWR), Lampeter-Aberayron (ex-GWR), Quaker's Yard-Merthyr (ex-GWR) and Kington-New Radnor (ex-GWR). The ex-L&NWR station at Oxford (Rewley Road) also met a similar fate on 1 October. The ex-NER engine shed at Cudworth (53E) also closed in 1951.

On the narrow-gauge front the Talyllyn Railway was reopened by the Talyllyn Railway Preservation Society from Towyn to Rhydyronen on 14 May — only seven months after the society was formed to save the line.

Even more named trains were introduced in 1951. These included the 'Red Rose' (Euston-Liverpool), the 'Heart of Midlothian' (King's Cross-York and Edinburgh), the 'Merchant Venturer' (Paddington-Bath and Bristol), the 'William Shakespeare' (Paddington-Wolverhampton, which had through coaches to Stratford-upon-Avon) and the 'Royal Wessex' (Waterloo-Bournemouth and Weymouth). In June 1951 the 'Thanet Belle' was renamed the 'Kentish Belle'.

Signalling was updated at York in April when colour-light signals were installed, and the last dc signalbox on the London Transport system was taken out of service on 17 November. Also on London Transport the first new tube stock to be built since the war arrived at West Ruislip, on 16 November — the first of 91 new cars destined for the Bakerloo and Northern lines.

Left:
Prior to the removal of the overall roof at Cannon Street station, Southern 'L1' 4-4-0 No 31787 prepares to leave the terminus with the 12.05pm Sunday working to Charing Cross in October 1951. These Maunsell locomotives, built in 1926, were all withdrawn between 1959 and 1961. *Brian Morrison*

Right:
The morning Class D fish train from Maiden Lane (King's Cross) heads north from Hadley Wood North Tunnel on a frosty 14 April 1951. LNER Gresley 'K3/2' class Mogul No 61868 pounds up the 1 in 200 gradient at around 30mph. A stipulation on Class D express freight, livestock, perishables or ballast trains was that at least one third of the wagons in the train should be vacuum-braked and connected to the locomotive. *E. D. Bruton*

Below:
On 16 July 1951, Eastern Region Class C13 4-4-2T No 67439 scampers through Romiley with a Manchester (London Road)-Hayfield working. The greater part of Manchester (London Road) station was utilised for LMS trains to Crewe, Liverpool and the northwest. *Tom Lewis*

Top left:
An interesting view of Camden Bank just out of Euston shows the LMS main line diesel No 10001 ascending the bank with the 5.05pm Euston-Blackpool express during 1951.
F. R. Hebron/Copyright Rail Archive Stephenson

Left:
The 'one-off' Gresley 'W1' class streamlined 4-6-4 locomotive No 60700 drifts down the 1 in 200 incline at Ganwick on a parcels train as it heads for King's Cross on 8 September 1951. This locomotive is the 1937 rebuild of the former 4-6-4 No 10000 of 1929, an experimental high-pressure four-cylinder Compound with a marine-type boiler. No 60700 is seen here in the BR experimental dark blue livery. *E. D. Bruton*

Above:
A typical Southern rural scene on 7 June 1951, as the 4.19pm Horsham-Brighton train arrives at West Grinstead hauled by Class D3 0-4-4T No 32372. This class was introduced by Billinton for the LB&SCR and by 1951 all surviving members of the class were fitted for push-pull operation. *E. C. Griffith*

Right:
Southern 'C' class 0-6-0 No 31724 heads a Holborn Viaduct-Dover freight, via Maidstone East, and is seen passing through Chislehurst in July 1951. These Wainwright locomotives were built for the SE&CR and one member of the class, No 31685, was converted to a saddle tank.
Brian Morrison

Above:
Hauling an extra long mixed Toton-Cricklewood freight, ex-LMS Beyer-Garratt 2-6-6-2T, No 47995 passes Chiltern Green, south of Luton, on 28 July 1951. *E. D. Bruton*

Left:
In the evening sunshine, Great Western 4-6-0 'Star' No 4042 *Prince Albert* leaves Bristol Temple Meads with the 5.32pm train to Weston-super-Mare in September 1951. The author was once the proud owner of one of the nameplates from this locomotive. The 'Stars' could be seen with steampipes 'tucked in', as in this view, with 'Castle'-style versions or with no steampipe visible. *J. D. Mills*

Below:
The Crewe Works shunter, 0-4-2ST No 47862, was difficult to capture on film but is seen here carrying out shunting duties within the works complex. This unusual locomotive, built by the L&NWR in 1901, is pictured on 28 April 1951. *H. C. Casserley*

Harrow & Wealdstone

Probably the event that first comes to mind when looking at 1952 is the dreadful Harrow & Wealdstone accident, which resulted in 112 people losing their lives and 354 sustaining injuries. Ten more died later from these injuries. This tragic day — 8 October — saw a double collision as the local passenger train from Tring to Euston crossed the up slow line to the up fast line stopping in the up platform. This commuter train was packed with 800 passengers with more waiting on the station when, pounding out of the patchy fog, came LMS Stanier Pacific No 46242 *City of Glasgow* having passed two signals at danger, hauling the Perth-Euston overnight sleeper, at almost 60mph. The standing commuter train was hit with such force that the last three coaches were compressed into the space of one. Although the Harrow signalman put all signals at danger he was too late to stop the Euston-Liverpool/Manchester express double-headed by Stanier Pacific No 46202 *Princess Anne* and 'Jubilee' No 45637 *Windward Islands*. This express struck the derailed *City of Glasgow*, mounted and crossed the down platform, cutting the electric current, stopping an approaching electric train. The impact created by the two express trains created wreckage 45yd long, 18yd wide and 30ft high between station platforms and at the bottom of this pile of wreckage was *City of Glasgow*. It was one of the worst British railway accidents of all time. No 46202, only named *Princess Anne* during the year on conversion from an experimental 'turbo' locomotive in the August, was damaged beyond repair as was No 45637 *Windward Islands*, but, remarkably, *City of Glasgow* lived on to October 1963 after over 1½ million miles in service. However, on paper *Princess Anne* was not officially withdrawn until May 1954!

Enamel station nameboards (totems) started to appear in 1952, each region having its own distinctive colour as follows: LMR (maroon), ER (dark blue), WR (chocolate brown), SR (green), NER (orange) and ScR (light blue). King's Cross station was 100 years old on 14 October 1952; in fact the name was taken from a large octagonal monument known as 'The King's Cross' which was erected in 1830 to commemorate King George IV and the House of Hanover. King's Cross station cost £123,000 to build.

From late September to early November certain platforms were lengthened at Euston and a new powerbox was installed together with colour-light signals and an improved track layout. This resulted in certain main line Euston-bound trains being directed to St Pancras and other services being temporarily withdrawn. Also on the London Midland Region, the ex-L&NWR engine shed at Wigan (Lower Ince) finally closed.

On 5 April the last passenger service over the ex-Stratford-on-Avon & Midland Junction Railway ran as the service from Stratford-upon-Avon and Blisworth was withdrawn — the end of another era as this was the final section of this interesting railway. Other closures to passengers included Wells-next-the-Sea to Heacham and Wellington to Coalport (2 June), the Framlingham branch (3 November), Kirkby Stephen to Tebay (ex-NER) on 1 December and, also on that date, the Canterbury to Whitstable line closed completely. The Whaley Bridge incline also closed to traffic, on 9 April 1952.

The appropriately named 'Bisley Bullet' was finally withdrawn on 19 July. This service from Brookwood to Bisley had, as usual, during 1952 operated during the National Rifle Association Shoot from 28 June with 23 trains operating each weekday. The author was on duty at the shoot and witnessed the last train, hauled by 'M7' 0-4-4T No 30027. It was a sad day and the band played 'Auld Lang Syne' and the two-coach train was decked with flags. In fact, the guard on the train was also the guard of the last train to run beyond Bisley to Deepcut in 1921, prior to the track being pulled up over that section.

On 3 February, electric locomotive-hauled freight and coal trains were introduced on the newly electrified Wath to Dunford sections of the Woodhead route, using Class EM1 Bo-Bo 1,500V dc electric locomotives which had been tried out on the Ilford-Shenfield route in Essex during 1950.

New locomotives introduced in 1952 included the first 'Clans', Pacific locomotives designed at Derby. Other members of the class planned but never built were earmarked for the Southern Region. As new 'Clans' appeared old 'Clans' disappeared, as the last 'Clan Goods' 4-6-0 was scrapped, No 57954 from Inverness, in October 1952, after 34 years of service. These locomotives, built for the Highland Railway, were fitted with Walschaerts valve-gear and were superheated.

On 21 January, the 'Fell' diesel-mechanical locomotive, No 10100, entered regular passenger service between Derby and Manchester although tests continued during the coming months, after which it was regularly used on Manchester-St Pancras trains.

From Swindon came the Class 3 2-6-2Ts in the '82xxx' series. Eventually these were scattered far and wide throughout the BR network. Work was also carried out at Swindon Works early in the year on two significant 'Castles' when the nameplates and numberplates from No 4082 *Windsor Castle* were transferred to No 7013 *Bristol Castle* to enable *Windsor Castle* to be used to haul King George VI's funeral train on 15 February. This was necessary as the original *Windsor Castle* was under general overhaul at the time and could not be made ready in time for the funeral. Having swopped plates for the occasion, they were never returned to their original locomotives.

The Western Region's second gas turbine locomotive, No 18100, commenced test runs from Swindon to the West Country in March, sometimes hauling up to 18 coaches. It was soon to be regularly seen on the down 'Merchant Venturer' and the up 'Bristolian'.

The ex-GWR streamlined diesel railcars were considered for possible use on the Eastern Region's Lincolnshire branches, where car No 20 commenced trials from Boston shed on 30 September. It operated on the Mablethorpe loop, the Skegness branch and the Woodhall Junction-Firsby loop, in addition to being used on the Boston-Sleaford-Grantham line and the Grantham-Lincoln branch — often with a trailing load. On 24 August No 20 was moved north and tried out between Leeds and Harrogate — a Reading driver was used.

On 9 November 1952, BR placed their order for the first 30 Standard '9F' 2-10-0s scheduled for introduction in 1953. These would include 10 which were to be fitted with Franco-Crosti boilers and allocated to the Western Region and the Eastern Region-allocated '9F's would be fitted with 6,000gal tenders. Although it was originally intended that the Southern Region would receive five '9F's, fitted with Westinghouse brakes, for working through Continental traffic, it was now decided that they would receive no '9F's at all.

Another new named train appeared on 2 July 1952. This was the 'Cunarder' which was to run between Waterloo and Southampton Ocean Terminal. It was a first-class express service to coincide with the arrival at Southampton of either the *Queen Mary* or *Queen Elizabeth*. The first 'Cunarder' was hauled by 'Merchant Navy' Pacific No 35004 *Cunard White Star*. Not to be outdone, on 8 July the maiden trip of another Southampton-bound train, the 'Statesman', introduced to meet the *United*

States liner, was 'all Pullman' and was hauled by 'West Country' Light Pacific No 34007 on its inaugural run as the 'Merchant Navy' Pacific, *United States Line* was in Eastleigh Works at the time. Both newly-named trains carried roof boards and decorated white shields on the front of the engine.

On 29 November, the first push-button route-selecting signalling control system in Britain was brought into use by London Transport at Ealing Broadway.

Above:
Bulleid/English Electric diesel-electric locomotive No 10201 brings the 13.00 Waterloo-Plymouth express under Battledown Viaduct at Worting Junction, near Basingstoke, on 8 September 1952. Introduced in the previous year, No 10201 was constructed at Ashford Works and, machinery-wise, was generally similar to the 1,600hp Co-Cos Nos 10000 and 10001 of the LMS, but had a 1Co-Co1 wheel arrangement and engines rated at 1,750hp. The class of three locomotives was withdrawn in 1963 and eventually broken up at Cashmores of Great Bridge in 1968. *Brian Morrison*

Left:
Ex-Cleobury Mortimer & Ditton Priors Railway 0-6-0PT *Burwarton*, was numbered 29 when the CM&DPR was taken over by the GWR. Sporting its 'spark arrestor' chimney, No 29 rattles down the incline through Burwarton station with a train of empties from Ditton Priors on 18 September 1952. *Geoffrey F. Bannister*

Above:
Great Western 'Castle' No 111 *Viscount Churchill* was a rebuild of the GWR's only Pacific locomotive, *The Great Bear*, in 1924, retaining its old number, 111. Withdrawn in 1953 after spending its latter years allocated to Laira depot, *Viscount Churchill* is seen near Uphill Junction with a Sunday Plymouth-Paddington working on 13 April 1952. *J. D. Mills*

Right:
Ex-Great Northern Gresley 'N2' 0-6-2T No 69575 emerges from Copenhagen Tunnel during 1952 with empty stock from King's Cross. This locomotive was a left-hand drive version whereas 'N2s' built eight years earlier were right-hand drive locomotives. *F. R. Hebron/Copyright Rail Archive Stephenson*

Below:
Southern 'M7' 0-4-4T No 30048 leaves Bramber station on 27 August 1952 with a Horsham-Brighton train. This class of L&SWR locomotives was designed by Drummond and 105 were built between 1896 and 1911. No 30048 is fitted for push-pull working, an adaption which commenced in 1925.
E. R. Wethersett

Left:
A typical Scottish rural scene in 1952 showing ex-GNSR Class D41 Johnson 4-4-0 No 62248 leaving Craigellachie, with an Elgin-Keith freight train. This class of locomotive was to last only one more year and the line closed to passengers on 6 May 1968. *W. J. Verden Anderson/Copyright Rail Archive Stephenson*

Below left:
The 9.15am Charing Cross-Dover express heads south between Grove Park and Hither Green on 22 May 1952. At the head of the train is Southern 'Schools' class 4-4-0 No 30939 *Leatherhead* fitted with multiple jet blast-pipe and large diameter chimney by Bulleid. *Lewis Coles*

Right:
In the early 1950s, the first members of the 'Britannia' Pacific class, introduced in 1951, were allocated to the Eastern Region for East Anglian express duties. This view shows No 70003 *John Bunyan* recovering from adverse signals with a Liverpool Street – Norwich/Great Yarmouth express on 10 May 1952. The train is passing Mountnessing Junction where the Shenfield electrification originally ended, as can be seen. *Brian Morrison*

Below:
With Fell Head dominating the skyline at Dillicar and with the River Lune beside the railway, 'Clan' class Pacific No 72001 *Clan Cameron* storms north with a combined 'Scottish Express' from Manchester and Liverpool as it descends the 1 in 425 gradient in preparation for a water pick-up at Dillicar troughs before entering Tebay for the climb up Shap on 5 June 1952. *E. D. Bruton*

A 'Flood' of Closures

Due to terrible floods on 31 January and 1 February 1953, the Kent Coast line was cut between Faversham and Whitstable and between Herne Bay and Birchington. On the Eastern Region floods cut the Tilbury line between Benfleet and Leigh on Sea. Other BR lines cut by floods included Mablethorpe-Willoughby, the Fakenham-Wells-next-the-Sea, Beccles-Lowestoft and the Allhallows-on-Sea, the Brightlingsea, Clacton and Sheerness branches. Where tracks ran close to the sea in East Anglia, the severe gales coincided with a very high spring tide resulting in track being swept away as one high tide followed another – the army were called out to help. Both Yarmouth South Town station and shed were put out of action and Yarmouth Vauxhall station and shed were temporarily flooded. Some lines never reopened — a sad ending!

There were line closures in abundance during the year such as, on the London Midland Region, Low Gill-Clapham and Swadlincote Junction-Bretby; on the Eastern Region, the Mid-Suffolk Light Railway, in the northeast Malton-Driffield and Alnwick-Ilderton; on the Southern, Chichester-Midhurst; on the Scottish, Blantyre-Strathaven; and on the Western, Glastonbury-Wells, to name but a few. Passenger services were also withdrawn from Ruthin-Corwen (February), Highworth-Swindon (March), Cromer Beach-Mundesley (April), Bury St Edmunds-Thetford and the Gosport Branch (both June).

The last 'Saint' class 4-6-0, No 2920 *Saint David* was withdrawn from traffic in October 1953, its last passenger turn being on 1 October from Hereford to Worcester. Sadly, she was never preserved. Another 'last' was No 54650, withdrawn in September 1953 from Hamilton shed. This was the final ex-Caledonian 4-6-0 to succumb. The last 'Small Ben', No 54398 *Ben Alder*, also ended its days. This Highland locomotive, one of 20 designed by Peter Drummond, built between 1898 and 1906, was the final Highland engine in service to carry a name.

New locomotives appeared in the form of Standard Class 4 2-6-0s in the '76xxx' series, from Horwich Works, Class 2 2-6-0s in the '78xxx' series, from Darlington, and the Class 2 '84xxx' 2-6-2Ts, from Crewe. Nos 76000-04 were allocated to the Scottish Region on delivery, Nos 76005-19 to the Southern and Nos 76020-24 (which were built at Doncaster) to the North Eastern Region.

Modernisation of Sunderland station took place removing the 75-year old roof, replacing it with a modern glazed version and, on 24 August, after three months of closure due to flooding, the Ballachulish branch from Connel Ferry, near Oban, reopened 50 years after the line's original opening date.

Named trains were again in the news as the 'Pembroke Coast Express' from Paddington-Pembroke Dock was introduced. Others included the 'Elizabethan' — a non-stop London-Edinburgh express taking 6¾hr (from 29 June 1953). This train was the old 'Capitals Ltd' but was renamed in honour of Her Majesty Queen Elizabeth II in this year of her Coronation. Other newcomers were the 'Man of Kent' — from Charing Cross to Folkestone/Sandwich (in June 1953), the 'Manxman Express' from Euston to Liverpool to connect with sailings from Liverpool to the Isle of Man and the 'Empress Voyager' named in May 1953, which connected with Canadian Pacific Line sailings — a boat train also ran from Euston to Liverpool.

A 'named' freight service was reintroduced — the former prewar LNER 'Green Arrow' (another May introduction) which enabled traders to register full wagon-loads of freight to ports for export.

A new cheap overnight service from London to Scotland known as the 'Starlight Special' (departing on Friday nights) came into being from St Pancras-Glasgow St Enoch and from Marylebone-Edinburgh Waverley from 10 April, returning on the Saturday night. The return fare was 70s (£3.50p) as against the standard fare of 114s.8d (£5.73p). Today the normal fare in 1992 is £114 standard-class return. There again, in 1953, if you were earning £1,000 a year you were probably a company director — it is all relative, is it not?

From Eastleigh, new 2-EPB electric units were introduced to the Southern Region during 1953 and on 19 September a 4-EPB unit ran through the Cobham line bay at Guildford killing the assistant stationmaster. On 17 August, on the London Midland Region restoration of electric passenger services took place on the Lancaster, Morecambe and Heysham line after the change-over to 50 cycles ac, using ex-L&NWR electric sets.

On the signalling front, the last electropneumatic semaphore signal on the London Transport system was withdrawn on 21 November and further Metropolitan

Line electric locomotives received names. These were No 6 *William Penn* and No 11 *George Romney*.

A surprising locomotive transfer occurred in 1953 when, due to the Bedford Simplex petrol shunter, No 27, being out of action during April, Reading Signal Works received from South Wales the ex-Ystalyfera Steel Works 0-6-0 No 1 *Hercules* as it was found that the original replacement locomotive GWR 0-4-0PT No 1153 proved to be too heavy for the works track.

On 8 April, a fatal accident occurred on the London Underground when an eastbound Epping train collided with a stationary train in a tunnel and, on 8 August, the down 'Royal Scot' was derailed near Abington (between Carstairs and Beattock Summit), seven of the rear coaches leaving the rails. Incredible as it may seem, only seven passengers required hospital treatment. The first part of the train proceeded to Glasgow running four hours late. Other West Coast main line trains were directed over the Waverley route.

August was a bad month for accidents in 1953 as on 15 August the 7.36am train from Manchester Victoria to Bacup (hauled by a 2-6-4T locomotive) collided with an electric Bury-Manchester train. Sadly 10 were killed in this incident as the first coach of the electric train plummeted from the viaduct into the river, 90ft below. On 16 August LMS 'Jubilee' No 45699 *Galatea*, hauling an eight-coach train south of Tamworth, was thrown on its side after becoming derailed.

To end on an unusual note, in Eire, the CIE tested a turf-burning locomotive of a frightening appearance to create a design that could be steamed on turf or oil — needless to say Mr Bulleid was involved. Tests proved that the 'K2' 2-6-0 converted to peat burning used around twice as much peat as coal.

Above:
Near Penhargard on the ex-L&SWR Wenford Bridge-Wadebridge line, on 3 September 1953, one of the 2-4-0 Beattie well-tanks, No 30585, long associated with this line hauls the 10.03am Wadebridge-Wenford Bridge freight through the Cornish countryside. These fascinating 1874 Beattie-designed locomotives were, between 1884 and 1935, rebuilt by Adams, Urie and Maunsell. *S. C. Nash*

Right:
A push-pull working, under the control of ex-SE&CR 'H' Class 0-4-4T, No 31164 arrives at Hildenborough, just north of Tonbridge, in May 1953. The train is the 5.05pm Tonbridge-Dunton Green service. A typical Southern rural scene. *Brian Morrison*

Above:
With empty wagons, Great Western 'Dukedog' No 9001 hauls a Sunday engineer's train from Birmingham Snow Hill's down main platform on 13 September 1953. The train is a Class 'C' express ballast train forming a through working to Oswestry. The 'Dukedogs' incorporated parts from the 'Bulldogs', No 9001 carrying the frames of No 3412. No 9001 was withdrawn seven months after this picture was taken. *E. D. Bruton*

Right:
An ex-NER Class N8 Worsdell 0-6-2T, No 69390 attempts to move a heavy stock train from Newcastle Central on 24 June 1953. By now this class had reduced to eight members from a class that originally totalled 62.
K. W. Wightman

Right:
Carmine & cream-liveried Great Western railcars Nos 33 and 36 enter Bristol Temple Meads station in June 1953, still sporting the AEC crest on the front. These two AEC railcars were, as seen, flat-ended enabling a composite third to be placed between them to provide additional accommodation. In fact prior to No 35 being destroyed by fire Nos 35 and 36 would work together but after the withdrawal of No 35, railcar No 33 was adapted accordingly to work with No 36. *E. V. Fry/Copyright Rail Archive Stephenson*

Below:
The only 2-8-8-2T Beyer-Garratt locomotive was built for the LNER in 1925 — 'U1' class No 69999. It was fitted with Walschaerts valve-gear and is seen on 11 October 1953 on a test run with a 43-wagon load between Hadfield and Crowden on the ex-Great Central Woodhead route. Having recently been converted to oil burning, she hauls her load from Dewsnap Yard (Guide Bridge) to Crowden and back in order to test the locomotive's steaming capabilities. *Ian Allan Library*

Left:
Another unusual locomotive was 0-4-0ST No 41516, one of 28 of a class designed by Johnson for the Midland Railway and built between 1883 and 1903. They were built for dock shunting duties and for working in brewery yards, hence its appearance here on 15 May 1953 inside Burton shed, in 'ale' country. *H. C. Casserley*

Left:
Emerging from Copenhagen Tunnel on 11 July 1953 is ex-LNER 'V2' 2-6-2 No 60877, with an express for Hull. These impressive Gresley-designed locomotives were introduced for mixed traffic work but were extensively used on passenger duties. *Brian Morrison*

Below:
Excessive power for a three-coach train as ex-LNER 'B12/3' 4-6-0s, Gresley rebuilds of a Holden Great Eastern design, Nos 61569 and 61571 (piloting), pull out of Cambridge on 19 August 1953 with the 11.17am train for Ipswich. The collection of coaching stock in tow is certainly a 'mixed' bunch and appears to have been rustled together at the last minute. The stock is made up of a GNR brake composite, an NER clerestory third and an LMS vehicle. *Brian Morrison*

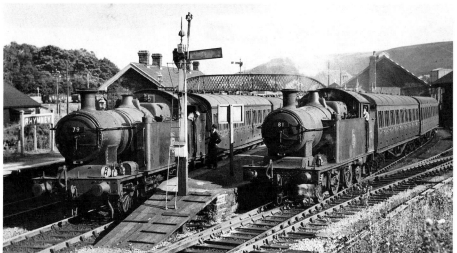

Top right:
Ex-Caley McIntosh 0-6-0T No 56331 shunts Perth North Yard during the summer of 1953. The stovepipe chimney was a later addition to certain members of this class. *W. J. Verden Anderson/Copyright Rail Archive Stephenson*

Right:
Two ex-Rhymney Railway 0-6-2T locomotives, Nos 79 and 81 (ex-RR Nos 36 and 38) await departure from Rhymney station on 1 August 1953. A total of 123 Rhymney Railway locomotives were absorbed by the GWR on 1 January 1922. The two pictured here were built in 1921 by Hurry Riches but acquired taper boilers later at Swindon. *W. Potter*

Below:
In 1949, British Railways Western Region introduced the new Hawksworth short-wheelbased 0-6-0 '15xx' class pannier tanks for heavy shunting duties. Only 10 of these locomotives were built and No 1502 is seen, near Kennington Junction, near Oxford with a Class K freight heading towards Hinksey Yard on 18 July 1953. *E. D. Bruton*

'The Duke's in Town

Built in 1954 as a prototype of the new Standard design for main line top-link duties, No 71000 *Duke of Gloucester* (now preserved) emerged from Crewe Works. This three-cylinder Pacific fitted with Caprotti valve-gear, originally allocated to the London Midland Region, was sadly the only one of its kind built due to the termination of the steam locomotive building programme on British Railways. 'The Duke' was withdrawn in 1962 — a very short life in service for this controversial Standard 8P Pacific – but its day would come!.

During 1954, a total of 312 new locomotives were built, comprising 237 steam, 69 diesel and 6 electrics. The electric locomotives, built at Gorton, Manchester, were numbered 27001-27006 and were introduced for working passenger services over the Woodhead route from Sheffield to Manchester. Over this route, during 1954, the new Woodhead Tunnel was opened on 3 June followed by the closure of the old tunnel on 14 June.

The inaugural service, on 14 September, was hauled by No 27000 (built in 1953) which reached speeds of up to 72mph at Deepcar. However this was almost upstaged by 'A4' Pacific No 60008 *Dwight D. Eisenhower* which hauled guests travelling from King's Cross to Sheffield for the opening ceremony as, despite a diversion at Potters Bar, a 30mph pw check at Corby Glen and a stop at Retford, she still reached Sheffield in 2hr 51min, just one minute slower than the best non-stop time recorded by the GNR when they were trying to outdo the GCR.

New steam locomotives constructed in 1954, in addition to 'The Duke', included 'Britannias' and '9F's from Crewe, '73xxx' and '80xxx' Standards from Derby, 75xxx, 77xxx and 82xxx Standards from Swindon, in addition to '16xx' class pannier tanks, '76xxx' and '80xxx' Standards from Doncaster, '78xxx' Standards from Darlington, '80xxx' Standard tanks from Brighton and one locomotive from Horwich Works, No 47009. From the Hunslet factory at Leeds came the '94xx' pannier tanks for the Western Region and Bagnalls produced 10 '84xx' class panniers, also for the Western Region.

Darlington produced 34 diesel shunters in the '13xxx' series, and Derby, 20 of the same type, all destined to work all regions except the Western. The third 2,000hp 1Co-Co1 locomotive, No 10203, emerged from Brighton Works; the Drewry factory produced five 0-6-0 200hp shunters for the

ER, numbered 11111-5; Hunslet built three 0-4-0 153hp shunters, Nos 11500-2, also for the ER and North British constructed Nos 11702-7, 0-6-0 200hp shunters for the Scottish Region.

On the rolling stock side 53,000 wagons were constructed, 1,820 passenger coaches and 930 non-passengers coaching stock vehicles.

New two-car lightweight diesel unit stock, painted in Brunswick Green with cream lining, appeared at Marylebone in April and made a 'demonstration' trip to Beaconsfield and back. This was followed by trials in the West Riding of Yorkshire where they were scheduled for services in the summer timetable. The vehicles were numbered in the 79xxx series and were built at Derby.

New two-car electric units were completed at Eastleigh Works in 1954 for South Tyneside services in the northeast.

Locomotives withdrawn during 1954 included the two last survivors of the Brecon & Merthyr Railway, Nos 434 and 435 (ex-B&M Nos 48 and 49). Also on the Western Region, the last ex-Cambrian 0-6-0, No 855, was withdrawn in October, and four old GWR favourites ended their days during the year — No 1 *Hercules*, No 5 *Portishead*, No 359 *Hilda* and ex-Cleobury Mortimer & Ditton Priors pannier tank No 29. Other significant withdrawals included LMS 4-6-0 No 54639 from 66C (Hamilton) — the last in its class, and No 46202 *Princess Anne*, out of use since the Harrow & Wealdstone disaster. GWR No 92 (ex-Rhymney Railway No 34), 0-4-4T No 58038 from 33A (Plaistow), LNER 'J2' 0-6-0 No 65020 and LNER 0-4-0T 'Y8' class No 68091 were also withdrawn, each the last in their class.

On the preservation front ex-L&NWR saddle tank No 1439 was painted by ICI Ltd in its original livery and presented to the British Transport Commission in June 1954.

In March colour-light signalling was completed from Norwood Junction to East Croydon as was the third stage of the London-Brighton resignalling scheme which commenced in 1950. This resulted in a new signalbox which replaced two manually-operated boxes housing 155 levers. Following the completion of a £300,000 improvement scheme at Euston, reconstruction work continued in 1954 on platforms 12-15, involving relaying of tracks and repositioning.

On 29 May, a commemorative plaque was unveiled at Paddington station to mark

the centenary of the station. Passenger services ceased in 1954 on the Ashbourne branch and on the ex-NER Hawes-Northallerton line and Beattock-Moffat services ceased in December. The 'Ally-Pally' passenger services also ended in 1954 when, on 3 July, LNER 'N7' No 69519 in an attempt to be the last train from Highgate, broke a coupling and left the eight coaches standing. Fortunately, No 69526 was on hand to take over. The push-pull units being used on this line were required for temporary service in the West Riding of Yorkshire pending the arrival there of the new Derby lightweight DMUs.

Depot closures included Plodder Lane (I0D), Moor Row (12E) and Bacup (26E) but it was announced that both Bradford (Hammerton Street) and Workington motive power depots were to be modified for the purpose of servicing diesel shunters and lightweight diesel trains.

The 'Cornish Riviera' celebrated its 50th birthday on 1 July 1954 and a commemorative headboard was carried in each direction during the day. The 'Bristolian' was reintroduced on 14 June to cover London to Bristol in 1¾hr. The train was hauled by No 6000 *King George V*. In June the 4.55pm Euston-Liverpool express was named 'The Shamrock' as it connected with the Belfast and Dublin steamship services. It returned from Liverpool at 8.10am.

No disastrous accidents occurred in 1954 apart from the occasional derailment, one of these, at Watford on 3 February, resulting in three Euston-bound expresses being diverted from Bletchley to Oxford, one of these trains continuing to Paddington being hauled by an LMS locomotive — No 45591 *Udaipur* — heading the 'Red Rose'. The incident at Watford involved the up 'Royal Scot' where the eighth coach was derailed in Watford Tunnel and continued for 1¾ miles before damaging paintwork at Watford Junction resulting in the ninth and 10th coaches becoming derailed, grazing an oncoming Wolverhampton express. The tunnel derailment was brought to the attention of the driver of the train by a passenger in the ninth coach pulling the communication cord.

On 12 November LNER 'J88' 0-6-0T No 68341, with a load three times that permitted for descending the bank on which it was travelling, plunged into the water at Kirkaldy Docks as she ran away down the incline. The breakdown crane, taking no chances, was held firm by three 'J88's. The retrieved No 68341 was scrapped.

Above:
Double-headed LMS 2-6-4T locomotives haul
the up 3.12pm Workington Main-Liverpool
Exchange stopping train, seen leaving Ravenglass
on 4 September 1954. The two differing designs
are clearly visible. Fowler '4MT' two-cylinder
2-6-4T No 42401 (one of a series introduced in
1933 having side window cabs with doors) is seen
piloting Stanier taper-boilered two-cylinder
'4MT' No 42427, a class introduced in 1935.
E. D. Bruton

Right:
On 1 January 1922, the GWR absorbed 275
locomotives from the Taff Vale Railway — a fleet
which included 209 0-6-2Ts. No 279, seen
shunting a freight train at Pengam Sidings in
January 1954, was a Riches '04' class locomotive
which was rebuilt by the Great Western.
S. Rickard

Above:
Dainton Bank, in South Devon, has proved to be a formidable task for locomotives over the years from Great Western days to the era of High Speed Trains. On 31 August 1954, Laira-based Great Western 'Hall' No 5964 *Wolseley Hall* climbs with comparative ease with a local train to Plymouth. *David S. Fish*

Right:
A Midlands freight working gives us a member of the small 3100 Class of 2-6-2 tanks. These five locomotives (3100-3104) were rebuilt from Class 3150 engines Nos 3173, 3156, 3181, 3155 and 3179 conversions involving replacing 5ft 8in driving wheels with 5ft 3in drivers. No 3102 leaves yards north of Wolverhampton on 20 July 1954, with a pick-up freight. *Brian Morrison*

Above:
New power for the Western Region arrived in 1949 in the form of the Brown-Boveri gas turbine locomotive No 18000. This was followed, in 1951, by No 18100, the gas turbine built by Metro-Vickers. The experimental No 18000 is seen working through Reading in 1954.
BR (Western Region)

Right:
Indicator shelters were fitted occasionally to certain locomotives to record, basically, performance. This took the form of a large box, on the front of the locomotive, with two 'circular' windows. The shelter would house one or two works engineers and equipment inside included, amongst other things, a pyrometer and chest pressure gauges. Readings would be taken in the 'indicator shelter' and one could imagine it to be 'quite warm' inside. Tests would be carried out over a few days and here we see Great Western 4-6-0 'County' No 1009 *County of Carmarthen* passing through Swindon, on 12 November 1954, on a trial run from Reading to Stoke Gifford. *R. C. H. Nash*

Right:
Great Western 'Grange' No 6817 *Gwenddwr Grange* descends the incline through the Glynn Valley with a freight on 21 April 1954. The two-cylinder Collett 4-6-0s were allocated, largely, for intermediate passenger work all over the Western Region. *B. A. Butt*

Below:
A Highbridge-Templecombe train leaves Cole, on the Somerset & Dorset line, on 4 June 1954, the two-coach train being hauled by ex-MR Johnson 0-4-4T No 58086. *W. Vaughan-Jenkins*

Above:
An LNER Pacific is seen in action near Grantshouse, just south of Penmanshiel Tunnel on 11 April 1954. No 60507 *Highland Chieftain*, an 'A2/1' 1944-rebuild, incorporating the 'V2' 2-6-2 boiler, makes easy work of a northbound freight. *W. J. Verden Anderson/Copyright Rail Archive Stephenson*

Right:
The Class Y3 four-wheeled Sentinel locomotives had two-speed gearboxes and were used by Lowestoft Engineers' Department, Ranskill Wagon Works, Boston Sleeper Depot, Cambridge Engineers' Depot and at Doncaster. In 1953 they were given departmental numbers and No 38 is pictured crossing the street in Lowestoft on 20 April 1954. *R. E. Vincent*

Below:
Having just emerged from Riddlesdown Tunnel, on 10 June 1954, Southern Maunsell-designed 'Q' class 0-6-0 No 30537 takes a train to Tunbridge Wells. The large diameter chimney was a modification included when multiple-jet blast pipes were fitted. *E. R. Wethersett*

Modernisation Programme

Early in May, the British Transport Commission announced its broad outline for the work to be put in hand in the first two years of its £1,200 million modernisation plan for British Railways. This included new diesel services, 170 new main-line diesels, Southern electrification and new fitted-brake freight wagons. One of the biggest items was for new diesel multiple units, comprising 844 vehicles, to replace steam services in East Anglia, Lincolnshire, Birmingham, Manchester, Hampshire, North Wales, between Edinburgh and Glasgow, Birmingham and Swansea, London and Hastings, Newcastle and Middlesbrough and between Birmingham and Lichfield. Diesel locomotive building plans included 40 locomotives of 600-800hp, 100 of 1,000-1,250hp and 30 of 2,000hp or over. A new railhead depot was planned for Ripple Lane and a new goods yard at Crawley in Sussex (both projects budgeted at £190,000 each). Goods yard improvements were projected at West Blyth and at Spekeland, near Liverpool.

Passenger station rebuilding plans were announced as being 'widespread' including Peterborough, Manchester Victoria, Barrow, Cannon Street, Banbury, Glasgow Central, Chichester, Weymouth and Gatwick Airport.

New rolling stock plans included 4,700 new passenger vehicles and 66,000 new freight vehicles for 1955 and around 70,000 for 1956.

In October 1955, the prototype 'Deltic' diesel-electric locomotive commenced trials. This powerful and impressive locomotive was designed by English Electric and was powered by two Napier 18-cylinder two-stroke high-speed engines of 1,650hp each. Initially, *Deltic* operated from Speke

Junction and it was soon to work Euston-Liverpool services.

On the 'steam' front, the 10 BR '9F' 2-10-0s fitted with Franco-Crosti-type boilers were delivered. Design work was carried out at Brighton but actual construction was carried out at Crewe with the majority of the Crosti '9F's being initially allocated to Wellingborough. The Franco-Crosti boiler was an Italian invention, which had been tested both in Italy and Germany, and the expected economics were in fuel consumption, where the exhaust gases were used to pre-heat the cold water in a separate 'boiler', thereby obtaining maximum heat from the fuel used.

The steam building programme for 1956 included more 2-6-0 and 4-6-0 '2MT', '4MT' and '5MT' Standards, '3MT' 2-6-2Ts, '4MT' 2-6-4Ts, '9F's and Western Region pannier tanks of '16xx' and '94xx' classes. Diesel shunters came from the Hunslet, Drewry, North British and Ruston & Hornsby stables, and 350hp diesel shunters were also built at Derby and Darlington works.

On the Western Region, Pullman cars returned to service — the first since 1929. The 'South Wales Pullman' made its inaugural run on 27 June 1955 having previously been postponed due to a footplatemen's strike. It was worked by Landore-based 'Castles', the initial run involving No 5016 *Montgomery Castle* to Swansea and No 5013 *Abergavenny Castle* on the return journey to London. The spotless Pullman rake used on the 'South Wales Pullman' included cars Nos 55, 171, 35, *Diamond*, *Cecilia*, *Zena*, *Auralia*, and No 54.

In April, Paddington station saw LMS Stanier Pacifics, the first being No 46237

City of Bristol heading the 'Merchant Venturer'. The LMS Pacific was sent to the Western Region to assess performances against Great Western 'Kings'. In May, *City of Bristol* worked the 'Cornish Riviera Express'.

The Scottish Region introduced an express freight train on 5 December. 'The Killie' was a nightly departure from Aberdeen to Kilmarnock. This train was for the rapid conveyance of merchandise traffic picking up and detaching traffic en route at Perth, Stirling, Glasgow and Irvine. Feeder services connected with 'The Killie' *en route*.

Passenger services that disappeared included those on the Tidworth branch, the Petersfield-Midhurst line, the Forfar-Arbroath line and the Rhyl-Denbigh line. In fact, the Tidworth branch from Ludgershall was taken over by the War Department on 25 November 1955.

A derailment at Sutton Coldfield on 23 January sadly resulted in 17 fatalities when a York-Bristol express was diverted to a secondary route due to track relaying on the normal route through Tamworth. Due to excessive speed, the locomotive left the track in the station with its six coaches in a tangled mess behind. Part of the station awning covered the derailed train whose engine lay on its side.

Good news for preservation occurred on 23 July when the Festiniog Railway reopened from Portmadoc to Boston Lodge following its closure eight years previous — the start of one of the most exciting preservation projects in Wales and now a tremendous tourist attraction.

On 21 November four-car lightweight diesel units commenced regular services between Middlesbrough, West Hartlepool, Sunderland and Newcastle interspersed with a few steam trains. The diesel units reduced the running times between Newcastle and Middlesbrough by up to 18min.

Left:
The Scottish hard winter is still apparent on 21 March 1955 as Brighton-built Standard '4MT' 2-6-4T No 80021 enters Ballater with the 8.11am train from Aberdeen. This branch line was closed to passengers on 28 February 1966 and prior to this Her Majesty the Queen travelled to Ballater by train when staying at Balmoral Castle, nearby. *W. J. Verden Anderson/Copyright Rail Archive Stephenson*

Right:
Still in Scotland, during the summer of 1955, the 12.30pm Mallaig-Fort William train pounds through picturesque countryside between Lochailort and Glenfinnan hauled by LNER 'K1/1' No 61997 *MacCailin Mor*. This was the only 'K1/1' locomotive, a 1945-built Thompson rebuild of a Gresley 'K4' Mogul. *W. J. Verden Anderson/Copyright Rail Archive Stephenson*

Below:
On 3 September 1955, station pilot duties at Perth are carried out by ex-Caley 0-6-0 No 57345. This large class of 'Jumbos' was introduced by Drummond in 1883 and perpetuated by Lambie and McIntosh in later years. Most of the class eventually received stovepipe chimneys as the one seen fitted here. *John Robertson*

Left:
The scene is Chinley North Junction surrounded by the rolling Derbyshire hills, and Fowler '7F' 0-8-0 No 49582 passes with an empty wagon train for the Sheffield line on 3 September 1955. *Tom Lewis*

Below left:
From the open countryside to the seaside where not only do we have the impressive sight of Great Western 'King' No 6025 *King Henry III* but what a wonderful array of 1950s motor cars parked in the car park. This September 1955 view shows the 'King' at Dawlish with an up express. *P. Ransome-Wallis*

Right:
On the West Coast main line, LMS 'Jubilee' No 45713 *Renown*, bearing a 68A shedplate denoting Carlisle (Kingmoor) prior to its 12A shedcode, climbs Beattock in 1955 with a northbound goods train. *W. J. Verden Anderson/ Copyright Rail Archive Stephenson*

Below:
On the East Coast main line, LNER 'A4' Pacific No 60021 *Wild Swan* climbs Holloway Bank from King's Cross with a down Leeds express on 9 July 1955. No 60021 was one of the eleven 'A4's fitted with a non-corridor tender. *D. M. C. Hepburn-Scott/Copyright Rail Archive Stephenson*

Goodbye 'Bertha'

In May 1956, the Lickey Incline on the Midland line, from Bromsgrove to Blackwell, lost its beloved 'Big Bertha' — the 0-10-0 Lickey Banker, No 58100. She was replaced by '9F' No 92079. The famous Lickey Banker had numerous nicknames, like 'Big Emma', or just plain 'Liz'. She was conceived at Derby Works during World War 1 but was not built until the end of 1919 running her first trial on 1 January 1920. The vast majority of her 36-year life was spent propelling trains up the 1 in 37¾ Lickey Incline and then coasting back down to Bromsgrove light engine. Her brief 'vacation' was in 1924 when she went to Wellingborough for trials on Toton-Brent coal trains. She also spent an entire year in Derby Works having a boiler change. Other Lickey Bankers included ex-L&NWR 0-8-4T No 7953 (1929-1930 winter), LMS Beyer-Garratt No 47998 (pitted against LMS 'Jinties' in 1934) and, in the 1950s, LNER Beyer-Garratt No 69999; 'Big Bertha', however, outlived them all on such work. Although most of her life she covered just short distances, she completed 838,856 miles and her classic four-cylinder bark will always be remembered by those who saw her in operation.

In March, the British Transport Commission announced that 25kV ac would be adopted for all future electrification schemes on Britain's railways with the exception of the Eastern and Central section of the Southern Region and on London Transport. Plans envisaged two types of electric locomotive; an express type of 3,000-3,500hp and a mixed-traffic type of 2,500-3,000hp, both initially for use over 495 route miles including the Euston-Manchester/Liverpool main lines, creating much faster trains over these routes.

On 31 December, electrification was completed on the Shenfield-Southend Victoria line in Essex, extending the scheme which had been completed from Liverpool Street to Shenfield in 1949. The new electric service to Southend provided 119 trains daily in both directions compared with 64 steam-hauled trains in the previous timetable.

On the day that the Southend extension saw its first electric service, the closure of an old favourite electric railway took place — the Liverpool Overhead Railway. This was the first overhead electric railway in the world and was born on 4 February 1893. At closure the line covered seven miles from Seaforth & Litherland, on the LMR's Liverpool-Southport line, to Dingle, passing beside the docks — a unique railway system in Britain and sadly missed.

Also on the electrification scene four new four-car corridor electric units were completed at Eastleigh Works, numbered 7101-7104 and designated '4-CEP'. These were prototypes designated for the forthcoming Kent Coast main-line electrification scheme. Trials involved twelve of the 16 cars, being used between Victoria and East Croydon, on the Brighton route, and to West Worthing and Littlehampton from London Bridge.

On the 'steam' front, one of the most innovative events of the year was the conversion of Bulleid's 'Merchant Navy' Pacifics from their streamlined state into a completely rebuilt version. This was felt necessary due to excessive coal consumption, poor accessibility during maintenance and the outshopping costs being three times as much as a normal express locomotive. From the start, these were controversial locomotives with their irregular-shaped smokebox, their special air-smoothed casing and their crankshaft, chain-driven from the driving axle. The first rebuilt 'Merchant Navy', outshopped from Eastleigh Works in February 1956, was No 35018 *British India Line*. The modified version was slightly heavier than the locomotive in its original state at 97.9 tons as against 94.75 tons. The tractive effort was reduced in 1954, from 37,500lb to 33,495lb when the class's boiler pressure was reduced from 275lb/sq in to 250.

Chocolate & cream coaches returned in 1956 on the Western Region and they ran in unmixed sets on the 'Torbay Express', 'Cornish Riviera' and 'Bristolian'. Each train carried roofboards in traditional GWR serif lettering and the word 'Limited' was returned to the 'Cornish Riviera' title — an appendage it carried from 1935-1946.

The 'Talisman' was introduced on 17 September between King's Cross and Edinburgh. The limited load of eight coaches included an ex-'Coronation' streamlined articulated set, repainted, like the rest of the rake, in standard maroon livery. Gresley Pacific No 60025 *Falcon* took the inaugural train as far as Newcastle where it handed over to No 60031 *Golden Plover* which had worked the southbound 'Talisman' from Edinburgh. The scheduled timing for the 'Talisman' was 6hr 40min incorporating one stop — at Newcastle.

Camping coaches were becoming more and more popular for holidays and in 1956 there were 187 available — the most since the war. One of the conditions of taking a holiday in a camping coach was 'travel by rail' and they could be found all around Britain's holiday regions at locations such as Robin Hood's Bay, Marazion and on the Cambrian Coast route.

On 3 June the abolition of third-class travel took place, being redesignated second-class on British Railways. The move was to conform with the two-class European passenger trains.

A new British Railways emblem appeared in June 1956. The rampant lion, holding a silver locomotive wheel between its paws and sat on a gold crown incorporating the English rose, the Scottish thistle, the Welsh leek and the Great British oak leaf. It first appeared on 'Britannia' Pacific No 70016 *Aerial*. This replaced the 'Ferret and Dartboard' emblem devised by British Railways after Nationalisation.

Thirty new '73xxx' Standard 4-6-0s were built at Derby Works during 1956, numbered 73125-73154 and fitted with Caprotti valve-gear. Ten each were to be allocated to the London Midland, Western and Scottish regions.

Steam sheds at Upminster (13E), Belle Vue (26G) and Louth (40C) all closed during 1956 and lines closed to passengers included the Princetown branch over Dartmoor and the Newport-Sandown line on the Isle of Wight. Ownership of the Cleobury Mortimer & Ditton Priors Railway was transferred to The Admiralty and the Welshpool & Llanfair Railway (now, of course, 'back in use') ended its days under British Railways ownership. The last train on the Welshpool & Llanfair Railway on 15 September comprised four drop-sided mineral wagons as 'open seconds' coupled between two brake vans and headed by No 822 *The Earl*. Station seats at Welshpool were used as 'stepping stones' to assist travellers to climb into the wagons. The journey to Llanfair Caereinion took 55min. The train then returned to Welshpool. On 5 November the Stephenson Locomotive Society ran a special train over the line involving 10 open wagons — fully laden with enthusiasts.

The Market Drayton and Leek branches closed to passengers on 7 May 1956. However, passenger services were reinstated on the East Grinstead-Lewes line after closure the previous year.

The Class 01 and 06 diesel shunters were constructed in 1956 and it was decided that a numbering scheme for diesel locomotives should commence from No 1, with a prefix

letter 'D', involving the renumbering of many diesel shunters.

On London Transport, the two oldest cars on London's Underground were scrapped after 50 years of service. They had formed part of the original fleet of cars used at the opening of the Piccadilly Line in 1906, and for many years they provided the shuttle service on the Aldwych branch. These two cars, Nos 5 and 30, were built in France and had open rear-end gates when constructed. When converted to air-door operation these two cars were renumbered 481 and 498.

Above:
Fresh on the scene in 1956 was the English Electric Type 5 Co-Co prototype *Deltic*, introduced, on loan, in the previous October and initially allocated to Speke Junction. Although never carrying the number, the locomotive was allocated DP1. Resplendent in her blue & white livery *Deltic* is pictured approaching Preston, in 1956, from the Blackpool/Fleetwood lines. She remained in service until March 1961 after which she was transferred to the Science Museum in London. *English Electric*

Right:
In 1956, Grimsby Fish Dock was being worked by a Drewry 0-4-0 diesel shunter (later Class 04), No 11152 (later No D2233). In this scene fish vans are being shunted past the port master's offices. *R. E. Vincent*

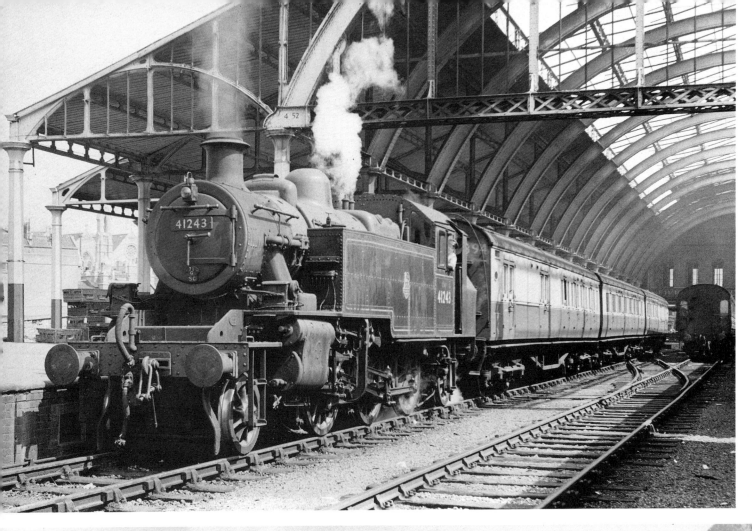

Top left:
The 12.43pm local to Bristol Temple Meads prepares to leave Bath Green Park station on 21 April 1956, behind Ivatt 2-6-2T No 41243. This splendid station was closed to passengers on 7 March 1966 on the closure of the S&D line. *Brian Morrison*

Left:
A Guildford-Redhill train pulls out of Betchworth during the summer of 1956 hauled by 'N' class Mogul No 31862. This line is scheduled for electrification under the Channel Tunnel scheme for the operation of freight trains. *M. R. Gailey*

Top:
The 3.40pm Didcot-Southampton Terminus train, hauled by ex-L&SWR Drummond T9 'Greyhound' No 30285, leaves Compton station, between Didcot and Newbury on 9 April 1956. These 4-4-0 locomotives were built in 1912, and superheated from 1915-17. *David J. Beaver*

Right:
During a period when Great Western 'Kings' were unavailable for duty due to a big problem with bogie failures, unusual motive power could be found working West Country expresses. Two LMS 'Princess Royal' Pacifics were enlisted to help out, amongst other invitees, and, on 10 February 1956, No 46210 *Lady Patricia* passes Stoneycombe Quarry, Dainton, in Devon, with the down 'Cornish Riviera' express, creating an impressive sight. This locomotive was one of the seven 'Princess Royals' of a class totalling only 13 locomotives, to carry a different name to that originally proposed — No 6210 changing from the proposed *Princess Alexandra*. *David S. Fish*

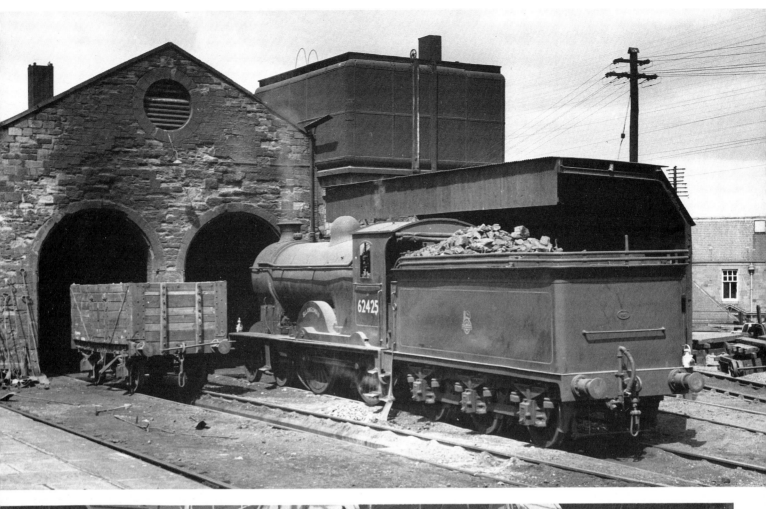

Left:
St Boswells shed was situated on the North British 'Waverley' route just north of Kelso Junction and was home for Jedburgh branch locomotives. On 22 June 1956 ex-NBR D30 Reid 4-4-0 'Scott', No 62425 *Ellangowan*, stands outside the original two-arch engine shed — a tight fit! *T. G. Hepburn/Copyright Rail Archive Stephenson*

Below left:
Tyseley roundhouse in 1956 with one of the three 'home' locomotives basking in the sun shining through the roof. In the centre is 'ROD' 2-8-0 No 3012, one of the original Robinson (ex-GCR) locomotives purchased by the GWR from the Royal Engineers in 1919. On the left is seen '51xx' class 2-6-2T No 4155 and, to the right 2-8-0 No 2856. *Ian Allan Library*

Top right:
More often that not, the Great Western Class 56xx 0-6-2Ts were used on freight duties, but on this occassion, 12 May 1956, No 6626 is pictured in the Rhondda Valley, near Llwynypia, on a passenger working. *S. Rickard*

Right:
On 4 April 1956, during the Welshpool & Llanfair Railway's final year of freight operations for BR, Great Western 0-6-0T No 822, now devoid of its nameplate (*The Earl*), hauls the daily freight to Llanfair Caereinion from Welshpool and is pictured crossing Raven Square, Welshpool. *Geoffrey F. Bannister*

Below:
The Liverpool Overhead Railway opened in 1893 initially from Alexandra Dock to Herculaneum and further extensions soon followed to Seaforth Sands, Dingle and in 1905 to Litherland. BR, it is said, played a part in its demise, as the ex-L&Y 'Pugs', although fitted with steel plates above their chimney, slowly deteriorated the metalwork of the structure which supported this overhead line. The line, an asset in the battle against traffic congestion, eventually closed on 31 December 1956. In this view a Dingle train, made up of one of the original two-car sets, with one coach added, is seen entering Clarence Dock station on 14 May 1956. *J. F. Davies/Copyright Rail Archive Stephenson*

Lewisham

On 4 December 1957, thick fog covered the southeastern suburbs of London. Running 45min late was SR 'Battle of Britain' Pacific No 34066 *Spitfire*. On passing a 'red' signal at St Johns (Lewisham) the driver made an emergency stop but it was too late as 138yd beyond the signal *Spitfire* piled into the rear of the Charing Cross-Hayes electric train, which was standing at a home signal. As the electric train was stood on an incline its brakes had been applied causing the train to telescope when it was struck. The impact caused the Pacific locomotive's tender and leading coach to strike a steel column which supported a bridge which collapsed on to the wrecked train. In this terrible disaster 90 lives were lost and there were 109 seriously injured.

At Welwyn Garden City, on 7 January an Aberdeen to King's Cross express was wrecked after colliding with a local train. This was another case of a train passing a signal at danger when the commuter train from Baldock to King's Cross had been given the right of way.

At Hexham in Northumberland, on 1 July, a four-car diesel unit, having just been relieved of its passengers, was severely struck by 'K1' 2-6-0 No 62029 hauling a 35-wagon coal train. The 'K1' was locked within the unit, was forced through the platform awning, and the fuel tank of the diesel unit exploded.

The first Gloucester Carriage & Wagon Works two-car diesel units built for the Scottish Region left the works and new diesel locomotives appeared in the form of Type 1 Bo-Bo and Type 2 A1A-A1A classes (later designated Class 20 and Class 31 respectively). The first English Electric Type 1s (later Class 20) were allocated to the first all-diesel depot — Devons Road, Bow and the Brush Type 2 (Class 31) diesel-electrics were initially built for the Eastern Region — the first 20 being allocated to Stratford and Ipswich. On 17 September an impressive new diesel depot was opened at Darlington. It included a three-road running shed, a totally enclosed heated repair shop, a carriage washing plant and four fuelling points.

On 6 May 1957, a diesel-electric multiple unit service commenced on the London-Tunbridge Wells-Hastings line. Vehicles were constructed at Ashford and Eastleigh — the underframes and bogies at Ashford and the coach bodies and interiors at Eastleigh. Hampshire diesel-electric multiple units were also introduced in November.

From 7 January, Swindon-built six-car cross-country diesel units came into service between Edinburgh Waverley and Glasgow Queen Street — a route that has seen a variety of traction both prior to this and in more recent years.

Doncaster Works completed the construction of its final steam locomotive on 16 October 1957. This was Standard Class 2-6-0 No 76114, although steam locomotives continued to be overhauled there. Construction of new locomotives at Doncaster now turned to 350hp diesel shunters. Also during the year, double chimneys were fitted to Class 4 Standard 4-6-0 No 75029 (now preserved) and four '9F' 2-10-0 locomotives.

Rebuilt 'Battle of Britain' and 'West Country' Southern Pacifics started to emerge in 1957 and No 34005 *Barnstaple* was the first 'West Country' to appear.

On 28 November 1957, LMS 'Coronation' class Pacific No 46245 *City of London* became the first to receive the London Midland maroon livery.

The shortlived change of name of the 'Morning Talisman' to 'The Fair Maid' in 1957, when the service was extended to Perth, lasted only until 1958. The inaugural run was in the hands of LNER 'A4' No 60015 *Quicksilver*, (which had recently been fitted with a double chimney), from King's Cross to Newcastle. From here to Edinburgh No 60027 *Merlin* took over to be replaced by a Perth South-allocated 'Black Five' for the final stretch of the journey.

Another London-Scotland named train was introduced in 1957. This was the 'Caledonian' — a Euston-Glasgow express stopping only at Carlisle with a scheduled running time for the entire journey of 6hr 40min.

On the Western Region the inaugural run of the 'Cathedrals Express' took place on 16 September. The Paddington-Oxford-Hereford train (7.45am ex-Hereford and 4.45pm ex-Paddington) was formed of chocolate & cream painted coaches.

A new all-electric signalbox was brought into use at St Pancras on 6 October. This was the first time a thumb-switched operated route-setting control panel was preferred to lever frames for a new box on the London Midland Region where colour lights were involved.

At Cannon Street box, on 5 April, a fire broke out and although the fire brigade arrived promptly, strong winds spread the flames quickly and half the box was burnt out. This virtually brought Cannon Street to a standstill as no power-operated points or signals could be used. However, less than five hours after the fire, a steam train entered the station from Hastings under hand signals and manual operation of the point motors but there were no electric services throughout the entire day.

Closures of engine sheds during 1957 included Stratford-upon-Avon (21D), Southend Victoria (30D), Dorchester (71C) and Newport, Isle of Wight (71E)

More positively, the Swansea & Mumbles Railway, widely regarded as the world's oldest passenger railway, celebrated 150 years of passenger service.

Top right:
After leaving Wellington, Somerset, with a down cross-country train to Paignton, denoted by the '411' train number, in 1957, Great Western 'King' No 6004 *King George III* bursts out from beneath a road bridge on its journey south. When studying the 'King' class one could test one's memory of history, as from Nos 6000 to 6027 they were in reverse order of ascendence to the throne from *King Richard I* (6027) to *King George V* (6000) — try it some time! *John Ashman/Copyright M. Esau*

Right:
A beautiful study of No 3440 *City of Truro*, brought back to service in 1957 after renovation, working many enthusiasts' specials and also service trains over the Didcot, Newbury & Southampton line until 1962. This fine record-breaking locomotive is pictured on 16 June 1957 storming Hatton Bank after returning from Swindon with an 'SLS Special' to Birmingham. *T. E. Williams*

Top left:
Sudbury station, in Suffolk, on 3 August 1957 and, as ex-GER Holden 'E4' 2-4-0 No 62789 prepares to leave with the 11.23am (SO) Cambridge-Colchester train, a 'J15' 0-6-0 No 65470 arrives from Mark's Tey with the 12.12pm (SO) to Cambridge. Under normal circumstances these trains would pass at Long Melford but on this occasion traffic conditions caused them to pass here. *G. R. Mortimer*

Left:
A Good Friday working (19 April 1957) and ex-GCR Robinson 'D11/1' 'Large Director' No 62666 *Zeebrugge* heads the 10.05am Sheffield Victoria-Nottingham Victoria train under 1,500V dc wires out of Sheffield. At this time Sheffield Darnall (41A) shared the allocation of the 'D11/1' 4-4-0s with Northwich (five each) with No 62668 *Jutland* being allocated to Trafford Park (17F). *K. S. Hudson*

Top right:
The '1366' class 0-6-0 pannier tanks were originally built to replace '1392' class tanks being withdrawn from Swindon Wagon Works duties, but when Nos 1367, 1368 and 1370 moved to Weymouth for working passenger trains to and from the quay, they were fitted with steam heating apparatus and a bell to warn the public of their approach. No 1367 is seen in September 1957 running along the quayside with a Channel Islands boat train. *T. G. Hepburn/Copyright Rail Archive Stephenson*

Right:
LMS 'Black Five' No 44964 prepares to leave Birmingham (New Street), on 29 June 1957, with the 8.05am Newcastle on Tyne train. A far cry from the Birmingham (New Street) we know today. *M. Mensing*

1958

Railbuses and Railcars

On 13 February, the first four-wheel lightweight railbus was delivered. This was the first of an order for 22 of these vehicles ordered by British Railways — two from Bristol Commercial Vehicles, five from Park Royal, five from Wickham, five from the German company, Waggon und Maschinenbau, and five from A C Cars, who had previously provided rolling stock for the Southend Pier line. The prototype from A C Cars (SC79979) commenced trials on the Speyside line in Scotland between Craigellachie and Boat of Garten. The second railbus came from the German company; all the German order arrived at Harwich in April and were destined for Cambridge. The remaining A C railbuses were earmarked for the Western Region for use on the Kemble-Tetbury and Kemble-Cirencester lines. Another railbus was destined for the Audley End-Saffron Walden-Bartlow branch, which closed to steam on 5 July. Park Royal versions worked between Bedford, Hitchin and Northampton, whilst Wickham railbuses, the last to appear, headed for Scotland. For service north of the border retractable folding steps were fitted. They worked between Crieff and Comrie and between Elgin and Aviemore.

Also in Scotland, on 21 April, the battery railcar two-car unit went into service on the Ballater branch. These railcars were Derby lightweight vehicles constructed in 1956 and converted at Cowlairs Works. Battery charging equipment was installed at Aberdeen Joint and Ballater stations.

The big steam news involved Standard '9F' 2-10-0 No 92250 when, on 15 December, she left Crewe Works to take up duty. This locomotive was the last of 7,331 steam engines to be built at Crewe since it was established in 1843 by the Grand Junction Railway, one of the original partners in the L&NWR. Crewe was again in the news when the first diesel maintenance depot to be specially built by the London Midland Region came into use. It was built to maintain, examine and service diesel units and housed both main line diesels and diesel shunters.

On the London Midland Region, at Guide Bridge station, on 21 August 1958, two electric locomotives were struck by lightning and on the evening of Friday

5 September, the southeast of England was hit by the 'storm of the century' — reported to be 'of tropical severity'. Lines were blocked by floods, landslides, subsidences and fallen trees. These closed temporarily every line between London and the southeast coast. A total of 120 'incidents' were reported from tons of rubble on the line at Sevenoaks to a 50ft deep, 12ft wide crater appearing between the tracks at St Mary Cray. Chaos reigned with bus and rail shuttle services being organised and some lines not reopening until the Tuesday. One diversion to a Charing Cross-Ramsgate (via Folkestone) train was routed through Haywards Heath, Polegate and Hastings and hauled by the normal rebuilt 'West Country' Pacific.

On 22 December, two Hastings-line diesel-electric multiple-units collided at Tunbridge Wells Central. In the new year the two damaged cars were conveyed to Eastleigh via Hove by 'H15' No 30476, an unusual locomotive for this route.

The first of 13 2,500hp main line electric locomotives for the Southern Region was completed at Doncaster on 24 December — this was No E5000. These locomotives (both for operation by third-rail or overhead electric current) were built for mixed-traffic duties, the electrical equipment being supplied by English Electric.

Also on the Southern, the closed Gatwick Airport station was replaced by a new station on 28 May which was a rebuild of the original Gatwick Racecource station. It was officially opened by Her Majesty the Queen on 9 June. Three months earlier, on 17 March, the Bluebell Railway (East Grinstead-Lewes) closed, for the second time, to passengers.

The main news on the Southern in 1958 was the closure of Brighton Works to locomotive and wagon maintenance. Locomotives were, however, stored there during the following year due to congestion at Nine Elms shed in July 1959.

Diesel locomotive construction included 'Warships', Type 2s (the future Classes 24 and 26) , Type 4s (Class 40) and the peculiar 'Metrovick' Co-Bo design (Class 28). 'Warship' No D800, the first of 38 of the future Class 42 to be built, was named *Sir Brian Robertson* at Paddington on 14 July.

These locomotives were based on the successful German Federal Railway V200 class, but due to loading restrictions the British version required a reduction in height of 10in and in width of 16in.

Derby Works turned out the first of 30 Type 2 diesels (Class 24), No D5000, built for the London Midland Region for mixed traffic work between London and Crewe. Fifteen of these locomotives were soon loaned to the Southern Region pending introduction of further Type 3s (later Class 33s) in 1961. The Class 24s were used on mixed traffic work in the Chatham-Faversham-Ramsgate-Dover area.

In July, the prototype 'Metrovick' Type 2 Co-Bo, No D5700, appeared. The entire class was earmarked for allocation to Derby.

On 26 November the first 25kV ac locomotive-hauled passenger trip took place over the 9½ mile line between Wilmslow and Mauldeth Road on the Styal route to Manchester (London Road). The converted Metro-Vickers gas turbine No E1000 (later E2001) — with its raised numbers — was in charge. The locomotive had recently been rebuilt from the Western Region's No 18100.

On the Western Region, the Ashburton-Totnes line closed to passengers on 3 November; part of the line, between Totnes and Buckfastleigh, is now fortunately preserved. In Wales the Brynamman-Pantyffynnon branch line also closed to passengers, on 18 August — Pantyffynnon being on the Central Wales line. The ex-L&SWR station at Plymouth Friary closed on 15 September; the station ended its life under Western Region jurisdiction. In June Abergavenny Junction station closed — once a busy location.

In the autumn of 1958 Cannon Street station in London closed during midday off-peak periods and after 10.15pm. It also closed after 3.15pm on Saturday and all day Sunday to enable the crescent roof to be removed due to age, corrosion and bomb damage.

Speed records for scheduled services changed hands during 1958. Firstly, the Western Region lost it to the North Eastern Region when the 5.5pm Newcastle-King's Cross (44.1 miles from Darlington to York in 39min) beat the 'Bristolian' by

0.2mph. However, in September, the Western Region recovered the record with the 1.50pm Bristol-Paddington covering the 41.3 miles from Swindon to Reading in 36min at an average speed of 68.8mph.

With the 1958 winter timetable the diesel-hauled Pullman 'Master Cutler' was introduced between King's Cross and Sheffield Victoria. Also on the Eastern Region, Stratford-allocated 'Britannia' Pacifics, being displaced by diesel power, commenced operation on fast Clacton services, including the 'Essex Coast Express'.

A variety of steam depots closed during 1958 as more and more diesels were constructed and new diesel depots built. These closures included Bradford (Hammerton Street) (37C), Dundee West (29C), Walsall (3C), St Leonards (74E), Cardiff Cathays (88A) and Middlesbrough (51D) to name but a few and steam locomotive classes which became extinct in 1958 included the GWR 'ROD' 2-8-0s, the LNER 'G5' 0-4-4 push-pull tanks, the LNER 'F5' 2-4-2Ts,

the LNER 'F6' Holden 2-4-2Ts, and the original 'N15' Urie 4-6-0s built for the L&SWR — No 30748 *Vivien* being the last to go, one of 10 loaned to the LNER during World War 2 and used on freight trains between York and Edinburgh.

Finally, on a light-hearted note, 1958 saw a 100% price increase in the 'platform ticket' (from 1d to 2d). It had in fact been 1d since 1912!

Top left:
On 16 August 1958, the well-laden 11.15am Newquay-Wolverhampton train pulls out of Stratford upon Avon, double-headed, behind Great Western Mogul No 5341 piloting 'Castle' No 5070 *Sir Daniel Gooch*. Both locomotives were 'Midlands-allocated'; No 5341 to 84E (Tyseley) and No 5070 to 84A (Wolverhampton Stafford Road). *T. E. Williams*

Left:
The 4.30pm local service between Birmingham Snow Hill and Dudley was for many years operated by a Great Western diesel railcar. On 18 February 1958, this service, affectionately known as the 'Dudley Dodger' was worked by railcar No W14W and is pictured at Snow Hill waiting to cross to the down side of the station after performing its last duty for the day.
M. Mensing

Top right:
Heading for Liverpool Street, LNER 'B17/6' 4-6-0 No 61666 *Nottingham Forest* approaches an oncoming Class 306 three-car unit bound for Gidea Park in 1958. At this time electric current was 1,500V dc overhead, but is now converted to ac. *R. E. Vincent*

Right:
Ex-NBR LNER Class B16 Reid 4-4-2T No 67490 carries out shunting duties at Dundee West station in March 1958. These locomotives were a superheated development of the 'C15' class. *W. J. Verden Anderson/ Copyright Rail Archive Stephenson*

Above:
In July 1958, an ex-GER Class N7/1 0-6-2T, No 69632, climbs Holloway Bank after emerging from Copenhagen Tunnel with a King's Cross-Finsbury Park empty stock train. This class was rarely seen at this location but this particular example had made its way south from Hatfield (34C). *Brian Morrison*

Left:
In 1958, at a time when Bournemouth Central had four lines running through the station, a Class U Mogul, No 31808, passes through with an up freight. Bournemouth station has changed very little over the years and, as a listed building, was undergoing restoration and a clean-up in 1992. *R Hewitt*

Top right:
Another 'unspoilt' overall-roof station is St Pancras and, on 5 June 1958, Fowler '3MT' 2-6-2T No 40030, complete with condensing equipment, prepares to remove empty stock from the station whilst 'Black Five' No 44658 lies in wait before its next turn of duty which is a Nottingham express. *C. T. Gifford*

Right:
A classic Forth Bridge scene as, on 31 July 1958, Standard '5MT' 4-6-0 No 73106 crosses the river with an up express. Five members of this class have been preserved including one fitted with Caprotti valve-gear (No 73129). *E. R. Wethersett*

New Electrics

On 22 January, a trial trip for the new main-line electric locomotive, No E5000, the first of a class earmarked for the Kent Coast electrification, took place from Victoria to Newhaven. During the summer of 1959 these new electrics were put into service. The locomotives were stabled in the new depot specifically built for them at Stewarts Lane. Current inside the depot was picked up by overhead wires, as in the electric multiple-unit sheds. However, the multiple-units required a special trolley device to enable them to collect the overhead current whereas the locomotive could move freely in the depot with the use of pantographs.

For continental travellers to the Kent coast, where inadequate luggage space was available on multiple-unit stock, two special luggage vans, Nos S68001/2, which also carried mail, came into service in the summer of 1959. These first worked between Victoria and Dover Marine. On 21 February, work commenced on the partial reconstruction of Dover Marine station.

The 25kV ac line between Colchester, Walton-on-Naze and Clacton, the first in Britain to provide a regular passenger service, was officially opened by the Chairman of the Eastern Area Board on 13 April, although the new electric units had been operating over the line since 16 March. The entire line had been resignalled with searchlight colour-lights and continuous track circuiting. The steam locomotive shed at Clacton was converted into a temporary EMU inspection and maintenance depot. The new units were eventually destined for the LT&S line when this was electrified. The 112 four-car units to be built were constructed at Doncaster and York works.

This year also saw construction of the new 4-BEP electric multiple-units, to join the 4-CEP units for Stage One of the Kent Coast electrification. The 4-BEP differed from the 4-CEP units in that they contained a buffet car. The 4-CEP units were similar to the prototype built in 1956 apart from changes to the electrical and mechanical equipment. These changes provided greater acceleration partly for the 1 in 30 Folkestone Harbour branch, which was due for electrification in Stage Two. The rebuilding of Folkestone Central station commenced at the end of the year.

As electric traction was introduced on the Gillingham-Ramsgate line, on 15 June, the steam engine depot at Ramsgate (73G) lost its allocation of steam locomotives although stabling of overnight locomotives from other depots continued. Regular bedfellows there included 'West Country' Pacifics, LMR Class 3 2-6-4Ts, BR Class 4 2-6-2Ts and SR 'N' class 2-6-0s. Gillingham (73D) also suffered a similar fate, but still provided stabling for 'Q1s' and 'H' class 0-4-4Ts from Tonbridge.

On the London Midland Region, on 27 November 1959, the first of 25 25kV ac 3,300hp electric locomotives, No E3001, was officially handed over to British Railways at Sandbach by Associated Electrical Industries. Driver training commenced in December on the Styal line.

The electrification of the Birmingham main line brought inconvenience to Coventry travellers as all non-stop trains from London were suspended from 2 November for around three years. Journey times to and from London increased by 30min or passengers had to change at Rugby or Leamington. In fact the Rugby-Leamington Spa branch line had recently closed to passengers on 15 June.

Rolling stock on the Manchester-Bury line was replaced during 1959/60 by 26 new two-car electric units (later Class 504). These units replaced rolling stock built from 1915-21 for the L&YR, the new units being built at the ex-L&NWR works at Wolverton.

On the diesel scene, the first Derby Sulzer Type 4 (later Class 44), No D1 *Scafell Pike*, was completed in 1959 and underwent trials. Ten of these 2,300hp 1Co-Co1 diesel-electric locomotives were ordered, numbered D1-D10 and all were named after mountain peaks in the Pennines, the Lake District and North Wales. All were originally allocated to Crewe North depot awaiting the installation of servicing facilities at Camden and they were initially employed on fast passenger and parcels trains between Euston, Crewe, Carlisle and Glasgow. These locomotives ended their days 20 years later operating from Toton depot, working the route to Washwood Heath, Birmingham, previously operated by the LMS Beyer-Garratts.

Stratford depot on the Eastern Region received new Type 2 Bo-Bo diesels (later Class 21), constructed by the North British Locomotive Co, in 1959, numbered D6100-D6109. These 1,000hp locomotives were for allocation to Hornsey depot and their superstructure was constructed entirely of aluminium. From No D6110 (later Class 29), these locomotives were uprated to 1,100hp. These North British-built locomotives were transferred to Scotland, and some were fitted with token exchange equipment.

For the Western Region came a similar locomotive in design from North British. This was the Type 2 B-B (later Class 22) diesel-hydraulic locomotive. The first six, numbered D6300-5, were termed 'prototypes' and were first allocated to Swindon and Laira. The engine and transmission were based on the North British 'Warship' class locomotives.

The 'Baby Deltics' — all 10 of them — were introduced for use on the Eastern Region from April to June 1959. These operated from Hornsey depot primarily for short-distance passenger work. Their livery was dark olive green with a broad white line along the body side connecting with a similar band of red over the buffer beams.

For the Scottish Region the ex-'Coronation' beaver-tail observation cars were rebuilt in 1959 for use on the Glasgow-Fort William-Mallaig service. The rebuilding incorporated new rear windows, 28 movable armchairs in each coach and anyone wishing to travel on these luxury coaches was asked to pay an extra 3s 6d (17½p), or 2s 6d (12½p) between Fort William and Mallaig.

On 28 October 1959 the last British Railways 2-4-0 locomotive ran in service. This was LNER 'E4' class No 62785, which ended its days at Cambridge working Cambridge to Colchester trains.

Other classes which became extinct in 1959 included SR 'E6x', the final survivor being No 32411 (75C), LNER 'O4/5' (No 63851 of 41F), LNER 'N1' (No 69462 of 56C), GWR 0-6-0PT '2021' class (No 2069 of 6C), LNER 0-4-0T Sentinel 'Y1' (No 68150 of 50C), the last MR round-top 0-6-0 No 58246 (15D), SR '0395' class (No 30567 of 70B), SR 'E3' (No 32165 of 75C), diesel-mechanical shunter SR No 11001 (75C) and the Bo-Bo 800hp diesel-electric No 10800, allocated to Rugby (2A). Also withdrawn was LNER 4-6-4 No 60700.

Temple Mills freight yard, near Stratford, went into full operation in 1959 having been authorised in 1954. The yard received and despatched 250 trains each day. A unique feature of the Temple Mills 'hump' was the three-position semaphore signal, operated from the 'hump cabin' — a guide to crews working hump shunters. Initially the yard dealt with 3,000 wagons each day over the 'hump' but it had the capacity for 4,500.

Walsall motive power depot was converted late in 1959 to be exclusively used as a diesel maintenance depot for 100 diesel units. Sheffield (Darnall) electric depot was also converted to maintain 24 two-car diesel multiple-units employed on local services.

The Royal Albert Bridge at Saltash, near Plymouth, celebrated its centenary on 1 May 1959. The bridge, designed and built by Isambard Kingdom Brunel, was floodlit every night until 13 September.

Lines which closed to passengers during 1959 included Beccles-Yarmouth (South Town), the 'Last of the Summer Wine' Holmfirth branch, the Bristol-Radstock-Frome branch on the Western Region and the Aberfoyle branch in Scotland. One of the many lines which closed completely was the Hawes-Garsdale branch which met the Settle & Carlisle line at Garsdale.

There were depot closures in abundance, some of the more well-known ones being Coventry (2D), the three Great Yarmouth depots, Melton Constable (32G), following the closure of the M&GN Railway on 28 February, Fratton (71D), Faversham (73E) and King's Lynn and South Lynn depots in Norfolk.

On 20 May, the BTC Chairman formally opened the new stretch of track from Greenwood to Potters Bar on the Great Northern main line which had been widened to four tracks extending the four-track distance from King's Cross to 21 miles.

To end on a lighter note, an unusual sign appeared at Manchester (London Road) on 9 February 1959. It was the 58-letter nameboard from LlanfairPG station in Anglesey, having been screwed there by university students celebrating 'Rag Day' (using non-reversible screws)! It was wrenched off three days later.

Below:
Ex-LMS 0-6-0 4F No 44519, allocated to Spital Bridge (Peterborough), takes the L&NWR line at Seaton Junction, in Rutland, in May 1959, with a short freight, comprising an open wagon, two cattle trucks and a brakevan, en route for Peterborough. The train is pictured passing beneath the Kettering to Oakham MR line. The signals in the background control the lines from Uppingham and Stamford. W. J. Verden Anderson/Copyright Rail Archive Stephenson

Right:
A southbound local goods train heads towards
Perth as it pounds through wooded highland
country just south of Dunkeld & Birnam in June
1959. An ex-Caledonian '72' class Pickersgill
4-4-0, No 54486, heads the train in style.
W. J. Verden Anderson/
Copyright Rail Archive Stephenson

Below:
Having run round its train, ex-Caledonian
Railway 'Standard Goods' 0-6-0 No 57246 draws
forward into Killin station, in September 1959,
ready for its next run up to Killin Junction and
Crianlarich. These Drummond locomotives were
introduced in 1883. *W. J. Verden Anderson/*
Copyright Rail Archive Stephenson

Above:
A Cambrian scene, as an ex-GWR Collett 0-6-0, No 3213, hauls a short freight towards Llanbedr & Pensarn, south of Harlech, in 1959. At this time 'Cambrian' sheds at Oswestry and Machynlleth had an allocation of 27 Collett 0-6-0s and some even worked the coastal section of the 'Cambrian Coast Express' through to Pwllheli. *Mike Esau*

Left:
The 11.50am Tunbridge Wells-Brighton goods leaves Tunbridge Wells West Yard on 27 January 1959 in the hands of Southern Class K Mogul No 32341. *Derek Cross*

Below left:
On 19 July 1959, a Havant-Hayling Island train is hauled by the diminutive Class A1x Stroudley 'Terrier' 0-6-0T No 32640. It is pictured between Havant and Langstone. This locomotive is now restored and named *Newport* and can be seen in full working order on the Isle of Wight Steam Railway. *Les Elsey*

Top right:
The 1.25pm Paddington-Kingswear train approaches Newton Abbot on 4 July 1959 with Great Western 2-8-0 No 4706 in charge. Hackney Goods Yard can be seen in the background. These impressive Churchward mixed traffic locomotives were only nine in number and the sight of one of these in service was a bonus. *David S. Fish*

Right:
A 1959 view of a North British Class 22 diesel-hydraulic, No D6301, piloting a Great Western 'Castle' No 5028 *Llantilio Castle*. The pair is seen leaving Newton Abbot with the down 'Cornishman'. During this time, this scene was a regular sight as trains prepared to tackle the South Devon banks. *David S. Fish*

By 1959 the diesels were now part of the railway scene and looked fine (when clean) in their white-lined green livery. Brush Type 2 (later Class 31/0) No D5503 emerges from Audley End Tunnel on 8 September 1959 with an up goods. *E. R. Wethersett*

Left:
An interesting view at Stirling showing the transition period, in 1959, with 'Metrovick' Co-Bo No 5713 having just departed from the station with a Glasgow train. These locomotives were mostly remembered for their association with the fast freight service, 'The Condor'. *M. R. Gailey*

Blue is the Colour

The Bluebell Railway reopened from Sheffield Park to a point just short of Horsted Keynes station on 7 August and was operated by the Bluebell Railway Co. In fact the Bluebell Railway Preservation Society purchased two withdrawn locomotives from British Railways during the year — 0-6-0T 'A1X' No 32655 in May and 'P' class 0-6-0T No 31323 in July.

The new diesel-electric six-car Pullman set, known as the 'Blue Pullman' or the 'Midland Pullman', was unveiled at Marylebone station on 23 June. At the same time one of the three eight-car sets earmarked for the Western Region, ran to High Wycombe and back demonstrating its 90mph maximum speed on the descent to Denham. The interior of these Metro-Cammell-built units, with double glazing and venetian blinds, was second to none in Europe. The only rivals in style were the Italian 'ETR300' units used on the Rome-Milan 'Settebello' service. The 'Midland Pullman' made its debut in public service on 4 July operating on weekdays from Manchester Central to St Pancras — a journey time of 3hr 13min. On arrival at St Pancras at 12.03pm it made a St Pancras to Leicester round trip, finally returning to Manchester at 6.10pm. The Western Region 'Blue Pullmans' initially operated from Paddington to Bristol and Paddington-Wolverhampton (Low Level) but it was disappointing to find that the Bristol service did not equal the 'Bristolian' timings.

Services commenced on the Glasgow suburban electrified lines on 7 November 1960 operated by the 'Blue Trains'. These 25kV ac three-car sets had sliding doors, which, although unusual on BR stock, had been used earlier on the 1939-built Liverpool-Southport trains. These trains were built by Pressed Steel and operated from Springburn, Airdrie, Bridgeton Central, through the City of Glasgow to Milngavie, Helensburgh Central and Balloch Pier. The first stage of this electrification scheme covered 52 route miles mainly over ex-LNER lines. The rolling stock maintenance depot was at Hyndland with a carriage washing plant at Bridgeton. However, services were withdrawn from December 1960 to October 1961 after a series of mishaps and accidents.

Great Eastern suburban services went 'electric' on 21 November when electric trains came into operation from Liverpool Street to Hertford East, Bishop's Stortford-Chingford, Enfield Town and Cheshunt, leaving only five per cent of the Great East-ern's passenger services steam-worked. The new ac electric units, built at York and Doncaster, were four-car outer suburban sets (including first-class) and three-car 'all second' sets. Front ends were identical to the Crewe-Manchester units.

It was the 'blues' for the steam lovers as night fell for steam locomotive building on British Railways, but No 92220 *Evening Star* shone brightly as she was turned out from Swindon Works on 18 March 1960. The preserved Caledonian Railway 4-2-2 No 123 was sent to Swindon for the naming of *Evening Star*, together with many other fine locomotives, including No 3440 *City of Truro*, No 6003 *King George IV* and diesel-hydraulic 'Warships' Nos D817 *Foxhound* and D818 *Glory*. An 'unofficial extra' was Vale of Rheidol locomotive No 9 *Prince of Wales* which was already in 'A' shop. Guests travelled to the naming ceremony in a special train hauled by GWR 'Castle' No 7007 *Great Western*.

This was also the year of another 'last' on the Western Region as on 9 September the last slip coach was worked at Bicester, Oxfordshire. The Western Region was the last stronghold of slip coaches and as recently as 1956 there were still nine slips at five stations — Bicester, Didcot, Princes Risborough, Reading and Westbury — a service maintained by a fleet of 15 slip coaches. The final working at Bicester was off the 5.10pm Paddington-Wolverhampton train. Slip coach operation started in 1888 on both the LB&SCR and the SER, later to be joined during the same year by the GWR. By 1914, there were 170 slip coaches being detached from trains daily in England, Scotland and Ireland and the GWR was the largest user operating 79 slips at 24 different stations.

Another significant disappearance in 1960 was the oldest passenger-carrying line in the world — the five-mile Swansea & Mumbles Railway which closed on 5 January. During its 153 years of passenger service it used seven forms of motive power — horse, air, steam, battery, petrol, diesel and overhead electric. Passengers were first carried in June 1807 after four years of goods traffic. The large double-deck Brush-built electric cars which replaced steam in 1929 (the longest passenger-carrying road vehicles in Britain) were all eventually scrapped.

On 25 October the Severn Bridge, which carried the Great Western line from Berkeley Road in Gloucestershire to the Forest of Dean and Lydney, was struck by two barges, which demolished two spans after colliding with a pier in dense fog at 10.25pm. This incident occurred as the two petrol barges, *Arkendale H* and *Wastdale H*, missed the entrance to Sharpness Docks and were carried upstream by the incoming tide. On impact with the bridge the two tankers exploded bringing part of the bridge down into the river.

Other 'lasts' in 1960 on the Western Region were the Swansea Harbour Trust locomotives Nos 1143 and 1144, the last GWR '1101' class 0-4-0T No 1106 (87C), the last '31xx' 2-6-2T No 3103 (86A) and the last 'Dukedog' No 9017, which eventually went to the Bluebell Railway.

On other regions, classes which disappeared included 'A8'. 'B2', 'B17/6' (the last one being *Bradford City*), 'C13', 'C14', 'D30' (the last being *Cuddie Headrigg*) and 'J73', all from the LNER ranks, MR '1P' No 58086 and the Southern lost the last 'E1/R' 0-6-2T, No 32697.

On 12 September 1960 after three years work, the first stage of the electrification scheme of the West Coast main line from Crewe to Manchester Piccadilly and Liverpool Lime Street opened to Manchester. Of the 92 overbridges between Crewe and Manchester, 82 required major alterations to provide additional headroom for overhead wires. Many track rearrangements were necessary at locations such as Stockport, Cheadle Hulme and Wilmslow and stabling facilities at Alderley Edge and East Didsbury were provided for the electric units. Two batches of 15 sets of units were built at Wolverton Works for Manchester and 20 sets for Liverpool. Major station rebuilding was carried out at Crewe, Stockport and Manchester and electric locomotives and units were serviced at newly-built maintenance depots at Crewe and Longsight.

To cover the newly-electrified route, new Class AL1, AL2, AL3 and AL4 (later Classes 81, 82, 83 and 84 respectively) electric locomotives came off the production lines, some officially allocated to Longsight and some with a group allocation — AC Lines. These locomotives with their raised cab-side numbers were outshopped in special 'Electric Blue' livery.

A new diesel depot was completed at Leeds Neville Hill and finally opened on 17 June. Equipped to service 250 diesel multiple-units for the Leeds and York area, the depot's own allocation comprised 22 four-car sets, three triple and 12 twin units. Neville Hill's remaining steam allocation of 43 locomotives, including five LNER 'A3'

Pacifics remained huddled around the two remaining turntables in the 'half' steam shed.

On 11 April, the most modern marshalling yard in Europe (at the time) opened at Margam in South Wales. Fully automated, it covered 178 acres of what were formerly sand dunes and comprised 33 miles of running lines and sidings. The yard could 'hump' 30-35 trains over an eight-hour shift handling some 3,000 wagons.

The first Birmingham RC&W Sulzer Type 3 diesel, No D6500, was delivered to the Southern Region in 1960. These locomotives (later designated Class 33) proved to be extremely reliable. They were fitted with Crompton Parkinson electrical equipment. The last 12 locomotives of the order were to be designed for use on the Hastings line where there were restricted clearances. They were affectionately known as 'Slim Jims'.

Also introduced were the English Electric Type 3 Co-Co diesels (later Class 37), Nos D6700-D6703, which appeared in December 1960 and were first allocated to Stratford depot. The initial delivery heralded from the Vulcan Foundry. They have provided sterling work, particilarly in the field of freight, for many years.

As modernisation approached even more steam depots closed including Chester (84K), Peterborough (16B), Bristol Bath Road (82A) and Lowestoft (32C) and passenger services ceased on 4 January on the Northwich-Sandbach line in Cheshire and on the Blaenau Ffestiniog-Bala line in North Wales on 13 June. Victoria station at Barnstaple closed and the Dornoch-The Mound passenger services ceased. This was the line on which GWR Pannier tanks operated in its latter years. On 5 March the last passenger service ran on the Didcot, Newbury & Southampton line, a route operated by the reinstated GWR 4-4-0 *City of Truro*. The last up train, however, was hauled by ex-GWR 0-6-0 No 2240 (81E), the last down train being hauled by SR 'T9' No 30120 (71A), now preserved.

Below:
Double-headed Class 0415 ex-L&SWR 4-4-2T Adams Radials, Nos 30584 and 30583 climb towards Combpyne in June 1960 with the 4.36pm Axminster-Lyme Regis train. Built from 1882-85, only three of the 71 members of the class reached Nationalisation and all were allocated to Lyme Regis branch duties. *Ivo Peters*

Right:
In September 1960, the 11.45am Bristol-Paddington non-stop express awaits departure from Temple Meads station with Great Western 'Castle' No 5078 *Beaufort* in charge. Certain 'Castles' such as No 5078, were renamed after World War 2 aircraft, losing their previous names. The names they lost later appeared on 7000 series 'Castles', No 7005 taking on No 5078's original name, *Lamphey Castle*.
G. F. Heiron

Below:
Clifton Down station, on 7 June 1960, and a '57xx' class 0-6-0PT No 4660 potters through the station with a short ballast train. In the background, a two-car BR Derby-built diesel multiple-unit makes a scheduled stop with the 12 noon Severn Beach-Bristol Temple Meads service. *S. Rickard*

Top left:
With a running-in turn after overhaul at Swindon Works, ex-GWR 4-6-0 'County' No 1000 *County of Middlesex* leaves Steventon with a Swindon-Didcot two-coach stopping train on 16 February 1960. *Dr. J. A. Coiley*

Centre left:
'Schools' class 4-4-0, No 30927 *Clifton* is pictured at Ham Street & Orlestone with the 6.50am Sunday train from Hastings to Ashford on 31 July 1960. No 30927 was one of the members of this class to retain its original 1930 Maunsell design and its smaller chimney. *D. C. Ovenden*

Bottom left:
Rural Somerset, and two Standard 2-6-2Ts, Nos 82007 and 82044 stand beneath the unusual roof of the Great Western Cheddar station on 20 June 1960. As No 82007 arrives from Wells, No 82044 waits to propel a two-van 'Strawberry Special' to Draycott, the next station down the line. Passenger services on the line from Witham to Yatton, on which Cheddar was situated, ceased on 9 September 1963. *E. T. Gill*

Top right:
Emerging from Golgotha Tunnel on the Tilmanstone branch of the East Kent line, ex-S&ECR Class O1 0-6-0 No 31258 hauls an up coal train in April 1960. These Stirling locomotives were originally built with domeless boilers and rounded cabs but late survivors were converted as seen in this view. *Derek Cross*

Bottom right:
A relief train from York arrives at Scarborough on 27 August 1960 at a time when Saturday trains to the coast were packed with holidaymakers. On the platform, waiting to return home with all their luggage, holidaymakers watch ex-NER Raven 'B16/1' No 61459 arriving. *J. Cupit*

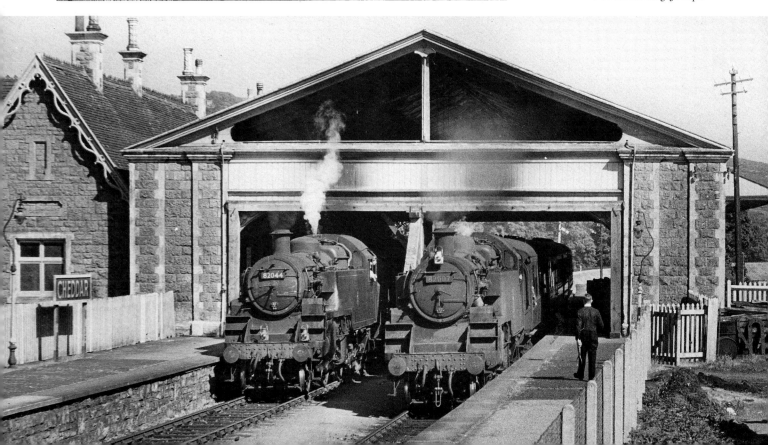

'Deltic' Power

The new English Electric Type 5 3,300hp 'Deltic' diesel-electrics emerged in 1961. These powerful beasts, with their 18-cylinder Napier engines, were built at Newton-le-Willows by Vulcan Foundry and the successful trials of *Deltic* inspired BTC to order 22 of these fine locomotives for the East Coast main line to take over the King's Cross-Scotland routes which had been the province of the 'A4' Pacifics. Initially, in June, only one was named — No D9007 *Pinza* — but eventually names were shared between famous racehorses, which had won the Derby, and British regiments. Allocation of the 'Deltics' was shared between Finsbury Park, Gateshead and Haymarket. Only six more 'Deltics' were named in 1961 after *Pinza* — these were *St Paddy*, *Meld* and *Alycidon* (in July), *Crepello* (September), *Tulyar* (October), and *Ballymoss* (November). The last 'Deltic' to be named was No D9019 *Royal Highland Fusilier* in September 1965. The 22 'Deltics' actually replaced 55 steam locomotives on express duties.

Other new locomotives on the scene in 1961 included AL5 electrics (Class 85) and more BRC&W Type 3 (Class 33) 'Cromptons'. The first diesel-hydraulic 'Western' (Class 52) emerged on 20 December — a class of locomotive which proved extremely popular with the enthusiast. The Yorkshire Engine Co produced *Taurus* in March 1961, a heavy shunting and transfer and trip working locomotive with a central driving cab — the forerunner of the 'D95xx' Paxmans used on the Western Region. Another diesel-hydraulic type produced in 1961 was the 1,700hp 'Hymek' Type 3, which was intended to replace steam locomotives in the West of England, west of Newton Abbot and in South Wales working passenger, freight and parcels trains to and from London. In fact, 500 main-line diesels were ultimately intended to replace 1,100 steam engines on the Western Region.

The first 2,700hp 'Western' numbered D1000 and named *Western Enterprise* was painted in an unusual livery of Desert Sand. Later members of the class appeared in a variety of liveries, including maroon, green and blue. For Scotland came the BRC&W Type 2 Bo-Bo locomotives (Class 27), 19 being produced in 1961. They started their life on the West Highland line and were similar in design to the previously-built Sulzer-engined Type 3 (Class 33s). The 23 earmarked for the Scottish Region were fitted with tablet-catching equipment for single line working and nine, which were to

be allocated to the North Eastern Region, were without train-heating boilers. Others were destined for the London Midland but all were commissioned at Doncaster prior to transference to their 'operating region'.

On the Southern, the Sevenoaks-Dover Priory line was electrified on 12 June and also the Ashford-Maidstone East line on 9 October, and early completion of Stage One of the new electrification scheme resulted in the urgency to provide new maintenance facilities at Chart Leacon, providing work for redundant staff from the Ashford locomotive shed. The extensively-glazed new repair shop — 496ft long, 220ft wide and 36ft high — could overhaul 300 four-car units each year.

The last steam-hauled 'Golden Arrow' ran on 11 June 1961. The final steam down working was operated by Bulleid Pacific 'West Country' class locomotive No 34100 *Appledore*. 'Golden Arrow' trains were now hauled by the Southern's 2,500hp electric locomotives in the E5000 series.

On 29 October, the privately-owned Bluebell Railway was extended into Horsted Keynes. The Bluebell now had four engines to meet their requirements with the recent arrival of Adams 'Radial' 4-4-2T No 488 (30583) to add to 'Terrier' *Stepney* (now fully restored in yellow livery), and two Class P tanks, *Bluebell* and *Primrose*.

The former Midland & South Western Junction Railway closed on 11 September apart from three sections which remained open for freight only. These were Cirencester-Swindon, Marlborough-Savernake, and Ludgershall-Red Post Junction, Andover (SR), with traffic on the Tidworth branch worked by the War Department. Cricklade, Marlborough and Ludgershall stations remained open for parcels traffic only. This railway was opened in 1872 as the Swindon, Marlborough & Andover Railway. It became the M&SWJR in 1884 and reached Cheltenham in 1891. In 1913 passengers could travel from Cheltenham to Waterloo by changing at Andover, using the M&SWJR, in 3hr 19min — almost as fast as the GWR route to Paddington.

On 9 September the last steam-hauled train in passenger service on London Transport's Metropolitan Line — the final steam-operated part of the Underground — ran and on 11 September Amersham became the terminus of the service instead of Aylesbury. Earlier in the year, the ex-Metropolitan Railway's Beyer-Peacock Class A 0-4-4T, No 23, of 1866, was delivered to Clapham Museum. It had been pre-

served at Neasden since 1948 after its withdrawal as departmental locomotive No L45. New stock for the Metropolitan Line was completed by Cravens in 1961. These units were of a completely new design with greatly increased standing space and 25% more seating accommodation. A total of 58 eight-car trains were ordered for completion in two years to replace existing EMU and locomotive-hauled stock used on the line.

On the narrow-gauge scene, Welshpool & Llanfair 0-6-0T No 822 *The Earl* was delivered to Welshpool from Oswestry Works and steamed through the town on 24 July. Two days earlier two narrow-gauge coaches and a number of narrow-gauge wagons were mounted on to standard-gauge wagons in the BR goods yard at Welshpool — all in preparation for the preservation society to reopen part of the railway in 1963. Also in Wales, the 4ft industrial Padarn Railway eventually closed on 27 October.

On 6 November, passenger-carrying electric trains commenced on the London, Tilbury & Southend line. These new trains were confined to non rush-hour periods due to insufficient stock being available. The fast acceleration of these new units resulted in trains arriving at Fenchurch Street sometimes 10min before platforms were available!

The first automatic level crossing on British Railways was installed near Uttoxeter, on the Churnet Valley line, on 6 February. Based on the French automatic barriers, the equipment was powered by constantly-charged storage batteries and should the main power supply fail, the batteries could supply power for up to 12hr.

On 2 January, the new Trans-Pennine diesel units went into service between Hull, Leeds, Manchester and Liverpool, incorporating 10 weekday trips each way between Leeds City and Manchester Exchange, five of these journeys being part of through services from Hull to Liverpool.

Prototype diesels No D0280 *Falcon* (forerunner of the Brush Type 4/Class 47), Brush 0-4-0 No D9998 and 4-6-0 Gas Turbine No GT3 all appeared on the scene in 1961. *Falcon*, although spending a great deal of its life on the Western Region, was originally allocated to Finsbury Park, and No D9998 went to Gloucester and disappeared off the scene after only 15 months. No GT3 began trials on the Shropshire lines around Crewe on 9 January. It was the first British gas-turbine locomotive to employ mechanical transmission. For many years these types of locomotives had been used in the USA for heavy freight duties and had proved to be very economical. No GT3 also carried out trials on the Great Central line between Marylebone and Leicester.

The steam depot that will always be associated with its impressive allocation of LMS Stanier Pacifics, Camden (1B) sadly closed in 1961 bringing the end of an era, as did Kittybrewster (61A) in Aberdeen, remembered for its LNER 'B1' 4-6-0s and its ex-Great North of Scotland Railway locomotives.

Above:
It was February 1962 when passengers could last change at Galashiels for Inverleithen and Peebles as this was a line that suffered the Beeching 'Axe'. In this July 1961 view, a Reid ex-NBR Class J38 0-6-0, No 64561, arrives at Galashiels with a pick-up freight from Edinburgh, via Peebles. *John C. Baker*

Right:
No 41769 was one of a class of 280 MR-built 0-6-0T locomotives, 95 of which reached Nationalisation. Staveley (Barrow Hill) had an allocation of six of these locomotives in 1961. This September 1961 view shows No 41769 on duty in the works yard. *Ivo Peters*

Left:
Ex-Great Western 'Hall' No 6916 *Misterton Hall* heads a Birkenhead to Paddington express out of Chester in August 1961. Certain Birkenhead-Paddington trains were 'King'-hauled between Wolverhampton and London. *J. R. Carter*

Below:
A 1942-built Bulleid Austerity 'Q1' class 0-6-0, No 33035, trundles along below the limestone cliffs through Folkestone Warren with a stopping train to Dover and Ramsgate in June 1961. The first withdrawal from the class was in 1963. *M. Pope*

Top right:
On 30 August 1961, the now-preserved LNER 'A4' Pacific No 60009 *Union of South Africa* leaves Edinburgh Waverley with the up 'Elizabethan'. Beside the 'A4' stands Class 45 'Peak' No D11 preparing to leave with the 1M88 up 'Waverley' express. A classic transition period view even incorporating 'vintage' LNER coaching stock in the background. *Bishop Eric Treacy*

Bottom right:
LNER Class O1 2-8-0, No 63773, leaves Manchester Victoria, in October 1961, with an Ardwick-Ordsall Lane goods train. This locomotive was a Thompson rebuild of a Robinson 2-8-0 and was fitted with a 'B1' boiler, side-window cab, Walschaerts valve-gear and a raised running plate. *J. R. Carter*

'Golden Oldies'

Yes, it was 'Gold' ... and it was 'Old'! Ex-Highland Railway 4-6-0 'Jones Goods' resurrected by the Scottish Region in 1959, continued to be used on specials in 1962, together with Great Northern 4-4-0 No 49 *Gordon Highlander* and North British 4-4-0 'Glen' No 256 *Glen Douglas*, hauling ex-Caledonian rolling stock. RCTS members were given the golden opportunity to travel behind these fine vintage locomotives in June over such routes as Perth-Inverness, Wick/Thurso-Inverness, and Aviemore-Craigellachie down the Spey Valley, on to Keith Junction and from there to Aultmore, one-time terminus of the Buckie branch, and then on to Aberdeen. This was an experience they would never forget.

In East Anglia, steam working ceased on 9 September 1962. One week later the remaining 27 Great Eastern-designed locomotives, from Classes J15, J17, J19, J20, J69 and N7 were condemned. Over their last months these ageing steam locomotives spent much of their time assisting their ailing diesel successors. Main line steam working into King's Cross effectively came to an end in 1962. No more was this impressive terminus station to be graced with the majestic 'A4' Pacifics, so much a familiar sight in the past.

On the Scottish Region, in January 1962, the last Class D11/2 4-4-0 'Director' No 62685 *Malcolm Graeme* was withdrawn from service. Built in 1924, 12 by Kitson & Co and 12 by Armstrong Whitworth, they were named in 1925 after Sir Walter Scott's literary characters. They worked principally between Edinburgh and Glasgow and in Fife. The last North British 'Glen', No 62496 *Glen Loy* also ended its days in 1962 after nearly 50 years of service. During their final years, the 'Glens' were, in the main, allocated to Kittybrewster, Edinburgh (St Margarets), Eastfield and Thornton.

On the Western Region it was the end for the GWR's pride and joy — the 'Kings' which finally ceased operation in service in December 1962, Nos 6000, 6011, 6018 and 6025 being the last to go. No more would these fine locomotives be seen hauling expresses from Paddington to the West Country. Designed by Collett in 1927, all were fitted with double-chimneys after 1955. Another class of locomotive to cease operation after December 1962 was the Southern 'Schools'. Seventeen members of the class were withdrawn in one fell swoop at the end of the year, ending the life of another popular class with the enthusiast.

Most of the 'Schools' ended their days at Bricklayers Arms and Ramsgate. The last 'King Arthur' No 30770 *Sir Prianius* was also withdrawn.

On the London Midland Region No 46200 *The Princess Royal* was the last of its class to go as was No 46170 *British Legion*, the LMS 'Royal Scot'. The latter was the rebuild of the Fowler compound No 6399 *Fury*, originally built in 1930 as an experimental compound locomotive with a super high-pressure boiler. Due to its lack of success it was later rebuilt as a three-cylinder simple with a taper boiler — a prototype to the 'Royal Scots'. Also in 1962 on this region the Fowler and Stanier 2-6-2Ts disappeared and the last War Department 2-10-0s were withdrawn, eight of the final nine being allocated to the Scottish Region — the other to Carlisle (Kingmoor).

On 24 November 1962, the Standard 'Caprotti' Pacific No 71000 *Duke of Gloucester* was condemned. Built in 1954 it was intended to be a prototype of a class of new heavy-duty passenger locomotives but then came the decision to concentrate on diesel locomotive construction. In fact it is said that No 71000 was born from No 46202 *Princess Anne* following the Harrow & Wealdstone disaster in 1952 as the loss of the 'Princess Royal' Pacific in the crash left the London Midland Region devoid of one '8P' Pacific — a necessity for their operational requirements.

At Wadebridge, in Cornwall, GWR locomotives replaced Southern 'Old Faithfuls' in the summer of 1962 as the Beattie well tanks were taken out of service and Great Western pannier tanks took their place. However, the GWR panniers Nos 1367, 1368 and 1369 which had arrived from Weymouth had to be patient for a while after their arrival at Wadebridge as, initially, the Beattie tanks were determined to carry on working for as long as possible; they lasted until August. The water tank in the woods at Wenford Bridge had to be raised for the use of the GWR panniers. All three Beattie well tanks Nos 30585/86/87 were scheduled for preservation, although only two in the event survived.

On the diesel and electric scene, more new locomotives appeared in 1962, including one prototype, No D0280 *Lion*, originally allocated to Wolverhampton (Stafford Road). Built by a consortium comprising AEI, BRC&W and Sulzer, it was hoped that orders from BR would materialise for a new Type 4 locomotive. It remained the property of the consortium. *Lion* was

painted white and trials commenced between Wolverhampton and Shrewsbury, and from 14 May 1962 it worked Wolverhampton-Paddington services.

In November 1962, the first three Brush Type 4 diesel-electrics (later Class 47), Nos D1500/01/02 were introduced — No D1504 also appearing before the end of the year. These were the first of a class of 512 2,750hp Co-Co locomotives built over a five-year period. They were eventually to become the mainstay of BR main line motive power, in one form or another. The first 20 of the class were delivered to the Eastern Region and allocated to Finsbury Park for working out of King's Cross.

For the Western Region came the Type 4 2,700hp diesel-hydraulic 'Westerns' in 1962, much loved during their comparatively short life of around 14 years. The prototype of this class, No D1000 *Western Enterprise* had already seen the light of day in December 1961 but now the fleet of these fine workhorses was in full production. Of the 74 built, 35 were constructed at Swindon and 39 at Crewe. Apart from No D1000 being outshopped in Desert Sand livery, No D1001 was painted maroon, and Nos D1002/3/4 were in green. In fact the Western Region organised a questionnaire amongst young railway enthusiasts to find out their preference in livery, the winner receiving a free trip on a 'Western'.

The first 'Claytons' appeared in 1962, also built to a new BR design incorporating a full-width central driving cab. They were initially for use on the Scottish Region, mostly allocated to Polmadie.

For the Southern came 14 Ruston & Hornsby 275hp diesel shunters for use at Southampton Docks, replacing the 14 0-6-0 'USA' tanks and six ex-LB&SCR Class 'E2' 0-6-0Ts. The first Class 73 electro-diesel, No E6001, emerged from Eastleigh Works on 5 February to commence trials and the second in the class, No E6002, ran trials from Eastleigh to Romsey on 13 March. No E6001 had a yellow band painted across the cab above the buffer beam but No E6002 was in plain green.

From 7 May, the Waverley route was diesel-operated, as far as Edinburgh-Carlisle passenger trains were concerned. These duties were taken over by BRC&W Type 2 diesels. These diesel locomotives invariably worked in tandem on freight workings over the route.

On 22 June, the Great Western Railway Museum at Swindon was officially opened, the building having originally been a Methodist church, erected at the suggestion of I. K. Brunel to serve railway workers in the town. This small museum housed *City of Truro*, *Lode Star*, as well as Nos 2516 and 9400. There was also a replica of the broad gauge single, *North Star*.

The new station at Plymouth opened on 26 March, a project taking six years and costing £1,800,000. But as this modern station complex was born in this bomb-scarred city, other stations in Britain died, as a mass of lines were closed to passenger workings. In January, it was the end for Barnard Castle-Penrith passenger trains together with the Rugby-Leicester line. In June it was the Fairford branch and in July, the Much Wenlock branch closed to passengers as did

the line from Dunstable to Leighton Buzzard. In September it was the turn of the Didcot-Newbury line, in October the Cheltenham (Malvern Road)-Kingham line closed and in November, the Helston branch. December brought about the last passenger train into Brecon.

Closures also hit locomotive works as BR announced, on 19 September 1962, that 12 of the 29 works would close within the next three years resulting in many redundancies. These were Bromsgrove, Caerphilly, Cowlairs, Darlington (Loco and Faverdale), Earletown, Gorton, Lancing, Stratford (Loco and Carriage), Walker Gate and Wolverhampton. Ashford Loco Works was already scheduled for closure by the end of 1962.

From 1 January 1962, the West Coast main line electric services were extended from Crewe to Liverpool, and more 'Blue trains' were introduced in Scotland as Glasgow suburban services using these units commenced south of the Clyde on 27 May. The Kent Coast Electrification Scheme was complete by June 1962 after three years of modernisation and resignalling bringing vastly improved services to the region.

Finally, from the winter 1962 timetable, the 'Pines Express' was rerouted from the Somerset & Dorset line (ceasing to serve Cheltenham and Gloucester) via Wellington, Birmingham (Snow Hill), Banbury, Reading and Basingstoke. The end of an era for this Manchester to Bournemouth train.

Left:
During its final year of service, ex-Great Eastern 'J19' 0-6-0 No 64673 shunts empty wagons at Goodmayes marshalling yard on 13 March 1962. Designed by Hill for the GER, the entire class was eventually rebuilt by Gresley, round-topped boilers being fitted. *M. Edwards*

Above:
Pacific power, as 'Princess Royal' No 46203 *Princess Margaret Rose* (later preserved) pounds up Beattock in August 1962 with a northbound express. The train comprises all-maroon ex-LMS coaching stock. *Peter J. Robinson*

Right:
The Torrington-Halwill line was part of the L&SWR's 'Withered Arm' route into North Devon and it closed to passengers on 1 March 1965. In this view, on 25 September 1962, Ivatt 2-6-2T No 41312 (now preserved) awaits departure from Hatherleigh with the 8.52am Torrington-Halwill train. These locomotives were fitted with Walschaerts valve-gear and the Southern coach attached to the locomotive is No S6728S. *R. C. Riley*

Below:
Standard '9F' 2-10-0 No 92082 heads an up freight through Hatton station, on the Paddington-Birmingham ex-Great Western line, in 1962. Hatton was the junction for the Stratford upon Avon and Alcester lines and is mostly remembered for scenes of steam operating up Hatton Bank. *M. Pope*

Left:
Pacific power in the form of 1954-built No 71000 *Duke of Gloucester*, which was fitted with Caprotti valve-gear. In this scene, 'The Duke' reaches the top of Camden Bank out of Euston with an evening Euston-Liverpool express in 1962. After years of hard work in restoration, *Duke of Gloucester* was back on Britain's main lines hauling steam specials from 1990 after ending its days in service just a mere derelict shell in the scrapyards of South Wales. *M. Esau*

Bottom left:
This splendid view, photographed on the Stranraer line, shows the breakdown train returning from a smash at Daljarrock in May 1962 hauled by ex-LMS 0 6 0 No 44281. Note the fascinating signalbox situated high above the road bridge in the background. *Derek Cross*

Right:
Western Region 'Warship' class diesel-hydraulic No D833 *Panther* passes Brecon Junction signalbox, Hereford, with the 9.10am Liverpool-Plymouth train on 1 May 1962. In the centre-distance is Ivatt Mogul No 46510 which has just come off the 10.45am service from Brecon and is turning round to take the return 12.42pm Brecon train. The Brecon curve can be seen to the top left of the picture. *Anthony M. Vickers*

Centre right:
The prototype diesel, No D0260 *Lion*, was built by the Birmingham RC&W Co and introduced in April 1962, as a Type 4 demonstration diesel. In fact it was only on loan to British Railways until October 1963 so pictures of this locomotive working are quite rare. *Lion* is seen near Twyford on 12 July 1962 with a down parcels train. *Cecil J. Blay*

Below:
USA 0-6-0T No 30066 hauls a train of vans from Southampton Docks on 15 September 1962 past an original Victorian grain warehouse. With the withdrawal of steam locomotive traction from Southampton Docks, Class 07 diesel shunters took over these duties. In this scene from the past is an early 1950s Southampton City Transport Guy Arab III double-deck with a Park Royal body. *L. Sandler*

The 'Beeching Axe'

On 27 March 1963, Dr Beeching made it clear in his *Reshaping of British Railways* report that the axe was to fall on many of Britain's picturesque branch lines. The aim was to save up to £147 million per year; up to £20 million by the elimination of steam, £18 million from the withdrawal of certain passenger services and up to £13 million by passenger line closures. It was hoped to save up to £12 million by the redirection of the wagon fleet and around £3 million by reducing the coaching fleet. To the enthusiast (and to people living in outlying areas) the news was devastating. The list was 'endless' for lines earmarked for early axing. On the Western Region there was Radley-Abingdon, Brent-Kingsbridge, Aylesbury-Princes Risborough, Taunton-Barnstaple Junction and Leominster-Kington to name but a few and on other regions lines such as Harpenden-Hemel Hempstead, Havant-Hayling Island, Grantham-Lincoln, and Barnard Castle-Bishop Auckland were scheduled for early closure. Britain's railways would never be the same again but financial losses were getting greater every year on British Railways and something had to be done. Only the previous year there had been proposals to reorganise the railway workshops in an effort to save £30 million. These necessary measures would reduce the workshops' labour force by 18,000 which naturally created bitterness in the NUR.

With the demise of steam and the Beeching cuts coming into force, there were many 'lasts' in 1963. In fact, by 1963, only 23% of passenger trains were steam-hauled. On the locomotive scene the 'lasts' included SR 'E2' No 32109, 'E4' No 32479, Powsland & Mason 0-4-0T No 1151, SR 'B4' 0-4-0T No 30096, LNER 'O2/2' No 63943, LNER 'J50' No 68988, GWR Class '54xx' 0-6-0PT No 5410, SR 'A1x' 0-6-0T No 32670, GWR '15xx' Hawksworth 0-6-0T No 1507, ex-CR Pickersgill '3F' No 57688 and diesel-electric 1Co-Co1 locomotives Nos 10201/2/3 — all the last survivors of their respective classes. On 7 January the last electric services ran on South Tyneside being replaced by diesel-multiple units and the last passenger trains ran on the Severn Valley line eight months later — two of the more significant changes of the year — and more steam depots closed in one year than ever before.

However, on an encouraging note, the Welshpool & Llanfair Light Railway was formally reopened to passenger traffic on 6 April by the Earl of Powys. The preservation society had now also secured No 823 *Countess* on 5 October 1962 in addition to *The Earl*. On the Isle of Man Railway the first ever Royal Train ran on 7 July when No 11 *Maitland* hauled Her Majesty the Queen Mother from Douglas to Braddan.

In February 1963, the weather in North Yorkshire took a turn for the worst when 15ft of snow blocked the Esk Valley line between Middlesbrough and Whitby.

A highly organised mail train robbery (now referred to as the Great Train Robbery) took place at Sears Crossing, north of Cheddington, Bucks, in the early hours of 8 August 1963 when a gang stopped the 6.50pm Aberdeen-Glasgow-Euston mail train bagging registered mail, banknotes and jewellery valued at £2,500,000. The train was hauled by English Electric Type 4 Co-Co locomotive (Class 40) No D326 and was stopped at signals which had been altered by the train robbers by masking the green light. The red light was produced by batteries brought by the robbers to the site. The robbers then uncoupled the first two coaches and forced the driver of the train to drive forward to Bridego Bridge where they unloaded the 'loot' from the two coaches. The crew was handcuffed and forced to lie down by the track. The train robbers were well clear of the scene before the sorters on the train became suspicious. Some of the robbers, when caught, received 30-year prison sentences.

On 14 January, No 60103 *Flying Scotsman* made her final official run for British Railways between King's Cross and Doncaster. King's Cross was packed with enthusiasts, the press, radio reporters, television cameramen and railway staff from the highest in office to the lower-paid. Platforms 1, 4, 5, 10, the signalbox, stairs and landings and a variety of other vantage points were swarming with photographers keen to get one final picture of this fine LNER locomotive. On arrival at Doncaster, six minutes early, *Flying Scotsman* was quickly taken off the train and moved to the bay platform surrounded once again by admirers. Fortunately for all lovers of this locomotive, Alan Pegler saved her from the cutting torch and she now looks as beautiful as ever nearly 30 years later. For those returning to King's Cross on this auspicious occasion soon after arriving at Doncaster hauled by *Flying Scotsman*, they were extremely fortunate to travel on the 'White Rose' hauled by 'A4' Pacific No 60022 *Mallard* also scheduled for preservation. On 20 April, *Flying Scotsman* made its first revenue-earning appearance since being purchased by Alan Pegler when it worked a Festiniog Railway Special after trials on 29 March from Doncaster to Barkston and back. She was resplendent in her LNER livery and bore the number 4472.

The big news for British Railways on the freight side was the signing of long-term agreements with six major oil companies for the conveyance of petroleum products. The six oil companies, Petrofina, Gulf Oil, Mobil Oil, Esso, Shell Mex & BP and Regent Oil were obligated to provide their own wagon fleets and terminal equipment. Contracts with six more oil companies followed in 1964 by which time over 200 block trains were conveying 90,000 tons of oil products each week.

More forward-looking freight policies resulted in a mammoth marshalling yard being built at Millerhill, Edinburgh, which was completed in May, the down yard opening on 8 April.

On the passenger side, the prototype Mk 2 coach (project XP64) was constructed. The coach was numbered W13252 and fitted with 'B4' bogies and went into use on the 'Bristolian', all stock on the train being similarly equipped.

The London Underground celebrated its centenary at Neasden on 23 May 1963. A parade of 15 trains, portraying steam and electric locomotives, and rolling stock, passed invited VIPs from New York, Toronto, Tokyo, Moscow and most European capitals, the parade being led by the 97-year-old Metropolitan Railway steam locomotive No 23.

On 23 April, the prototype English Electric diesel, *Deltic* made its way from the Vulcan Works factory for preservation in the Science Museum in London.

During the year, following the locomotive's withdrawal in April 1963, 'A4' Pacific No 60022 *Mallard* was being restored at Doncaster to its original livery and old number — 4468. Regarding preservation, the asking price in May 1963 for ex-Metropolitan Railway 0-6-2T No L52 was £500!

Above:
LMS 4-6-0 'Patriot' No 45532 *Illustrious* climbs past Clifton, near Penrith, with the morning pick-up freight from Carlisle Yard to Harrison's Sidings, Shap, during May 1963. The Ivatt version of the Fowler design incorporated a larger tapered boiler, new cylinders and a double chimney uprating these 'Patriots' from 6P5F to 7P. *Peter J. Robinson*

Right:
An all-out effort from ex-GWR 0-6-0PTs Nos 8409 and 9493 as they bank a northbound freight up the Lickey Incline in Worcestershire on 2 March 1963, which is headed by ex-LMS '8F' No 48363. Banking on this incline has passed through various hands over the years from the LNER Beyer-Garrett locomotive No 69999 to 'Hymeks' and Class 37 diesels, but none more successful and reliable as ex-MR 0-10-0 No 58100 'Big Bertha'. *R. H. Postill*

Above:
By 1963, LMS 'Duchesses' were demoted to freight duties and, in December of that year, Upperby-allocated No 46238 *City of Carlisle* heads south from Carlisle with a meat train for Broad Street, London. Originally streamlined, No 6238 had her streamlined casing removed in November 1946. *Peter J. Robinson*

Left:
Sporting its English and French flags, the down 'Golden Arrow' emerges from Knockholt Tunnel, early in September 1963, with rebuilt 'Battle of Britain' Pacific No 34088 *213 Squadron* in charge. The title 'Golden Arrow' was bestowed on the 11.00am London Victoria-Paris train in 1929 and the service was then exclusively 'Pullman' but, in the train's latter years in service, only four Pullman cars were included — the rest of the train was second-class. This prestige service ended its days in 1972. *Derek Cross*

Above:
An idyllic rural scene in the Forest of Dean as Great Western 0-6-0PT No 4624 climbs towards Coleford, on 20 December 1963, with a short mixed freight. This ex-Severn & Wye Railway line from Coleford to Parkend closed to passengers as long ago as 8 July 1929.
B. J. Ashworth

Right:
The severe winter of 1962/63 created havoc on Britain's railways and this 'cold' scene tells it all. The snowploughs are out near Sourton between Okehampton and Tavistock in North Devon and British Railways staff endeavour to clear the line manually in an almost impossible situation. In January 1963, two Drummond ex-L&SWR Class 700 0-6-0s, Nos 30689 and 30697, provide mechanical assistance. *Ian Allan Library*

Right:
A 1963 view of the up 'Birmingham Pullman' approaching West Ruislip. The train in this scene is an eight-car set, three of which were built. There were also two six-car sets. Often referred to as 'Blue Pullmans' due to their attractive 'Nanking Blue' livery, these units originally carried the name 'Midland Pullman' on the leading car. *Lewis Coles*

Left:
Five AC railbuses were introduced in 1958 and, on 12 June 1963, No W79978 is seen at Tetbury prior to working the 7.30am train to Kemble. The AC railbuses were the first of five types introduced on BR and were fitted with 'basic' buffers, four marker lights and a central headlight. Four of these vehicles were allocated to the Western Region and one, No SC79979, to the Scottish. *A. Swain*

Below left:
Departing Scarborough for Hull on 22 August 1963, a Gloucester RC&W unit (later Class 100) passes Class 03 shunter No D2151 shunting stock in the adjacent platform. *P. H. Wells*

Freight Progress

Merry-go-round trains were introduced in 1964 when the new galvanised 26/32-ton capacity HOP AB 18ft 3in-wheelbase hopper wagon trains came into being for the conveyance of coal from pits to power stations. A major advance in unloading technique was created where lineside apparatus engaged fitments on the hopper wagon which automatically discharged their load of coal at the power station whilst the train moved slowly forward at ½mph. Special slow-speed-control was fitted to certain Brush Type 4 diesel locomotives earmarked for these trains. The CEGB, in turn, designed new base load coal-fired power stations initially at West Burton, Ferrybridge, Eggborough, Ratcliffe-on-Soar, Fiddler's Ferry and Cottam to accept the new MGR workings. Also, other power stations were modified to accept these trains. All this coupled with a long-term agreement between the CEGB and the BR Board set up a secure future for this important part of BR's freight operations. Each power station's estimated requirements were 20,000 tons of coal per day and the new apparatus could handle a train with a load of 2,000 tons, bringing the expected tonnage of coal to power stations each year to 60 million. Unfortunately, the National Coal Board were unprepared to modify existing pithead installations to cater for the new MGR wagons other than at BR's expense.

This year also saw the introduction of Cartic trains conveying new cars from factories and the dockside. These comprised twin-decked four-section articulated vehicles. This 'Cartic 4' wagon was designed with the help of the Ford Motor Co and the wagons could take Ford's entire range of cars. Both decks could be loaded at the same time, old coach underframes being adapted to provide a mobile ramp. The Cartics were also suitable for car-sleeper services but their open sides sadly led to vandalism. The Ford Motor Co initially chartered over 60 Cartic trains per week, each train comprising five or more vehicle sets, each articulated set having the capacity to carry between 24 and 34 cars, depending on size.

The Roadrailer equipment completed technical trials in 1964. This was, basically, an ordinary road trailer container with two pairs of wheels, one for rail and the other for road use. Compressed air altered the wheel configuration and a length of track was set into the road surface. Unfortunately the idea did not result in the anticipated success as the breaking up of trains took far

too long and the fact that the new wagons were not compatible with other rolling stock restricted their use.

There was also 'freight' news on a much smaller scale in 1964. The railways had used genuine 'horse-power' for many purposes, even shunting wagons, over the years and in June 1964 the last LMS horse, 17-year-old *Prince*, retired from his workplace at Stoke on Trent to a farm near Peterborough. *Prince* was a familiar sight at Stoke station with his fine high-sided cart and shining LMS horse brasses.

Under the project number XP64, British Railways unveiled their eight-coach train of the future when, on 28 May, it was hauled by Brush Type 4 diesel No D1733 from Marylebone to High Wycombe and back. Designed at Derby the new Mark 2 coach with its new 'B4' Type bogies was five tons lighter than the existing BR Mk1 stock. The coaches were painted in a livery of 'rail blue' and light grey. On 15 June, the eight-coach train went into service on the 'Talisman' and from the winter 1964 timetable was used on King's Cross-West Riding of Yorkshire services.

Derby's new laboratories of BR's Engineering Research Division were opened on 14 May 1964. Their main objective was to obtain better knowledge of equipment design, to improve reliability whilst at the same time reducing manufacture and maintenance costs, and to investigate new proposals concerning railway equipment and operation. Initial projects included marshalling yard design using Dowty Automatic Wagon Control. Computer calculation at the new research establishment would ascertain the best design for the booster-retarders to be installed in marshalling yards. These booster-retarders controlled wagon speeds in the marshalling yards, in order to reduce heavy repair costs on wagons caused by excessive shock whilst being shunted. Other future projects included the vibration problem in general, checking the strength of integral coach body shells, wear and tear of trackwork, and locomotive stress.

New locomotives in action during 1964 included the Paxman 0-6-0 diesel-hydraulic centre-cab shunters, which were also designed for pick-up freights. The 1964 deliveries (D9500-24) were allocated to Worcester (85A), Bristol Bath Road (82A), Cardiff Canton (86A) and Old Oak Common (81A), Nos D9500-05 emerging in July. They ended their days on BR as early as 1969, after an extremely short life, but

not before many had been transferred to Hull Dairycoates, from December 1966, where they had taken over the roundhouse prior to withdrawal from this region in 1968. Most were sold, many to the National Coal Board and the British Steel Corporation. Some even went to Belgium and Spain and several are now preserved in Britain.

The three original 0-6-0 diesel shunters built for the Southern Railway, Nos 1, 2 and 3 (15201-03) ended their days in service in November/December 1964, although it was five years before No 15201 was cut up and 1964 also saw the demise of *Taurus*, which ended its days at Stratford.

May saw the end of the GWR '47xx' class 2-8-0s built by Churchward in 1919 and in November the last surviving Hawksworth GWR 'County' No 1011 *County of Chester* ended its days at Cashmore's scrapyard in Newport as the end of steam drew nearer for the Western Region.

The last '7F', No 53807, was withdrawn from the Somerset & Dorset on 5 September. This coincided with the withdrawal of night freight services over this route. No 53807 was one of 11 ex-S&D 2-8-0s built in 1914 and taken over by the LMS in 1930. Two of the type, Nos 53808 and 53809, are now preserved. We also saw the end of the Johnson ex-Midland Railway '3F' 0-6-0s, introduced in 1885 and affectionately known by enthusiasts as the 'Duck Sixes' — a class which once boasted 935 locomotives.

The Southern's last 'M7' 0-4-4T also disappeared in the guise of No 30667 as did the LNER's last 'B16/2' 4-6-0 No 61435 and the last LMS 0-6-0 dock tanks, Nos 47164/5. However, the saddest news was that concerning the end of the LMS 'Duchesses' that graced the West Coast main line for so many years. They were one of the finest sights to see and those who were lucky enough to see them in their 'streamlined' state prior to 1949 (like the author) had an extra bonus.

On 4 September, the 'Atlantic Coast Express' — now 38 years of age — performed its final steam run at over 60mph. The last down 'ACE' was hauled by 'Merchant Navy' Pacific No 35022 *Holland America Line* and looked immaculate. Diesel-operated 'ACE' trains commenced on 7 September, hauled by Western Region-allocated 'Warships'.

As more and more lines closed following the Beeching cuts during the year all over Britain, lightly-loaded electric trains from the Manchester-Crewe line were released for use on the newly-electrified Crewe-Nuneaton line from 2 March. The new electrically-operated signalbox at Rugby was brought into use in September following electrification of the line from Crewe, replacing 22 manually-operated boxes. The section from Lichfield to Nuneaton was energised on 3 January.

Replacement Lickey banker BR '9F'

2-10-0 No 92223 was withdrawn in February. In fact the first diesel to be used on this duty operated on 3 July when English Electric Type 3 No D6938 was sent there for crew training in anticipation of a further four locomotives of this class arriving by 31 August. Initially, this trial was booked to be operated by a diesel-hydraulic 'Hymek' locomotive.

It is interesting to compare today's prices for railway relics with those from 1964 as locomotives were being withdrawn. In 1964 Swindon Works were offering GWR 'Hall' class nameplates for sale at £15 each, brass cabside numberplates at £7 10s 0d each and cast-iron cabside numberplates at £1 each — what would they fetch today?

Left:
On 29 August 1964, Great Western 2-6-2T tank No 4113 travels over ex-MR metals and works the Worcester to Bristol service. It is pictured at Bredon passing a fine example of a Midland Railway signal box. *Derek Cross*

Bottom left:
The 8.00am Gloucester train waits at Chalford on 24 April 1964 with Great Western 0-4-2T 'Coffeepot' No 1444 in charge. The entire '14xx' class was fitted for push-pull working. *B. J. Ashworth*

Right:
Consett Steelworks in 1964, a scene not to be repeated owing to the closure of the works in the early 1980s. With its chimney stacks towering above the railway, ex-NER Raven 'Q6' 0-8-0 No 63379 waits impatiently at the signal whilst preparing to pass through with empties. The 'Q6s' together with the 'J27s' were the last surviving LNER pre-Grouping classes, some lasting into 1967. *W. J. Verden Anderson/ Copyright Rail Archive Stephenson*

Below:
A December 1964 view sees Staveley 0-4-0T locomotive No 41528 working over the Staveley Coal & Iron Co's lines. Ten of these locomotives were built between 1907 and 1922 to a design by Deeley for the Midland Railway and by June 1964 only three survived, two to be found at Staveley and No 41535 allocated to Neath on the Western Region. *W. J. Verden Anderson/Copyright Rail Archive Stephenson*

Top left:
During the final years of BR Western Region steam, the 4-6-0 'Manors' worked predominantly over Cambrian metals alongside BR Standard 4-6-0s. On 29 August 1964, No 7821 *Ditcheat Manor* ascends Talerddig Bank, between Llanbrynmair and Carno, with the 10.40am Aberystwyth-Manchester train. No 7821 is one of the nine members of this class now preserved. *Gerald T. Robinson*

Left:
Ex-Great Western 2-6-2T No 6148 hauls the 17.00 coal train from Radstock, in April 1964, and is seen making the climb from Pensford. Up until the early 1950s, this class could only be found in the London area, all members being allocated to '81' sheds and 34E Neasden. *Ivo Peters*

Above:
BR Standard '2MT' 2-6-0 No 78038 leaves Crystal Palace Tunnel with the LCGB 'Surrey Wanderer' railtour whilst running between Tulse Hill and Beckenham Junction on 5 July 1964. These locomotives were similar, in almost all respects, to the Ivatt LMS design Moguls of 1946. *Brian Stephenson*

Right:
An ex-GWR '45xx' class 2-6-2T, No 4564, heads for Gloucester with a goods train and is pictured on the Cinderford branch on 28 August 1964. These locomotives were developed from the '44xx' class smaller-wheeled 2-6-2Ts and a further development, the '4575' class, incorporated larger tanks for greater water-carrying capicity. *B. J. Ashworth*

Above:
A Rosyth-Thornton workmen's train restarts from Dysart in March 1964 headed by Standard 2-6-0 '4MT' No 76111. These Doncaster-built locomotives were allocated to all regions with the exception of the Western at this time.
W. J. Verden Anderson/
Copyright Rail Archive Stephenson

Left:
A northbound parcels train headed by ex-GWR 'Modified Hall' No 7920 *Coney Hall* approaches Craven Arms on the Central Wales line, on 5 June 1964. The 'Modified Halls' differed to the original 'Hall' class by the fitting of a larger superheater, a 'one-piece' main frame and a plate-framed bogie. *Derek Cross*

Top right:
The 11am Victoria-Brighton non-stop 'Brighton Belle' passes through Wandsworth Common on 15 November 1964. The train carries the umber & cream Pullman livery and the elongated Pullman crest introduced in the early 1960s which replaced the traditional version. Changes to lining-out also took place at the same time. There were four 'Brighton Belle' Pullman trains in each direction from September 1963, the final daily departure from Victoria (11pm) stopping *en route* at Haywards Heath. *Brian Stephenson*

Right:
A Park Royal-constructed two-car diesel unit (later Class 103) forms a train for Wolverhampton in 1964 and is pictured near Hammerwich, between Lichfield and Brownhills. This unit sports the half-yellow warning panel – the precursor to the present-day all-yellow front end seen on the majority of motive power. *M. Mensing*

Below:
During a morning rush-hour in 1964, commuters from Woking pack the corridors of a train comprising three 4-COR units led by set No 3115. These one-eyed 'Nelson' units were originally introduced in 1937 to coincide with the electrification of the Portsmouth route. In this view another commuter train, from Shepperton formed of 4-SUBs with set No 4744 leading, runs parallel on the up local line. *Brian Stephenson*

Western Steam Finale

The end of regular steam working on the Western Region was commemorated by a special 'Farewell to Steam' train run by British Rail on 27 November 1965. This was the last steam train from Paddington and was hauled by the last surviving GWR 'Castle', No 7029 *Clun Castle* (now preserved), which departed at 9.18am for Swindon, Bristol, Gloucester (Eastgate) and Cheltenham (St James). The return journey to Paddington was via Gloucester Central and Swindon. Regular steam working from Paddington, in reality, had ceased some months previous. Although the actual train covered the route stated, the part of the journey from Gloucester to Cheltenham and return was diesel-hydraulic 'Western'-hauled, by No D1006 *Western Stalwart*, whilst *Clun Castle* was being serviced at Gloucester, and, from Swindon to Paddington on the return journey, two Brush Type 2 (Class 31) diesels took over.

GWR named classes which survived to the end of steam on the Western Region included 'Castles', 'Halls', 'Granges' and 'Manors', the last survivors (in addition to *Clun Castle*) being No 7925 *Westol Hall* (81F), No 6872 *Crawley Grange* (85A) and No 7829 *Ramsbury Manor* (85B). In fact the last 'Castle' to be given an overhaul at Swindon Works prior to the end of steam was No 4079 *Pendennis Castle*.

The last 'booked' steam passenger train from Paddington left for Banbury on 11 June, also hauled by *Clun Castle*, packed, as you might have imagined, by enthusiasts. From then on one could no longer see from the train that impressive sight of 'Castles' and 'Kings' simmering near the turntable at Ranelagh Bridge Yard as one approached and departed by train from Paddington.

As steam ended on the Western Region in June 1965, a number of 'train names' in the new timetable were discarded. These included the 'Bristolian', the 'Royal Duchy', the 'Mayflower', the 'Red Dragon', the 'Capitals United Express', the 'Inter City' and the 'Cathedrals Express'.

At Bristol (Temple Meads) the old train shed ceased to be used from 6 September, part of the area being converted into a car park.

In June, contractors' cranes were to be found at the famous Crumlin Viaduct in South Wales, dismantling this amazing structure which once carried the Great Western Railway line from Pontypool Road to Neath. Five different companies attempted this mammoth task, including one German firm, but the job was finally completed by Birds, who built a Bailey bridge and moved it along as each section was demolished. At Lydbrook, in the Wye Valley, two cranes worked from ground level to dismantle the GWR 120ft-high viaduct there in August 1965.

An abundance of Western Region line closures took place during 1965, including the Carmarthen-Aberystwyth line on 22 February and the Calne branch on 18 September (after 102 years of service). Passenger workings ceased on the Kemble-Cirencester branch on 4 October.

On the London Midland Region in the Midlands, three routes closed to passengers on 18 January. These were the Coventry-Nuneaton and Coventry-Leamington Spa lines and the Wolverhampton-Walsall-Lichfield-Burton route.

On the North Eastern, the passenger service between Sunderland and South Shields terminated on 3 May 1965 and all passenger services to Whitby Town were withdrawn except that from Middlesbrough, via Grosmont. This had a dramatic effect on the number of visitors to Whitby during the summer. Passenger services from Grosmont to Malton — the North York Moors line — also ceased in 1965.

From the start of the year, the BR Standard '9F' 2-10-0s, a familiar sight on iron ore trains from Tyne Dock to Consett, gradually ceased operating, their duties being taken over by BR/Sulzer Type 2 diesels.

In Scotland there were no more passenger workings timetabled over the ex-G&SWR Stranraer-Dumfries line from 14 June 1965, the only way open to Stranraer for the Irish sea crossing to Ireland now being via Ayr. The picturesque Crianlarich Junction-Killin Junction line also lost its passenger services on 28 September. Another important and beautiful route in Scotland which had its passenger services terminated, this time on 18 October, was the Speyside line from Aviemore to Forres, in whisky distillery country.

Sussex closures on the Southern included the 'Cuckoo' line between Eridge and Hailsham, on 14 June 1965, the Guildford-Horsham line, on the same day, and on 29 November, the Axminster-Lyme Regis branch lost its passenger service.

Following a temporary closure of Bournemouth West station on 4 September 1965, the station faced permanent closure on 4 October resulting in Somerset & Dorset line trains terminating at Bournemouth Central.

Work was well underway by the end of 1965 on the electrification programme for the Waterloo-Bournemouth line. From September to November 1965 relaying of track between Brookwood and Farnborough and from Basingstoke to Eastleigh was progressing well, and during electrification of the line from Bournemouth Central station to the depot at Branksome, S&D line trains terminated at Branksome, special buses conveying passengers to and from Bournemouth West. The stock ordered for the Bournemouth electrification included 11 3,200hp four-car motor units (4-REP), 28 unpowered four-car corridor units with driving compartments at each end (4-TC) and 20 four-car 4-VEP sets. A 4-REP with two 4-TC sets was planned to work as a 12-car set.

On 10 May, there was a complete suspension of services in and out of Waterloo due to a problem with Clapham Junction 'A' signalbox which spanned two main lines. During the morning 'peak' services, part of the structure at the Windsor lines end of the box dropped 3-4ft at one corner. Chaos reigned as some trains, such as those from Bournemouth, terminated at Surbiton or Woking (their steam locomotives being turned using Byfleet Junction) and some trains terminated at Wimbledon. Windsor trains terminated at Twickenham and Barnes. The gantry supporting the signalbox was erected in 1905.

Sir Winston Churchill made his final journey by rail on 30 January 1965 when his funeral train was hauled from Waterloo to Handborough in Oxfordshire, for his burial in Bladon churchyard, by, appropriately, 'Battle of Britain' Pacific No 34051 *Winston Churchill*. The train comprised Pullman parlour brake No 208, van No S2464 and Pullmans *Carina*, *Lydia*, *Perseus* and *Isle of Thanet*. The hearse van, No S2464, was painted in Pullman livery in 1962.

Steam locomotives continued to flow to scrapyards all over Britain during 1965 to locations such as Barry Docks, now starting to burst at the seams, Bridgend, Long Marston, Newport (Gwent), Kettering, Hull, Troon, Beighton, Great Bridge (Staffs), Killamarsh, Motherwell and at Airdrie.

From 4 January 1965, an official ban on steam power for through workings south of Crewe had been put into practice. Steam locomotives banned south of Crewe could always be recognised as they carried a yellow diagonal stripe on their cabsides. The last 'Royal Scots' and 'Patriots' were withdrawn on 31 December 1965, No 46115 *Scots Guardsman* and No 45530 *Sir Frank Ree* being the last survivors.

As more and more steam locomotives ended their days on the London Midland Region, new locomotives emerged from August 1965 in the form of the AL6 (Class 86) electrics. These locomotives carried only one pantograph. An improvement for maintenance purposes over the AL1-AL5 (Classes 81-85) electrics was the increased headroom in the between-cab sections.

Test runs also began with the four-car AM10 ac electric multiple-units during the summer of 1965. These were the first multiple-units to be fitted with standard disc brakes and they were for use on the Euston-Bletchley-Rugby-Birmingham semi-fast services at peak periods operating in sets of eight or 12. On 27 September the line was energised to Willesden from the north and

to Euston on 25 October and new power boxes were built at Euston, Willesden, Bletchley and Wolverhampton.

After extensive trials the first new Brighton line 4-CIG express units entered public service on 29 March with morning and afternoon peak services to and from London Bridge. Push-pull trials were carried out towards the end of 1965 on the Central Division of the Southern Region with electro-diesel No E6007 and push-pull set No 601, which was made up of former 6-PUL/4-COR stock.

As many steam depots closed during 1965, a brand-new diesel depot opened at Old Oak Common on 20 October, but, to the delight of enthusiasts, the turntable was retained.

A new BR symbol, the double arrow (cruelly nicknamed the arrow of indecision), based on the idea of two-way traffic, emerged in 1965 and the new BR blue livery was applied to a diesel locomotive for the first time — Brush Type 4 No D1733 being the 'guinea pig'. Also Western Region Brush Type 4 Diesels started to be named when, on 20 March, *North Star* and *Isambard Kingdom Brunel* appeared. Their nameplates carried Great Western style lettering.

On the freight side, a new hump yard at Tinsley was opened in October where the three 700hp master-&-slave diesel shunters operated — these were converted from six 0-6-0 shunters and were to become Class 13 under the TOPS system. These locomo-

tives were fitted with cab signalling apparatus and VHF radio.

On 15 November, Freightliner services started from London to Glasgow using the all-new container stock. The heaviest train ever to be hauled on BR, a 240-ton power-station boiler drum, 122ft long and 26½ft in circumference, travelled from Ettingshall Road (Staffs) freight depot to Eggborough (Yorks) in June.

But, in all, the main 'scare' of the year was Dr Beeching's proposals to cut trunk routes on Britain's railways from 7,500 miles to 3,000. If the plan had materialised, lines beyond Plymouth or Aberdeen would have probably been singled, as would the North Wales coast route to Holyhead, and Mid-Wales would have been left bereft of a railway system. In addition, the lines to Fort William, Oban, the Kyle of Lochalsh, Wick and Thurso would have disappeared by now — a fine Centenary gift for the Highland Railway which was 100 years old in 1965.

Below:
In Scotland, the Edinburgh-Carstairs local train hauled by double-headed 'Black Fives' Nos 44700 and 44956, makes an exhibitionist departure from Edinburgh Princes Street station on 29 May 1965. This fine ex-Caledonian Railway station closed to passenger traffic on 6 September of that year. *Derek Cross*

Left:
Steam on the Western Region ended in 1965 and on 29 March of that year an exceedingly 'short' freight provides few problems for ex-GWR 0-6-0PT No 9711 as it crosses the River Wye after leaving Lydbrook for Ross-on-Wye.
B. J. Ashworth

Below:
Leslie, in Scotland, was situated at the end of the ex-NBR branch from Markinch and was a typically rural branch line. This view shows a Gresley-designed 'J38' 0-6-0, No 65901, hauling a freight over one of the primitive road crossings on the line in April 1965. It is noticeable that one of the gates has come off its hinges — an unacceptable state of affairs on today's railways.
W. J. Verden Anderson/Copyright Rail Archive Stephenson

Above:
Ex-LMS 'Jubilee' No 45660 *Rooke* heads north from Carlisle with a St Pancras-Glasgow express on 7 August 1965. The line converging from the right is the ex-NBR Port Carlisle branch. The main line north from Carlisle to Glasgow is ex-Caledonian and the train will soon be passing Carlisle Kingmoor locomotive shed.
Peter J. Robinson

Right:
The last portion of the 'Lakes Express' leaves Penrith for Keswick and Workington in July 1965 behind Ivatt Mogul No 46426. After a wartime break, the 'Lakes Express' returned to service leaving Euston at 11.50am, calling at Crewe, where it released the Barrow and Whitehaven section. Then, rather strangely, the rear portion train followed the front portion, each part calling at Wigan, Preston and Lancaster, both trains appearing in these stations together, before going their separate ways.
Peter J. Robinson

129

Top:
Steam on the Isle of Wight in September 1965, and Class O2 0-4-4T No 27 *Merstone* is seen near Smallbrook Junction with a Ventnor train. This line closed to passenger traffic, temporarily, seven months later. *A. R. Thompson*

Above:
Steam, diesel and electric traction at Rugby on 27 March 1965. This view of the north end of Rugby Midland station pictures LMS 'Black Five' No 45349 having terminated at Rugby with a passenger service whilst 'AL5' (Class 85) electric No E3059 waits to take over the parcels train brought down by Type 4 (Class 40) diesel No D313. *J. B. Groycott*

Left:
The Great Eastern's East Suffolk line, on 4 September 1965, and Type 2 Bo-Bo No D5039 eases to a halt to pick up holiday-makers at Oulton Broad South, with the 11.52am summer Saturdays Yarmouth South Town – Liverpool Street train. In the background can be seen a blue 'camping car', No CC9. *G. R. Mortimer*

Goodbye to the S&D

The Somerset & Dorset Railway has always been one of the more popular lines with railway enthusiasts, along with the M&GN and the Cambrian, but, sadly, as 1966 approached, the end was nigh for the S&D. The date earmarked for closure was 7 March 1966 and many enthusiasts, anxious to travel over this picturesque route before the chance disappeared, crowded trains from January to the final day. Services were greatly reduced, many in the hands of BR Standards such as Nos 73001, 75072, 80041 and 82041. Enthusiasts' 'Specials' were in abundance during the line's last week of activity with the RCTS employing 'Merchant Navy' Pacific No 35028 *Clan Line* on 6 March. Two Ivatt 2-6-2Ts were also on duty that day — Nos 41283 and 41249 on the Highbridge branch. On 5 March the LCGB hired Nos 41283 and 41307 for the Highbridge section and Nos 34006 *Bude* and 34057 *Biggin Hill* from Evercreech Junction to Bath and back to Bournemouth. The Great Western Society, using Stanier '8F' No 48706, and the SLS, using No 80043, also ran specials — everyone wanted a part of the action! But the RCTS had the last word (southbound) as far as Templecombe using rebuilt 'West Country' *Okehampton* double-headed with unrebuilt 'Battle of Britain' *Biggin Hill* on Sunday 6 March. By then the S&D line at Radstock had been cut to allow the connection to the North Somerset branch to be completed. This was the end of a 'very special' railway.

On 5 September, another sad closure took place. This was the Great Central main line. Yes, the last main line to be built became the first to be closed. North of Aylesbury, only the Rugby to Nottingham Victoria service remained. The railway village of Woodford Halse, once thriving, seemed to die as the engine shed, where locomotives from all the Big Four companies could often be seen together, was destined to be demolished. However, for those who watched television news around that time, you will recall that Woodford Halse did not give up that easily. Explosives were set to demolish the shed buildings but, when detonated, this was not to be as only the windows fell out. The second try only brought the roof down. Yes, it took three attempts to bring Woodford Halse depot to its knees! With the closure of the line, gone were the 'Master Cutler' and 'South Yorkshireman'. The last up and down trains were the 5.15pm Nottingham-Marylebone and the 10.45pm Marylebone-Manchester

(well, the last as far as the enthusiasts were concerned, as these were the last steam-hauled). There were, in fact, two later trains each way but the 'pull' of steam power drew the crowds. Both up and down trains were hauled by Colwick-allocated 'Black Five' No 44984 with eight coaches. It was intended that 'Black Five' No 44825 should make this last run having been highly polished at Colwick but she had 'failed' and even LMS 'Jubilee' No 45562 *Alberta* was considered. Crowds of enthusiasts lined the route at various locations, some with their tape recorders, which one day would give them happy memories of the 'Great' Great Central.

Steam disappeared in 1966 on the Isle of Wight. On 18 September, services ceased between Ryde Pier Head and Ryde Esplanade and on 31 December all the Island's steam engines (one of which is now preserved) were withdrawn from service for, on 1 March 1967, the line from Ryde Pier Head to Shanklin was to be electrified in preparation for electric services to run from 20 March. Ex-London Underground tube stock to replace steam-hauled trains arrived on the Island on 2 September in readiness for its new life. The Cowes-Newport line was never to see this change as it closed on 21 February 1966.

Other lines closed to passengers during the year included Ballachulish-Connel Ferry (ex-CR), Lanark-Carstairs and the ex-GNSR branch from Ballater to Aberdeen, a route once used by the Royal Family when travelling to Balmoral Castle in Scotland. The Keswick-Workington line closed on 18 April, and Wadebridge-Okehampton on 3 October.

Important stations closed to passengers during the year included both Glasgow St Enoch and Glasgow Buchanan Street and Southampton Terminus, and steam depots closed included Carlisle Upperby, Doncaster, Leicester (Midland) and Llandudno Junction.

A full timetable for electric trains was introduced for Euston-Manchester/Liverpool trains on 18 April following electrification to Euston. Journey times were cut by up to one third and services included eight Pullman trains daily.

In January 1966, one of the most unusually-designed locomotives, the Southern's 'Q1' 0-6-0, ended its days; the last examples being allocated to Guildford. It was also the finale for the LNER 'A1', 'A2', 'A3' and 'A4' Pacifics.

As British Railways continued to flood the scrap merchants throughout Britain with withdrawn locomotives, Woodham's scrapyard in Barry Docks, by the midsummer of 1966, was lined with well over 150 steam engines including GWR 'Castles', 'Halls' and tank locomotives, SR Bulleid Pacifics and 'U's and LMS 'Black 5s' to name but a few types. Mr Woodham was constantly being sought out by enthusiasts wishing to purchase locomotives for preservation, negotiating over the 'weight' of the locomotive desired and the price of cast iron per ton. Fortunately in most cases agreement was achieved, with many of the locomotives which stood at Barry rotting away having now been preserved or in the course of restoration.

Sir William A. Stanier, who from 1922 to 1932 was principal assistant to the CME of the GWR and from 1932 to 1944 was CME of the LMS, sadly passed away at the age of 89 in 1966. His fine locomotives will always be remembered. Fortunately some of them, like No 6201 *Princess Elizabeth*, can still be seen today, preserved, as he would have wished to have seen them.

Left:
War Department 2-8-0 No 90678 powers her way up the 1 in 70 incline to Copy Pit Summit and is seen near Cornholme on 30 July 1966. The train is assisted at the rear (unseen) by ex-LMS 2-8-0 '8F' No 48079. Banking locomotives for this incline were supplied by Rose Grove shed. *David D. Gouldthorp*

Below:
On Christmas Eve 1966, a down Crewe-Carlisle goods powers up Shap, near Shap Wells, with 'Britannia' Pacific No 70020 *Mercury* in charge. The 'Britannia' is ably assisted at the rear by a Fairburn 2-6-4T. A powerful scene in a Christmas setting. *John M. Boyes*

Right:
BR Standard '4MT' 4-6-0 No 75051 vigorously attacks the climb out of Carlisle with the 7PO4 Carlisle Yard-Skipton freight, near Cotehill in May 1966, over the Settle & Carlisle route. *Peter J. Robinson*

Below:
Until 1966, trains on the former Cromford & High Peak Railway worked from both Buxton and Middleton Top to Friden. Trains would then be exchanged at this point. Shown in this view of 22 July 1966, are ex-LMS Ivatt Mogul No 46465 waiting to return to Buxton and ex-Ministry of Supply 'J94' 0-6-0ST No 68006 with the Middleton train. The 'J94s', introduced in 1943, on loan, were purchased by the LNER in 1946. *L. A. Nixon*

Bottom:
'EM2' electric locomotive (later Class 77) No 27006 *Pandora* passes Hadfield, on 5 July 1966, with the 16.10 Manchester Piccadilly-Sheffield Victoria service. This 1,500V dc locomotive, although introduced in December 1954, did not receive its name until May 1959 and was one of the seven locomotives of a class built specifically for passenger work over the ex-GCR Woodhead route. No 27006 was exported to Holland with the rest of the class, for use on the Netherlands Railways, in September 1969. *C. R. Whitfield*

Above:
The LNER Class J38 mineral locomotives, with their 4ft 8in driving wheels, were allocated to Scotland. No 65921 passes Benarty Hill, near Kelty, with the 9.25am goods train from Thornton to Milnathort, in September 1966, taking the southern ex-NBR route. *S. C. Crook*

Left:
On 20 May 1966, the final train on the Wisbech & Upwell Tramway was hauled by Class 04 diesel-mechanical shunter No D2201. The locomotive was fitted with a cowcatcher and side-sheets, obligatory on unprotected tramway lines. This final freight train carried boxes of flowers in the brake van. *L. Sandler*

Below left:
A local service for Glasgow Queen Street awaits departure from Grangemouth in March 1966 headed by 'Black Five' 4-6-0 No 45359 and is passed on the freight line by North British diesel-hydraulic 0-4-0 shunter No D2776 hauling a long train of timber planking.
W. J. Verden Anderson/
Copyright Rail Archive Stephenson

Top right:
King's Cross station on 13 May 1966 and Brush Type 2 (Class 31) No D5604 is seen departing with the 5.53pm to Cambridge as a Cravens diesel multiple-unit from Hatfield awaits departure from the York Road platform for Moorgate. A fine view of a now vastly-changed area. *Brian Stephenson*

Right:
Condemned brake vans line the route on the approach to Brentford Central as the prototype 4-SUB electric unit No 4101 works a Waterloo-Brentford-Richmond service on 10 September 1966. No 4101 first entered service late in 1941 on the Victoria-Orpington line but it was not until 1944 before the second 4-SUB, No 4102, appeared, production models being introduced in 1945. *Brian Stephenson*

Bournemouth goes Electric

As 1967 approached, the scheme to electrify the Southern Region's main Waterloo-Bournemouth line neared completion. On 18 January 1967, the stretch of track between Swaythling, near Southampton, and Lymington Junction was energised and a test train of two 2-EPB units, Nos 5769 and 5772, electro-diesel locomotive No E6025 and three coaches of 4-EPB unit No 5129 ran from Wimbledon Park to Brockenhurst and back. March saw the section electrified from Bournemouth Central and Branksome, where the depot was situated, certain carriage sidings there also being energised. Prior to electrification, in 1966, six Brush Type 4 diesels (Nos D1921-26) had been allocated to Bournemouth duties mainly for use on boat trains to and from Weymouth. From 3 April a variety of motive power could be seen over the Bournemouth route including Brush Type 4s (Class 47), electro-diesels, 'West Country' and 'Merchant Navy' Pacifics, Birmingham RC&W Type 3s (Class 33) and REP electric units with TC stock and even double-headed Standard Class 4 2-6-0s and 4-6-0s.

The last 'Pines Express' runs took place on 4 March with Brush Type 4 diesel Nos D1700 and D1653 performing these duties. Traditionally associated with the S&D, the 'Pines' was rerouted via Oxford and Basingstoke in September 1962, linking Liverpool and Manchester with important places such as Southampton. The first day of electrification on the Lymington branch resulted in passengers having to revert to road transport until midday as the 5.30am Eastleigh-Lymington Town service operated by a 2-HAP unit failed at Brockenhurst. Unfortunately, in these early days, electric services to Bournemouth proved very unreliable with failures of REP, HAP and VEP units and also the electro-diesels.

The final day for steam on the Southern was 9 July and the Southern Region's own 'Farewell to Steam' specials ran on 2 July. 'Merchant Navy' Pacific No 35008 *Orient Line* hauled 11 coaches to Weymouth and No 35028 *Clan Line* with 10 coaches went to Bournemouth. On the return journey *Orient Line* was paired with No 35007 *Aberdeen Commonwealth* as far as Bournemouth. On the same day the regular 9.33am Waterloo-Bournemouth excursion was operated by 'West Country' No 34025

Whimple. Two 'specials' were found to be ample as the response was poor due to high fares and inadequate publicity. Originally, five trains had been planned.

Disaster struck the Southern Region between Grove Park and Hither Green on 5 November 1967, when a train from Hastings was derailed resulting in 49 fatalities and 78 injuries. The derailment was due to a broken rail outside Hither Green's Continental Freight Depot. The 12-car train split in two at 70mph, the front section continuing for some distance before stopping, the driver being unaware of the situation behind him. The derailed rear portion lay slewed across the main line.

Only the previous month the Southern suffered a tragic disaster at Sevenoaks when 13 were killed and 61 injured, and on 28 November a Waterloo-Farnborough and Guildford newspaper train was derailed at Raynes Park.

On 1 January the Eastern and North Eastern regions of British Railways merged to form one region — the Eastern. Mr G. F. Fiennes was made Chairman of the Eastern Region Board — he was also General Manager of the region.

Another 'S&D' closure in 1967 was the historic Fighting Cocks section — a distance of 1¾ miles across the East Coast main line from Albert Hill Junction to Fields Crossing — of the Stockton & Darlington Railway, which closed completely on 21 May.

The English Electric diesel prototype, No DP2, completed in 1962, one of the privately-sponsored contenders for the Type 4 diesel orders, came to a sad end in July 1967 when she collided with the derailed wagons of a cement train at Thirsk. She looked a sorry sight after the collision with the left hand side of her front end completely demolished. From the prototype DP2 came the English Electric Type 4 (later Class 50), ironically in the same year as the prototype ended its days. Rather than purchase the 50 locomotives of the type outright, a leasing agreement was entered into with English Electric which helped BR to spread the locomotives' costs over their entire lives. No D400, resplendent in her new blue livery, appeared in October 1967, Nos D401, D402 and D404 appearing before the end of the year. The entire class of 50 locomotives was initially allocated to the London

Midland Region and all carried a small oval plate inscribed, *This locomotive is the property of English Electric Holdings Ltd*. They first operated north of Crewe and performed excellently on trains such as the 'Royal Scot'. 'Hoover Power' had arrived — a class which proved to be a 'favourite' with all diesel enthusiasts.

As the 'Hoovers' moved in on the London Midland Region, sadly the LMS 'Jubilees' moved out. One of the last 'Jubilees' to work regular trains was No 45593 *Kolhapur* (still with the name spelt wrongly on one side); the other was No 45562 *Alberta*. Both were allocated to Leeds (Holbeck) and at this time one could still capture there that old magic which only a steam roundhouse could offer — a feeling never to be forgotten.

The last steam locomotive on the Eastern Region was withdrawn in December 1967. This was the LNER 2-6-0 'K1' No 62005 (now preserved). Introduced in 1949 the 'K1' class was a Peppercorn development of the Thompson 'K1/1' No 61197 *MacCailin Mor*.

By the end of 1967 all remaining 'Britannia' Pacifics, with the exception of No 70013 *Oliver Cromwell*, were withdrawn from Carlisle (Kingmoor). Their last duties included freights to Tinsley and Skipton, parcels trains to Manchester and Ayr and a passenger working from Manchester to Leeds worked by *Oliver Cromwell*.

Yes, it was the final curtain for the big boys in 1967, including the War Department 2-8-0s and Bulleid Pacifics. On 6 March 1967 the main line electrification on the London Midland Region was extended to Birmingham and on 5 June, the Glasgow suburban electrification was extended to Gourock and Wemyss Bay.

On the Western Region, BR opened their first Freightliner terminal in Wales at Cardiff. Three 1,200ft lengths of track adjoining roadways spanned by a gantry crane were capable of handling 10 trains per day. Initial services ran to and from Manchester and Liverpool from June followed by London services in July. From 1967 even bananas were being transported by Freightliner trains from Southampton Docks to Scotland in an effort to speed up deliveries. Still on the subject of freight, the first 100-ton bogie tank wagon was completed to convey Shell Oil products. From now on trains of these wagons were to become a familiar sight.

The final Tyneside electrics in the Newcastle area were replaced by diesel multiple-units during the summer as the sub-stations and conductor rail installation had become life-expired and it had proved uneconomical to renew it. These electric units, built for the LNER, had had a life of 30 years.

From the Western Region in December, were withdrawn the entire class of North British-built Type 4 diesel-hydraulic 'Warships' Nos D600-604 (A1A-A1A Class 41). These locomotives spent the majority of their lives allocated to Plymouth (Laira) working between there and Penzance.

As steam on BR neared its end, 'Preservation' was the word on everyone's lips. Funds were being set up all over Britain to 'save' engines from the cutter's torch. Some of the classic locomotives had already been saved — such as *Flying Scotsman*, *Clan Line*, *Princess Elizabeth*, *The Great Marquess*, *Clun Castle*, *Green Arrow* and *Mallard* — but enthusiasts were keen to restore to duty as many classes as possible and to reopen many of the closed lines — a mammoth task requiring vast amounts of money. The Bluebell Railway and Welshpool & Llanfair in particular, being early starters, were well on the way to success but a great deal of hard voluntary work was required. Even the Isle of Man Railway was saved when, from 3 June 1967, under new (leased) ownership steam trains ran from Douglas to Peel seven days a week during the summer.

The only form of BR power that could not be preserved and used again was *Charlie*, BR's final shunting horse who retired from his duties at Newmarket, after 18 years of service, in February 1967. He retired to pastures new in the fields of Somerset, to create yet another extinct class on Britain's railways. *Charlie* died there at his new home on 29 October 1968 at the grand old age of 29. *Charlie* was genuine horse-power!

Below:
The River Wear at Monkwearmouth is spanned by adjacent road and rail bridges. On 29 August 1967 ex-NER Worsdell Class J27 0-6-0 No 65894 crosses the river with a coal train for South Dock, Sunderland. The view shows two excellent examples of both stone and steel architecture. *Brian Stephenson*

'God Save our Gracious Steam'

It was a Saturday evening — on 3 August 1968 — and Preston was overrun by fanatical railway enthusiasts to mourn the end of steam in normal main line service on British Railways. The final two steam-hauled passenger trains were packed with enthusiasts — the ordinary passenger anxious to get a seat, wondering what it was all about. The penultimate train was the 20.48 Preston-Blackpool South and the very last steam-hauled passenger train was the 21.25 Preston-Liverpool Exchange. These were hauled by 'Black Fives' Nos 45212 and 45318 respectively. The cheers were deafening as each engine arrived in the platform at Preston from Lostock Hall shed, both departing to a similar ovation. Tripods were tested and cameras and tape recorders were checked and checked again. Enthusiasts with cameras jockeyed for position — this was the one they could not afford to get wrong.

At Blackpool South, enthusiasts clamoured for autographs from the engine's crew of No 45212. As No 45318 arrived at Liverpool with corridors bursting at the seams with enthusiasts she was greeted with renditions of *Auld Lang Syne*, *God Save our Gracious Steam* and chants of *Steam! Steam! Steam!*. It was like an FA Cup Final. Fanatical enthusiasts wept, completely overcome by the occasion — no one really believed it was happening. Under the direction of a man in a top hat and cloak, enthusiasts joined in and sang *John Brown's Body lies a mouldering in the Grave, but Steam goes marching on*. The man, together with his friends, then raised a coffin, which they had brought from Preston, as they rendered yet another chorus. The songs and chants went on and on and even passengers, young and old, and the crew, joined in as a bottle of Martini was poured over the front of the locomotive. It was yet another 'Liverpool Sound'.

Although BR ended steam-hauled services on that Saturday night in August, there were numerous 'Steam Specials' on the following day. Lostock Hall shed was again an active steam depot as the highly-polished locomotives, prepared by enthusiasts for the day's specials, simmered on shed. The locomotives used were 'Britannia' Pacific No 70013 *Oliver Cromwell* which worked with 'Black Five' No 44781,

two more 'Black Fives' which worked double headed, Nos 45017 and 44874, named 'Black Five' No 45156 *Ayrshire Yeomanry*, Stanier '8F' No 48476 which worked in tandem with Standard 4-6-0 No 73069 and 'Black Fives' Nos 44871, 44894 and 45305. Of these locomotives, No 44781 later met with a tragic end when, disguised as a Malayan engine, it was 'destroyed' by a terrorist attack in the film *The Virgin Soldiers*. The film required the locomotive to be tipped over and it was subsequently scrapped.

On the following Sunday, BR ran more steam specials for a fare of £15 15s 0d which included meals and an inscribed scroll, using virtually the same locomotives. As on the previous Sunday, these trains brought out crowds of lineside photographers and sightseers.

On the preservation scene, the Keighley & Worth Valley reopened for business on 29 June — the result of extremely hard work by enthusiasts who were determined to reopen this line in the heart of the Pennines. The inaugural special was double-headed by Ivatt 2-6-2T No 41241 and SR 'USA' 0-6-0T No 72. The opening of the line followed the filming of *The Railway Children*. The K&WVR initially operated a weekend and Bank Holiday service through the summer of 1968 connecting with incoming BR trains to Keighley from Leeds and Bradford with BR connections meeting their incoming trains from Oxenhope.

The Bluebell celebrated the purchase of the freehold from British Railways of the Bluebell Line from Sheffield Park to Horsted Keynes and the Festiniog Railway opened their extension to Dduallt on 19 June. This railway was now becoming a booming tourist attraction as it approached ¼ million passenger journeys a year. Also in Wales, the Vale of Rheidol Railway was re-aligned into Aberystwyth's main line station. The VoR's three 1ft 11½in gauge locomotives — Nos 7, 8 and 9 — were now the only remaining steam locomotives in BR ownership following the end of standard gauge steam. The old standard gauge steam shed at Aberystwyth was relaid with narrow gauge track to accommodate all VoR rolling stock.

The Association of Railway Preservation Societies was growing in strength by the

day and locomotives such as *Clan Line*, *Blackmore Vale* and Ivatt 2-6-2T No 41298 were stored at Longmoor Military Railway. The Wight Locomotive Society purchased the last ex-L&SWR 'O2' tank on the Island — No 24 *Calbourne* , and LMS 'Jubilee' No 5596 *Bahamas* was overhauled by the Hunslet Engine Co in Leeds at a cost of around £5,000. The North Norfolk Railway purchased the ex-L&Y directors' saloon No 1908 for transportation to Sheringham. The North Eastern Locomotive Preservation Group purchased their second locomotive; it now owned both 'J27' 0-6-0 No 65894 and 'Q6' 0-8-0 No 63395. The Talyllyn Railway experienced its record Easter to date and negotiations started to save the North York Moors Railway from extinction before BR lifted the track — 'preservation' was now the name of the game!

As lines continued to close and passenger operation ceased, one actually 'reopened' to passengers in Devon in 1968. This was the Barnstaple Junction-Bideford line which was reopened from 9-22 January to provide service access across the river after the road bridge had collapsed. The line had previously closed to passengers on 4 October 1965. Lines which closed to passengers during the year included Cheltenham (Lansdown) to Stratford upon Avon, in March, Bere Alston to Okehampton in May and Dunfermline to Stirling in October. Lancaster (Green Ayre) station closed to all traffic on 8 January and the small station at Shap closed on 1 July. The last train ran on the Wembley Loop on 18 May.

On 6 January, the 11.30 Manchester-Euston train collided with a 120-ton transformer at Hixon automatic half-barrier level-crossing between Stone, in Staffordshire, and Colwich. The train was hauled by Class 81 electric No E3009 whose front cab was completely destroyed. Three masts carrying electric wires were brought down in the incident. At the moment of impact the road tractors were on each side of the track and were not damaged but the first five coaches of the train were demolished. Sadly three crew members in the locomotive's cab were killed together with eight passengers — another 44 passengers were injured. The transformer was on the crossing travelling at 2mph, attended by walking tractor crew members, when the crossing lights began to flash, the barrier descending on the transformer.

No HS4000 *Kestrel* left Brush Works, Loughborough, for Derby Works on 20 January 1968 resplendent in its yellow & brown livery and grey roof. *Kestrel* carried out trials on the Eastern Region between Shirebrook and Whitemoor. This 4,000hp diesel-electric locomotive hauled the heaviest freight train drawn by a single locomotive (at the time) during trials between Mansfield and Lincoln — 2,000 tons.

The first of the 'Baby Deltics' were withdrawn in the latter part of 1968, the majority of them being cut up at G. Cohen's of Kettering.

On 14 October, the rebuilt Euston station was opened by Her Majesty the Queen. Rebuilding had resulted in the demolition, in the early 1960s, of the historic 'Doric Arch' which created an uproar but attempts to save it were in vain. The old London terminus with its original building and black smoke from the 'Royal Scots', 'Princess Coronations' and 'Jubilees' had made way for a new ultra-modern Euston where blue & white electric locomotives would stand on their trains at the end of the platforms awaiting departure in this new clean environment.

Also in London, the first section of the new Victoria Line on the London Underground was opened between Walthamstow Central and Highbury on 1 September, using automatically-driven trains. New tunnelling methods were used and the entire line was in twin tunnels each around 12ft in diameter. The new rolling stock was constructed of aluminium bodies and was built by Metro-Cammell. Eight-car sets, which could be separated into two four-car sets, operated on the new line. At first, there was apprehension from certain members of the public when they learnt that the trains were automatically driven. These new tube trains had previously carried out trials on the Central Line between Woodford and Hainault.

As a footnote GWR nameplates sold at Sotheby's on 13 December 1968 realised £165 (*Saint Patrick*) and £95 (*Saint Andrew*) ... still, they were probably purchased for a mere £15 from BR!

Below:
The local Nottingham-Grantham services were diverted to Nottingham Midland with the closure of Nottingham Victoria station. This January 1968 view shows the 10.30 Grantham service formed of two two-car diesel units with car No E56043 (later Class 114) leading. This excellent view clearly shows the fine Midland Railway signal box and the vast expanse of this junction with the Great Northern line. *J. Cupit*

Right:
Steam's final days are summed up in this study of LMS 'Black Five' No 44894 awaiting departure from Lancaster Castle station on 15 February 1968. Soon this scene was to be no more — what would these men be doing this time next year? How would the end of steam affect them? *J. Seddon*

Bottom right:
The last 'Britannia' Pacific to remain in BR service was No 70013 *Oliver Cromwell*. This locomotive is now preserved, owned by the National Railway Museum and housed at Bressingham Steam Museum in Norfolk. Obviously, No 70013 was a popular choice for steam specials as the end of steam drew near and on 9 June 1968, *Oliver Cromwell* passes Chinley North Junction with the BR 'Midland Lines Centenary Special' returning from Manchester to St Pancras via the Hope Valley line with the 'Britannia' Pacific working only as far as Nottingham. *Brian Stephenson*

Left:
North British Type 1 diesel-hydraulic No D6346 is seen near Pangbourne on 10 October 1968 with an up parcels train. From 1968, these locomotives were phased out due to the decision to abandon diesel-hydraulic transmission. *J. H. Cooper-Smith*

Below centre:
Class 21 North British-built diesel electric locomotives were first allocated to the Eastern Region but, between November 1965 and September 1967, most were refurbished and reclassified '29', the entire class eventually being allocated to the Scottish Region. Whilst based in Scotland, some of these locomotives were fitted with single-line token catchers. In this scene, No D6101 awaits departure from Oban with a Glasgow train, on 20 April 1968. *Derek Cross*

Bottom:
The Class 71 electric locomotives were introduced in 1958 for express passenger and freight duties on the newly-electrified Kent Coast main line. These duties included the 'Night Ferry' and the 'Golden Arrow'. On this occasion, on 27 May 1968, No E5011 is pictured leaving Hither Green with a freight for Bricklayers Arms. Passing in the opposite direction is a Hastings-bound train. *J. H. Cooper-Smith*

Right:
From 1964/65, the 'Midland Pullman' carried a standardised livery of blue & grey (the new BR corporate identity) and from the summer of 1967 worked 'South Wales Pullman' services from Paddington to Swansea, stopping only at Newport, Cardiff, Bridgend and Neath *en route*. A 'South Wales Pullman' is seen on 10 October 1968, sporting both old and new liveries, between Tilehurst and Pangbourne. *J. H. Cooper-Smith*

Below:
In a 1968 scene at Wormit, a two-car Cravens-built diesel unit, bearing differing liveries, takes the single line to Newport with a service from Dundee after crossing the Tay Bridge. This scene is now no more as the line closed to freight on 14 August 1967 and to passengers on 5 May 1969. *T. G. Hepburn/Copyright Rail Archive Stephenson*

New Signalling

A number of new signalling schemes were completed in 1969, including those at Old Oak Common, Swindon, Gloucester, Trent, Derby and Saltley. All these schemes resulted in the closure of many existing signalboxes and the new Old Oak Common powerbox now controlled 13½ route miles (67¼ track miles) disposing of 18 boxes. Gloucester controlled 94¾ route miles and the Midland line resignalling at Trent, Derby and Saltley covered 242 route miles, closing 180 redundant boxes with the loss of 560 staff. Unfortunately progress often brings redundancy! The 1969 schemes brought MAS to an area from Chesterfield in the north to west of Reading in the south.

The Great Eastern's Lea Valley line was electrified in 1969 extending the suburban line from Liverpool Street a further nine miles from Copper Hill Junction (Tottenham) to Cheshunt. Services commenced on 5 May — no new electric stock was built for the extension but redeployed 'AM5' units (Class 305) were used over the route.

The Woodhead route suffered severe snow storms and blizzards in February, resulting in the line being blocked in places and a Sheffield Victoria-Manchester train was stuck in a snowdrift for five hours. The 'EM2' Class 77 electric locomotives built to haul passenger trains over the route found a new home in 1969 when they were sold to the Netherlands Railway. All seven locomotives travelled to Holland but only six were required for service as No 27005 was dismantled to provide spare parts. Nos 27000 and 27001 have since returned to Britain and a third is preserved in the Netherlands.

In the west of England on 19 February, at a time when severe blizzards were hitting the north of England, a force nine gale coupled with high spring tides ripped up most of the planking on the down platform at Dawlish station and dislodged coping stones. Ballast was also washed away between the station and Kennaway Tunnel causing single-line working between Exminster and Teignmouth. The gales were followed by heavy snow and drifts blocked the line between Plymouth and Totnes. These severe weather conditions created many train cancellations and trains that ran suffered lengthy delays, especially night trains, one Paddington-Plymouth overnight train arriving 4hr 5min late. February 1969 was an extremely bad month for weather in the West Country, creating constant chaos.

In Hampshire it was a similar story in a county which invariably escaped severe weather, with snow and ice creating havoc both here and on the Isle of Wight. The blizzards and freezing conditions resulted in very few trains entering or departing from Waterloo owing to frozen or blocked points.

On 9 January, the 'Waverley Route' from Carlisle to Edinburgh, via Hawick, finally closed. Approaches were made to BR with a view to purchase the 100-mile-long main line but after lengthy negotiations the privately-owned Border Union Railway Co, which hoped to reopen the line before the winter of 1969/70, failed to save the line from complete closure and demolition which commenced on 1 April 1971. The asking price for the line was £1,750,000.

On 10 August, the heaviest and largest concrete single-span bridge ever to be placed into position by BR was installed to carry the Runcorn-Frodsham line over the M6 Motorway, which was at that time under construction. The bridge weighed over 4,000 tons and was of a type thought to be unique in Europe. It was actually built beside the track at Frodsham.

Work continued on the conversion of the Euston-Watford and Broad Street-Richmond dc electric lines of the London Midland Region from third and fourth rail to outside third rail. Between Gunnersbury and Richmond the centre rail was retained for London Transport District Line trains.

The flood of line closures which had hit the railways of Britain after the Beeching proposals had dwindled to next to nothing by 1969. On 4 May, the line from Lewes to Uckfield officially closed to passengers although from 24 February a special bus service had been provided by BR. In December, the Yate-Bristol Temple Meads line (via Mangotsfield) ceased passenger workings and from 6 October, in Norfolk, the Dereham-Wymondham line saw passengers no more. Services to and from Manchester Central to places such as Fairfield, Trafford Park (ex-CLC), and Chinley ceased on 5 May as this historic station eventually closed to passengers. Manchester Exchange was also closed. On the Isle of Wight, the Ryde Pier Tramway ceased operation on 26 January bringing to an end the life of this 105-year-old line. The original electric trams were replaced with Drewry petrol cars by the Southern Railway in 1927, the petrol engines later being replaced by diesel ones. Services were replaced by the new electric trains that had recently been introduced to the Island's one remaining railway route.

Preservation news included two new privately-owned items of stock being delivered to the Bluebell Railway in January. These were BR Standard 4-6-0 No 75027 and Caledonian corridor third No 3339, restored to its original livery by BR. At the Severn Valley Railway, the Stanier '8F' Preservation Society's engine No 48773 moved to Bridgnorth on 4 January and No 5 *Shannon*, the Wantage Tramway locomotive built in 1857, arrived at Didcot. On the K&WVR there was a welcome return for No 69023 *Joem* after an absence of nearly a year and on the Bluebell Railway GWR 4-4-0 No 3217 *Earl of Berkeley* returned to traffic at Easter after a lay-off of three years. The Great Western Society saved another two GWR locomotives from the cutter's torch early in 1969. These were Mogul No 5322 and 0-6-0PT No 3650. The former had previously been part of the Woodham collection of locomotives stored in Barry docks, whilst the latter had been in industrial service since 1963.

No 4472 *Flying Scotsman* ran mystery tours from St Pancras in February which ended up in Cleethorpes and the LNER 'A2', No 60532 *Blue Peter*, arrived at Doncaster Works on 1 April for repainting in LNER Apple Green livery.

A crowd of 15,000 visited Dinting on their steam weekend in April to see LMS 'Jubilee' No 5596 *Bahamas* in steam for the first time since preservation and on 28 May preserved LMS 'Royal Scot' No 46115 *Scots Guardsman* was delivered to Dinting where extensive work on the locomotive was to be undertaken before the 'Royal Scot' could again be steamed.

Twelve locomotives were now at Carnforth, from a Peckett saddle tank to 'Black Five' No 44871. Also in the north, an offer for the 18-acre site of Embsay station by the Yorkshire Dales Railway Society was accepted.

In Wales, the Talyllyn Railway topped their previous best passenger journey figure in 1969 by 8% by reaching 131,993. The Welshpool & Llanfair Railway also increased their passenger journeys to 32,000 — an increase of 20%.

On 19 September, the country said farewell to the beloved *Flying Scotsman* as she set sail for the USA on board the ship *Saxonia* on a trade promotional tour. Her stay there was longer than enthusiasts had hoped; she did not return until 1973.

Above:
The 'Baby Deltics' were introduced in 1959 and they were just 10 in number. Built by English Electric, they had a lifespan of around 10 years and they proved to be expensive to operate and not at all reliable. On 1 July 1969, four months before withdrawal from service, No D5902 arrives at Welwyn Garden City with the 08.43 Royston train from King's Cross. *P. R. Foster*

Right:
In January 1968, the Type 5 prototype Co-Co, No HS4000 *Kestrel* appeared on the scene. Brush Electrical and Sulzer joined forces to build this 4,000hp diesel locomotive, with its semi-streamlined cab, assisted by Hawker Siddeley sponsorship. However, due to BR's lack of interest, *Kestrel* was eventually sold to the Soviet Railways where it was used for research purposes until 1988. On 22 October 1969, *Kestrel* is seen about to leave King's Cross with the 16.20 train for York. *Hawker Siddeley Group*

Left:
A wintry scene at Twyford on 10 February 1969 as a Class 52 'Western' powers through the station with a South Wales-Paddington express. A Class 117 diesel multiple-unit waits in the station with a stopping train for Reading. Twyford still holds some of that Great Western 'magic' in its architecture. *J. H. Cooper-Smith*

Bottom left:
British Thomson-Houston Type 1 diesels (Class 15), with their Paxman engines, spent their lives on the Eastern Region after the 10 pilot scheme members of the class had a spell allocated to Devon's Road, Bow (1D). They were chiefly used on station pilot duties and cross-London transfer freights. On 3 September 1969, No D8242 approaches Ipswich with an up cement train. *J. H. Cooper-Smith*

Right:
Steam operation had ended in 1968, but steam was by no means dead. Ex-BR steam locomotives could still be found carrying out sterling work at industrial installations throughout Britain. In this 1969 scene, ex-LMS 0-6-0 'Jinty' No 47445 passes beneath the ex-L&YR Crigglestone Junction-Healey Mills line as it crosses Blacker Lane, Calder Grove, on its way to the canal staithe with a trainload of coal. *Peter A. Hogarth*

Below:
As standard gauge steam ended on BR, many enthusiasts turned their interests towards the existing industrial steam scene and organised trips to NCB collieries took place. As with BR steam, preservation also took place in this field and many ex-industrial locomotives can be seen today on Britain's preserved railways. On 2 February 1969, the now preserved Kitson 0-6-2T No 29 (4263/1904) faces wintry conditions at Bournmoor, County Durham, with a full load from Philadelphia to Penshaw. *Ian Krause*

Stranded Diesels

On 23 May, the Britannia tubular bridge, linking Anglesey with mainland Wales, was severely damaged by fire. The wrought-iron structure, built by Robert Stephenson, was lined inside with tarred felt which was set alight by vandals. The intense heat distorted the girders and the line closed until January 1972 resulting in diesel locomotives and stock being left stranded at Holyhead. Despite BR examining the possibility of a single-line bridge whilst repairs were carried out, this was not to be. 'Stranded' diesel locomotives were Class 08 shunters Nos 3004, 3174, 3175 and 4137; Class 24s Nos 5034, 5044 and 5083; Class 40s Nos 219 *Caronia*, 231 *Sylvania*, 232 *Empress of Canada*, 233 *Empress of England*, 241, 307 and 390; and Class 47s Nos 1724, 1851 and 1940. All locomotives, with the exception of Nos 219, 5034, 5083 and the diesel shunters, were taken by sea and rerailed at Barrow by 24 June 1970. This 'disaster' brought about the reopening of LlanfairPG station (the first station on Anglesey) to where buses from the mainland conveyed passengers for transfer to a two-car diesel multiple-unit from there to Holyhead. Also at Holyhead were the two Class 01 0-4-0 diesel-mechanical shunters Nos 2954 and 2955, which were on the breakwater. The Holyhead breakwater line was not connected to the main line.

Other news from North Wales was the closure of the Bangor to Caernarvon branch on 5 January. On 1 July 1969, this line had been used when Prince Charles went to Caernarvon for his investiture as Prince of Wales. The train was hauled by Class 47 diesel No 1719 which had taken over the 12-vehicle train from electric locomotive No E3112 at Crewe.

On the Welshpool & Llanfair Railway, an Austrian locomotive appeared coupled with rolling stock from the same country. The 0-8-0T (No 699.01) was built in 1944 for German military use as a tender engine and was rebuilt as an 0-8-0T in 1957. This entire Austrian train on the W&L comprised ex-Austrian Zillertalbahn coaches. The locomotive was later named *Sir Drefaldwyn* (Welsh for Montgomeryshire).

On the Severn Valley Railway, the inaugural train, hauled by Collett 0-6-0 No 3205, ran on 28 June. There were now 11 locomotives at Bridgnorth with a further nine expected shortly. Those ready for use included four industrial engines, three ex-GWR, two ex-LMS and two BR locomotives built to an LMS design. Trains ran between Bridgnorth and Hampton Loade.

The reopening of the line followed payment of the balance due by the Severn Valley Railway to BR on 25 June. In January, BR 2-6-4T No 80079 was chosen by the Severn Valley from the 14 members of the class being held on the scrapline at Barry Docks by Woodham Bros, pending full payment of £3,000.

During 1970 regular approaches were being made to Dai Woodham for the purchase of locomotives, and bids were made for 'West Country' Pacific No 34016 *Bodmin* (which finally departed in 1972), and GWR 2-6-2T No 4588 by the Dart Valley Railway. On 16 June, GWR 'Manor' No 7827 *Lydham Manor* arrived from Barry scrapyard at the Dart Valley Railway almost one year after purchase and another locomotive arrived at the Great Western Society's premises at Didcot from Barry. This was GWR 'Castle' No 5051 *Earl Bathurst*.

In Scotland, following a landslip in November 1969 at Strathcarron which had closed the route to the Kyle of Lochalsh, the line reopened on 16 March 1970 after the clearance of the debris and the building of a shelter. Falling rocks on the Oban line in Scotland are detected by wires connecting signals which appear at frequent intervals in the area around Ben Cruachan. As falling rocks touch the wires this turns all signals to danger. A similar problem occasionally occurs on the Dover-Folkestone line, as it did in the early part of 1970, and this resulted in the Southern Region installing a similar system of sensitive wires along the track which rang alarm bells in signalboxes at both ends placing signals at danger.

On 2 May local passenger services came to an end over the Settle & Carlisle route and all stations en route, except Appleby and Settle, closed. Often the crews of the two-car diesel multiple-units used in stopping trains over the route would outnumber the passengers. However, new scaffolding appeared at Ribblehead Viaduct and work was being carried out at Blea Moor Tunnel, so all was not lost — as we were to realise in later years.

Passenger services ceased over the Woodhead route between Manchester and Sheffield on 3 January 1970. Many railway enthusiasts turned up to pay their last respects to the former Great Central line. The last westbound train was hauled by No E26053 *Perseus* and the last eastbound by No E26054 *Pluto*. Passenger services, however, continued over the 1,500V dc routes from Manchester to Hadfield and Glossop west of the Pennines, and a diesel multiple-unit service remained over the section from Penistone to Sheffield Midland, passing through the increasingly derelict remains of Sheffield Victoria station en route. Life also went on for the Class 76 electrics, hauling regular coal trains over the route for another 11 years.

Passenger services also ceased in October 1970 from Cambridge to St Ives and from Peterborough to Boston, and on 2 February passenger workings were also terminated on the 11-mile branch from Colne to Skipton.

Following a collision at Chertsey on 1 June 1970 involving Class 74 electro-diesel No E6109, the entire class was temporarily taken out of service for thorough examination of brake block stack adjusters, but the majority were released by 4 June.

Two new named trains emerged in 1970, although neither was shown as such in the timetable. Both trains covered the north-east-southwest route, the 'Severn-Tyne' working from Weston-super-Mare to Newcastle and the 'Torbay-Tyne' from Paignton to Newcastle and return. The 'Severn-Tyne' carried WR-style side-boards and the 'Torbay-Tyne' was formed of Eastern Region stock.

On 13 May, as container traffic grew from strength to strength at Felixstowe Docks, a new 650yd spur was opened to enable container trains to run direct from Ipswich to the docks without having to reverse at Felixstowe Town station.

In Somerset, a new line, three-quarters of a mile long was opened on 19 August to Merehead where Foster Yeoman were quarrying vast quantities of stone for construction of our motorways. This line was linked to the surviving section of the ex-GWR Cheddar branch. Initially, eight trains per day used the line, being formed of conventional four-wheel wagons.

Above:
A breakdown train, hauled by Class 43 'Warship' No D847 *Strongbow* is overlooked by Bath's impressive tiered terraces on 29 April 1970. By now, the days were numbered for the 'Warships', No D847 being withdrawn in March 1971.
J. H. Cooper-Smith

Left:
The Somerset & Dorset line was being lifted during 1970 and a weekly engineer's train, in connection with the lifting past Corfe Mullen, is propelled by Class 33 No D6506 on 4 April 1970. Track removal continued until September 1970. *John H. Bird*

Above:
The ex-GCR Woodhead route across the Pennines saw 1,500V dc electrified services from 4 February 1952 but passenger services ceased on 5 January 1970. Freight continued until 1981. On 14 March 1970 Class 76 No E26032 passes Torside with a coal train. The majority of the class were sent to C. F. Booth's scrapyard at Rotherham on withdrawal, most of them lying there for around two years before being cut up. One was, however, preserved as part of the national collection. *G. W. Morrison*

Left:
Altrincham MSJ&AR depot yard on 3 May 1970 and two three-car electric sets, with No M28581 (ex No 11) on view, lie stabled with other stock. Electric services using 1,500V dc traction commenced over the 8½-mile route from Altrincham to Manchester London Road on 11 May 1931. From 3 May 1971, 25kV ac services commenced following electric current conversion. *N. H. Spilsbury*

Bottom left:
London Transport acquired ex-Great Western pannier tanks for operation from their Neasden depot, numbering them in their own sequence. No L90 (ex-GWR 0-6-0PT No 7760) returns from Moorgate to Neasden with a materials train on 26 April 1970 and in this view the disused line to Blackfriars is seen converging from the right. No L90 was one of the last three ex-GWR locomotives to remain operational with London Transport. *Brian Beer*

Top right:
One of the ex-GWR pannier tanks which ended up under National Coal Board ownership working the South Wales coalfields was No 9600. Now devoid of numberplate, the locomotive is pictured at Merthyr Vale Colliery, during 1970, remembered for the tragic Aberfan disaster. Other GWR 0-6-0PTs ending their working life in these collieries included Nos 1607 (Cynheidre), 3650 (Gwaun-cae-Gurwen), 7714 (Penallta), 7754 (Elliot) and 9792 (Mardy). *C. J. Machin*

Right:
On 1 September 1970, Hudswell, Clarke-built outside-cylinder 0-6-0T *Fryston No 2* powers a train of empty coal wagons from the canal basin at the National Coal Board's Fryston Colliery, near Castleford, Yorkshire. *G. T. Monks*

Push-Pull Power

In an effort to speed up the service between Glasgow (Queen Street) and Edinburgh (Waverley), new-style trains were introduced in 1971. Twelve Class 27 diesels were converted for push-pull working by fitting a small additional diesel engine and generator set in place of the boiler, covering over the boiler water tank filler point and gauge, and by fitting ETH jumper leads on the nose ends to replace steam pipes. These locomotives were reclassified 27/1 and operated one at each end of six Mark 2a coach trains. Average speed was in excess of 70mph — a vast improvement on the Swindon-built diesel multiple-units previously used, cutting the journey time by over 10min. This involved two stops *en route*, at Falkirk High and Haymarket.

The demise of the 'Baby Deltics' was complete in March 1971 when No 5909 was withdrawn from Hitchin depot after only 12 years in service. Their life included a period when the entire class was out of traffic probably for longer than any other class — this was from June 1963 to July 1964. This was due to what was termed as 'major failure' usually meaning crankcase fracture or damage to cylinder liners and connecting rods caused by seizure. During service, workings included King's Cross to Cambridge, Baldock and Royston and a regular double-headed working in 1966 on the Naphtha trains from Fawley to the new plant at Cadwell, north of Hitchin.

No HS4000 *Kestrel* was handed over to Russia's railway authorities at Scherbinka on 16 July. For those who visited Crewe prior to this date, they had the opportunity of seeing her for the last time having been fitted with new bogies in the works for her trip to Russia. *Kestrel* was used for research in the USSR until 1988 and was eventually cut up in March 1989.

As the high-density 4-PEP prototype units commenced trials in 1971 over the Alton line, the 2-BIL and 2-HAL sets, introduced in 1935, ended their days, three 2-BIL units straying, on 25 September, to the North London line, to Euston and to Broad Street. The two original 4-PEP units, with their pairs of powered sliding doors on each side, were numbered 4001 and 4002 and were the forerunners of Classes 313, 314, 315, 507 and 508 EMUs. During trials, passenger services were also undertaken by the prototype 4-PEP units over the Shepperton, Hampton Court and Chessington branches. The powered sliding doors were incorporated to help reduce the risk of accident.

On 1 October, after 22 years of operation, the Bulleid eight-coach 4DD double-deck train was withdrawn. This train had covered 700,000 miles over the Dartford line. Introduced in 1949 to cope with increased rush-hour traffic the experiment proved unsuccessful, as loading and alighting proved to be a lengthy process, and trains were increased in length instead.

Advanced Passenger Train news was that the first power coach for the train was delivered to Derby, minus bogies, on 21 May where the first two coaches were nearing completion. Track testing of the first three bogies commenced on 20 September on the test track between Melton Junction (Leicestershire) and Edwalton (Notts). The APT was expected to be the first train in the world to travel at speeds of up to 155mph over existing routes as the specially-designed bogie and suspension system would, it was assessed, result in speeds on curves 50% higher than with conventional trains as wheel flanges did not come into contact with the rails. It was later realised, after trials, that there were serious problems and these eventually caused the entire project to be abandoned.

On 12 July, the first of the new Mark 2d air-conditioned coaches went into daily service over the King's Cross-Newcastle route. These vehicles, of which there were 350, were the last of the 1969 order for 600 Mark 2c coaches, the Mark 2ds being fitted with lower ceilings to accommodate air-conditioning equipment.

At the beginning of May 1971, work commenced on the electrification of the West Coast main line between Glasgow and Weaver Junction, where the Liverpool line diverged north of Crewe. The 25kV electrification of this 235-mile stretch of line had been estimated to cost £25 million and a more simplified form of overhead wiring from that used on the Euston to Manchester/Liverpool routes was being installed.

Also on the West Coast main line, the last lineside postal apparatus, just north of Penrith, ceased operation on 4 October when the last mail bags were dropped at speed from a train. This system had been in use for 133 years. Netting apparatus fitted to TPO vehicles was removed but the body-side recess where it once was fitted was still apparent.

On London Underground, Brixton came on to the map on 23 July when the Victoria Line was completed to this new station on the line from Walthamstow Central. This new 3½-mile-long tube extension also incorporated stations at Vauxhall and Stockwell, with another station at Pimlico opening during the following year. Brixton had been served by the LC&DR line since 1862.

In April, work started on London Transport's Heathrow link — the first section of the new 3½ mile Piccadilly Line extension to the airport and, in contrast, the last steam-hauled working on London's Underground, hauled by ex-GWR 0-6-0PT No 7752 (LT No L94) ran from Moorgate to Neasden depot, on 6 June, with an engineers' departmental train. Special electric trains were laid on at Moorgate for all enthusiasts to arrive at Neasden prior to the steam train's arrival. At both ends of the route there was not a space to be found as photographers flocked to the event.

As lines closed, such as the Sandbach branch in January and the Mangotsfield-Bath line in May, the Blackburn-Hellifield line reopened to passengers on 7 February and, on 7 June, the Peterborough to Spalding line, closed to passengers only the previous year, reopened with the support of three local authorities who agreed to subsidise the service to the tune of £16,000 per year. The old Sidmouth Junction station also reopened as Feniton on 3 May for local Exeter trains.

In Liverpool, the Riverside station known to thousands travelling to and from the River Mersey closed to trains after 76 years in existence. The station was built to give passengers direct access to liners using the adjacent Liverpool landing stage.

Saturday, 2 October 1971 saw the return to steam of GWR 'King' No 6000 *King George V* on BR metals, the first steam locomotive allowed to run over BR track since the end of BR steam in 1968 apart from Alan Pegler's *Flying Scotsman*. After a series of Pullman excursions, where tracksides were packed with photographers and overbridges were bursting at the seams with enthusiasts, *King George V* returned to Bulmer's at Hereford for the winter on 8 October.

Right:
Eastbound coal empties from Moston to Healey Mills pass through Todmorden on 2 June 1971 headed by Class 37 No 6942. This was one of the locomotives originally allocated to Worcester and tried out on Lickey Incline duties.
J. H. Cooper-Smith

Left:
By 1971 a number of diesel locomotives had lost their 'D' from their cabside numbers and demonstrating this, but still carrying the two-tone green livery, Class 25 No 7561 leaves York Yard with a southbound train of hoppers on 8 September 1971. *J. H. Cooper-Smith*

Below:
Class 55 'Deltic' No 9001 *St Paddy* leaves York on 8 September 1971 with a King's Cross-Edinburgh service. *St Paddy* was one of the eight members of the class to be named after Derby winners. *J. H. Cooper-Smith*

Right:
Still resplendent in its original Electric Blue livery and sporting its raised aluminium numbers and BR crest, Class AL6 (later Class 86) electric No E3143 arrives at Manchester Piccadilly with a train from Cardiff on 30 March 1971. In September 1972, this locomotive was given its first TOPS number, No 86203, and in July 1974 became No 86103. In January 1981 it was named *André Chapelon. J. H. Cooper-Smith*

Bottom right:
On 10 April 1971, Class 17 'Clayton' No D8586 passes Polmadie depot, Glasgow, with a load of pipes. This was the last year of operation for these locomotives, which had only entered service between 1963 and 1965. *N. E. Preedy*

Above:
During the last day of operation on the section of the Dart Valley line from Buckfastleigh to Ashburton in Devon, the DVR's Great Western 0-6-0PT No 1638 arrives with a freight on 2 October 1971. Whatever happened to those lovely signs? *John H. Bird*

Below:
The impressive sight of preserved Great Western 'King' No 6000 *King George V*, complete with bell, in action on the main line again was a sight to behold. The 'King' was housed at the H. P. Bulmer premises at Hereford and on 3 October 1971 made the historic trip that restored main line steam working to British Rail. It is seen emerging from the Severn Tunnel resplendent in its GWR Brunswick Green livery and hauling a rake of Pullman coaches. This was one of the early successes of the preservation scene. *R. O. Coffin*

Exit 'Southern Style'

The farewell journeys of the 'Brighton Belle' Pullman took place on 30 April 1972, the 18.50 from Brighton offering a cheese and wine party and the return 22.30 from Victoria offering a champagne meal. This was the end of Pullman services over the Brighton lines, services which had spanned 90 years. The 'Brighton Belle' entered regular service (as the 'Southern Belle') on New Year's Day 1933 and was reported as 'putting the *trains de luxe* of the Continent definitely in the shade'. When the Brighton and Worthing lines were electrified there were 38 Pullman services introduced, 23 of which being withdrawn during 1965/66, when 6-PUL units made way for 4-CIG/BIG sets. When introduced on 1 January 1933, to cheering crowds, this was the first all-electric Pullman multiple-unit express in the world. When the units were repainted in standard InterCity blue & grey livery during 1968/69, the six first-class Pullman cars sadly lost their names bestowed on them in 1933. The names were *Doris*, *Hazel*, *Audrey*, *Vera*, *Gwen* and *Mona* — all third-class coaches were merely numbered. 'Brighton Belle' coaches were sold and used as restaurants, and by innkeepers in Cheshire and Yorkshire, and Allied Breweries purchased three parlour cars for £22,500.

The year 1972 also saw the end of another Pullman service on the Southern, as the 'Golden Arrow' Pullman made its final run, hauled by Class 71 electro-diesel E5013 on 30 November, marking the end of Pullman travel on the region. The locomotive carried the 'Golden Arrow' emblem, headboard and flags as was the tradition, and the train included first-class Pullman cars *Perseus* and *Phoenix*, now both restored and part of the VSOE stock. The 'Golden Arrow' London-Paris Pullman express was, since the war, regularly hauled by streamlined and rebuilt Bulleid Pacifics. During the 1952/53 timetable the outward sailing of the 'Golden Arrow' services was transferred from Dover to Folkestone.

It was also farewell to the Southern Region's 4-COR units in 1972 as, on 30 September, they performed their last public duties. Unit No 3102 worked the 08.35 Haywards Heath-Seaford and the 09.50 Seaford-Brighton trains on the day which was quite fitting as it was the oldest 4-COR unit in service at the time.

The tragic Eltham crash occurred on the Southern on 11 June 1972, when an excursion, returning from Margate to Kentish Town, hauled by Class 47 diesel No 1630, became derailed, killing four people (including the driver) and injuring 129. The derailment was put down to excessive speed over a 20mph restriction area.

During 1972, the controversial APT-E appeared on the scene, when in July the prototype gas-turbine-powered four-car set emerged from Derby Works and commenced slow-running trials (around 40mph) on the Chesterfield main line before moving to the trial track at Melton for higher speed trials.

Trials of the new High Speed Train, with its Paxman Valenta engines of 2,250bhp, had been intended to start in 1972 but these were 'blacked' by ASLEF together with APT-E trials. The new Mark III coaching stock built for use with the new trains incorporated air-cushioned disc-braked bogies for smoother running and, during the summer, the new coaches commenced trials on the West Coast main line. On 22 November, the first of these coaches were introduced on the King's Cross-Edinburgh service. The prototype HST carried the reversed standard livery of grey & blue, similar to that of the Pullmans but production models were painted in the standard livery.

West Coast main-line electrification between Crewe and Glasgow progressed as the year went on and, from the Scottish end, wires had reached Carstairs South Junction by the end of the summer. From the Weaver Junction end electric locomotives were used on freight and parcels trains as far as Warrington by the late summer.

Following computerisation of BR operations (TOPS), London Midland Region electrics carried the new five-figure numbers by the summer of 1972, the West Coast electrics being classified 81-86. The first refurbished Class 86 electric, No 86201 (E3191), was fitted with new bogies in Crewe Works of a design earmarked for the forthcoming new Class 87 locomotives, and was reclassified 86/2.

Station news in 1972 gave us a rebuilt station at Oxford which opened on 1 August. Bristol Parkway, a new idea in station design, being situated 'outside the town', with ample parking thereby avoiding congestion within the town, opened on 1 May and the closure of the historic GWR station in the centre of Birmingham — Snow Hill — took place on 4 March. Prior to its final demise it had become the 'world's largest unstaffed halt', having seen, during its history, platforms packed with holidaymakers, trains hauled by GWR 'Kings', 'Castles' and 'Halls', and an abundance of suburban trains to the Black Country and beyond. Main line use of Snow Hill had ceased in 1967.

Elsewhere, Huddersfield's Victorian station was restored and the station at Matlock Bath in Derbyshire was reopened on 27 May for pay-trains to operate between Derby and Matlock, having been closed since March 1967. Shotton Low Level station (ex-L&NWR) also reopened to passengers on 21 August after a closure of 6½ years.

Lines which closed during the year included the Swanage branch, on 3 January (now, thanks to the efforts of volunteers reopened from Swanage to Harman's Cross), and the Penrith-Keswick line in Cumbria which closed to passengers on 6 March. This latter line was part of the original Cockermouth, Keswick & Penrith Railway.

It was with great delight in 1972 that agreement was reached between those involved in preservation and British Rail regarding steam-hauled specials over five main-line routes from June. Routes included Birmingham-Didcot, Newcastle-Carlisle, York-Scarborough, Newport-Shrewsbury and Carnforth-Barrow. Locomotives passed for duty included No 7029 *Clun Castle*, No 6000 *King George V* and 'A4' Pacifics No 4498 *Sir Nigel Gresley* and 60019 *Bittern* — and enthusiasts both crowded on to these excursions and lined the track to see again these fine locomotives back in full flight.

In Wales, the Welshpool & Llanfair Railway extended their line to Sylfaen on 15 July after months of hard graft but sadly vandalism struck the Vale of Rheidol Railway causing a derailment to No 9 *Prince of Wales* in August.

Woodham Bros of Barry reported that 20 locomotives had now left the scrapyard there including nine GWR, two Southern, seven LMS, S&D No 53808 and Standard tank No 80079 and a further 20 were set aside pending final purchase from a variety of organisations.

As the diesel-hydraulic 'Warships' ended their working life in 1972, No E26000 *Tommy*, the original Woodhead electric locomotive, was cut up in Crewe Works in October.

Above:
Class 52 'Western' diesel-hydraulic No 1068 *Western Reliance* passes beneath Ranelagh Bridge, providing the 'classic' railway photograph, on 25 April 1972, with the 1C47 Paddington to Cardiff Central express. *Brian Morrison*

Left:
After a 'retimed' departure of 08.25, the diverted 09.40 Edinburgh-Plymouth train, hauled by Class 47 No 1987 in original two-tone green livery, passes Wylam, on 24 July 1972. The diversion was via Carlisle and Hexham to Newcastle and was due to engineering works at Dunbar. *I. S. Carr*

Top right:
By the time this picture was taken half the Class 35 'Hymek' diesel-hydraulics had been withdrawn from service. Despite this, these popular locomotives still found regular employment on Western Region services to the south coast. No 7084, with its 'raised D' obliterated, leaves Salisbury on 20 May 1972 with a Portsmouth-Cardiff service. *G. F. Gillham*

Right:
This scene on 25 July 1972, near Duffield, shows the first test run with the gas turbine experimental advanced passenger train, APT-E. The articulated bogies joining the 70ft carriages are clearly visible and this test run took place on the stretch of track between Derby and Duffield. *Colin J. Marsden Collection*

Above:
Emanating from Tolworth coal depot, Class 74 electric locomotive No E6106 heads back to the Western Region with empty hoppers, via Kensington Olympia, on 15 August 1972 and is seen in Clapham Cutting. Renumbered to 74006 in February 1974, this locomotive was the first of the class to be withdrawn, in June 1976.
Brian Morrison

Left:
On 8 June 1972, Class 24 Bo-Bo No 5095 takes the coastal route over ex-NBR metals through Kinghorn, south of Kirkaldy, with northbound coal empties. No D5095 was one of the 59 members of the class to start its life allocated to March depot (31B). *J. H. Cooper-Smith*

Britain's High Speed Trains

On 11 January 1973, trials and crew training of the prototype High Speed Train commenced between Derby, Trent and Wigston involving Class 41 power-car No 41002 and two Mark 3 coaches. Trials continued into February with a power-car at each end running from Derby to Kettering. Trials later commenced from Leeds (Neville Hill). On 6 June the prototype HST broke the British speed record set by *Mallard* of 126mph when it achieved 131mph for a distance of one mile between Tollerton and Thirsk and only five days later reached 141mph, increasing this to 143mph the following day. The previous world record of 133mph was set by a German diesel train on 23 June 1939. The High Speed Train was scheduled to enter service on the 'North Briton' from 13 August but this event was delayed due to an unsettled drivers' pay claim. Production units eventually entered service on the Western Region first in 1976.

On the Old Dalby test track the APT-E reached 125mph only six weeks after technical trials had commenced there in October 1973. The train was fitted with a tilt system providing the facility to travel at high speeds on the curves on existing BR tracks. However the tilt system was not fitted in the same way to power cars due to the movement of the roof pantographs making the train de-wire, so a complicated anti-tilt system was devised. Tests continued on the West Coast main line until 1979, sometimes achieving speeds of up to 160mph.

Speed and efficiency was now the order of the day and 100mph running over almost 80% of the East Coast main line route between King's Cross and Newcastle was made possible by Stage 2 of the Eastern Region's line speed improvements programme. At Peterborough, at a cost of £2½ million, speed limits through the station were increased from 20mph to 100mph by the simplification of the track layout. This also involved the complete rebuilding of the station.

On 23 July, Stage I of the Weaver Junction-Glasgow electrification scheme was completed as far as Preston. This facilitated a locomotive change from electric to diesel for northbound trains at Preston instead of Crewe, (apart from those not scheduled to call there) which improved timings considerably. By September, the Scottish Region's contribution to West Coast main line electrification to Glasgow was almost complete with overhead wires installed, apart from a few short sections.

By mid-June the prototype Class 87 electric locomotive, built at Crewe Works and with a power rating of 5,000hp, was in action and, just one month later, Nos 87002/3/4 were also in service. Any drivers conversant with the Class 86 could drive one of these new locomotives, introduced for the forthcoming Euston-Glasgow electrified route. The Class 87 locomotives were fitted with GEC cross-arm pantographs, similar to those carried by the Class 86 electrics at this time.

The electrification of the Eastern Region's Great Northern section from King's Cross and Moorgate to Royston via Welwyn Garden City and via Hertford North was progressing well, and by early October most of the electrification masts had been erected between Bowes Park and Enfield Chase.

On the freight scene encouraging new contracts were signed including one for five years with British Aluminium for transporting 40,000 tons of aluminium per year from the smelter in Invergordon to the company's rolling mill in Falkirk, and for 50,000 tons of alumina, arriving by sea at Invergordon, to the Lochaber and Kinlochleven works.

Esso Petroleum renewed their contract for a further 10 years in 1973. Movement of petroleum products had become one of the most successful freight activities of the past 10 years, increasing over the period from 5 million tons per year to 21.5 million and now employing around 10,000 privately-owned rail tankers.

On 4 May, Western Region Pullman services ceased operation. This was the end of the top-quality diesel multiple-units — the 'Blue Pullmans'. Introduced as the 'all-first' six-car 'Midland Pullman' in July 1960, these were increased to eight-car sets for the Western Region's 'Bristol Pullman' and 'Birmingham Pullman'. These were joined by the 'South Wales Pullman' in September 1961. The 'Bristol' and 'South Wales' Pullmans were the last survivors.

More 'new look' stations appeared in 1973 when, on 25 June, the new passenger concourse at King's Cross was opened. Another 'Parkway' station opened, in Nottinghamshire — Alfreton & Mansfield, similar to Bristol Parkway. In Southport a new station, incorporating a large shopping centre and large car park, was constructed. New stations were also opened at St Albans and Stevenage and a new Bradford Exchange station replaced the old one. The busy Blackfriars station in London commenced a rebuilding programme on 23 July which would last for around 3½ years. The original station (named St Paul's) was built by the LC&DR in 1886.

Line closures in 1973 included the Alton-Winchester line on 5 February. Freight-only lines to disappear included the Teifi Valley branch lines from Carmarthen to Lampeter and Newcastle Emlyn, which closed on 30 September.

On 19 December 1973, the 17.18 Paddington-Oxford train was derailed between Ealing Broadway and West Ealing. All 11 coaches left the rails and the train's locomotive, No 1047 *Western Lord*, ended up on its side. The driver of the train escaped serious injury but sadly 10 passengers were killed and 53 injured. The derailment was caused by an open battery box on the locomotive striking lineside apparatus.

The first 'Deltic' to cover two million miles in service was No 9010 *The King's Own Scottish Borderer*, on 15 January 1973 — all were to achieve this landmark by the end of the following year.

On the Lickey Incline, banking power, having been in the hands of just one locomotive ('Big Bertha') for many years, was provided by at least 36 different Class 37 diesels, used in pairs, in the last six weeks of 1973.

TOPS locomotive renumbering to five digit numbers continued during the year and, from 6 May, the traditional shed code incorporating a number and a letter (eg 12A), introduced by the LMS in 1935, was abolished being replaced with a two-letter code (eg KM).

On 23 April, the British Museum of Transport at Clapham closed in preparation for the transfer of exhibits to the impending new National Railway Museum at York; the old York Railway Museum, situated on the other side of the main line, near the station, closed on 31 December 1973. The new NRM was created by converting the former steam locomotive roundhouse at York into the main exhibition hall, a project which was to last for about two years. All Clapham exhibits could not be accommodated at York and provision was required for the flood of new exhibits which were to follow.

The North York Moors Railway Company reopened the line from Pickering to Grosmont on 22 April 1973 and, on 5 May, the Lakeside & Haverthwaite Railway ran a public service for the first time on the short Cumbrian line, using Fairburn 2-6-4T No 2073. The North York Moors Railway is now one of the main attractions for railway enthusiasts and tourists alike visiting the area.

Left:
Class 81 electric locomotives made regular appearances on 'Cartic' trains over the West Coast main line. The Class 81s were the first ac locomotives built for the London Midland Region and the first member of the class appeared as long ago as November 1959 — allocated to Longsight. No E3096 is seen here at Wembley in June 1973 in charge of the 14.00 Silcock & Collins Group 'Cartic' to Garston, Liverpool. *Brian Morrison*

Bottom left:
The same style 'Cartic' wagons were also used at the rear of Motorail trains to Scotland and, during the summer of 1973, Class 25 No 7660, in ex-works livery, hauls empty 'Cartics' through Kensington Olympia station. These Motorail departures from Kensington Olympia were diesel hauled to Mitre Bridge Junction, near Willesden, where electric traction took over before proceeding north. *Brian Stephenson*

Right:
The twin-engined Brush locomotive, No D0280 *Falcon* was the forerunner of the Class 47 Brush Type 4 diesel and was the first of three Type 4 prototypes introduced, being similar in design to *Lion*. Designated Class 53 (and being the only member of the class), in December 1970 *Falcon* was renumbered D1200 and, after losing its 'D' is seen at Newport, on 25 April 1973, with a steel train. Newport was where *Falcon* ended its days of service in October 1975. *J. H. Cooper-Smith*

Below:
Double-headed Class 24/2 diesels Nos 5120 and 5124, seen here running well over an hour late, haul the down 'Night Capitals' (23.15 King's Cross-Aberdeen) past Ferryhill, Aberdeen, on 21 March 1973. The two Class 24s would have replaced a failed Class 40 , the normal motive power for this overnight sleeper. *Brian Morrison*

Left:
When one associates 1970s' power with the Eastern Region one's thoughts immediately go to the 'Deltics'. The East Coast main line powerhouses had a lifespan in service of around 20 years and six of the 22 built have been preserved, to the delight of modern scene enthusiasts. No 9003 *Meld* is seen on 12 September 1973 climbing Holloway Bank with the 'Tees-Tyne Pullman'. The Pullman coaches are at the rear of the train.
Brian Morrison

Below:
On the Western Region, 1970s' power is associated with the diesel-hydraulic Class 52 'Westerns' with their unique design, the GWR-style lettering on their nameplates and, over the years, their varying liveries of Desert Sand, Golden Ochre, green, maroon and blue. On 25 April 1973 a train headed by two 'Westerns' approaches Paddington from the West Country with '14 up'. The train is hauled by No 1045 *Western Viscount* piloting No 1069 *Western Vanguard*. Seven 'Westerns' have also been preserved. *Brian Morrison*

Top right:
With the winter sun attempting to reflect from its grimy flanks, Class 08 0-6-0 diesel shunter No D3904 approaches Perth, on 14 November 1973, with a short train of empty wagons. *Brian Morrison*

Centre right:
The 'AM10' electric units (Class 310) were introduced in 1965 for 'Little Euston' services and electrified London Midland branches. They could be coupled only to units of Classes 304 and 312 and comprised four-cars. On 6 June 1973, No 076 emerges from Primrose Hill Tunnel with a 'Little Euston' service from Birmingham (New Street). *Brian Morrison*

Below:
Prior to the English Electric Class 50 diesels being transferred to the Western Region, they worked expresses to Scotland over the West Coast main line. On 1 April 1973, No 419 is seen near Garsdale, on the Settle & Carlisle route, with the 10.25 Euston-Glasgow express after being diverted from the WCML. Should the constantly threatened closure of the S&C ever take place, WCML diversions would require rerouteing via Newcastle — a much longer route. *J. H. Cooper-Smith*

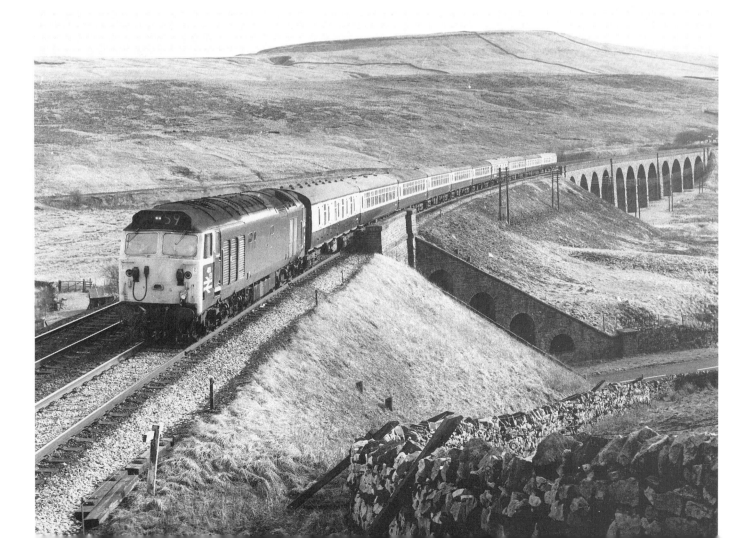

Electric: London-Scotland

On 6 May 1974, accelerated services commenced between Euston and Glasgow over the newly-electrified West Coast main line, using the new Class 87 electric locomotives. Electrification of this route reduced running times over the 401 miles by almost one hour on six trains per day, completing the journey in 5hr 5min. The 'Royal Scot' regularly achieved that magical five hour schedule, including a stop at Preston — an average speed of more than 80mph. A new daytime service via Birmingham was introduced — the 'Clansman' — which served the Midlands en route. Lack of availability of air-conditioned stock resulted in only three sets being used at the commencement of the new service.

The introduction of electric traction over Shap and Beattock meant that for the first time in history 12-coach trains (hauled by a new Class 87 electric locomotive) could sustain speeds of up to 96mph, unassisted, during the climbs, Beattock being graded at 1 in 88/69. Even the powerful 'Duchesses' when in their prime would be down to 30mph as they reached Beattock Summit. The new accelerated services over the entire Euston-Glasgow electrified route increased passenger journeys by 57% over the previous year with Bristol/Birmingham-Glasgow/Edinburgh trains hitting 116% increase.

With the introduction of the new Class 87 electric locomotives, this paved the way for the English Electric Class 50s to be transferred to the Western Region for West Country express duties as the diesel-hydraulic 'Westerns' faced withdrawal. By 28 April, the last Class 50 locomotives had been despatched from Crewe diesel depot to Bristol Bath Road and Laira. For the journey they were routed via Craven Arms coupled in pairs or threes, but they experienced a considerable number of failures in their early days in their new environment. The introduction of the Class 50s to the region was a stop-gap measure pending the arrival on the Western Region of the new High Speed Trains.

By the end of May 1974, the prototype High Speed Train had ended the first stage of its evaluation programme by completing 100,000 miles, involving regular runs at 125mph between York and Darlington and 100mph between Leeds and Edinburgh.

In preparation for HSTs being allocated to the Western Region, two major depots to accommodate these trains had reached the halfway stage of construction by midsummer. These were at Old Oak Common and at St Philips Marsh, Bristol. When completed they comprised three-road fully-pitted maintenance sheds, 700ft in length, with outside fuelling points.

On 11 December, the prototype High Speed Train began trials on the Western Region between Reading and Bristol. HST production sets were now being built in preparation for taking over from diesel-hauled trains on main Western Region InterCity routes from 1976.

Over the weekend of 4/5 May, the final and major stage of the Western Region's £1 million resignalling scheme in the West Country was completed — on schedule. This provided multiple-aspect signals over the 32 route miles between Totnes in Devon and St Germans in Cornwall.

The first stage of the resignalling scheme controlled from the Southern Region's new £6 million signalbox at Feltham was switched into operation on 8 September 1974. Less than a month later, on 5 October, the second stage was inaugurated resulting in the replacement of the last of the region's semaphore signalling in the southwest London suburban area by colourlights. The new box at Feltham replaced 45 signalboxes and controlled 351 colour-light signals and 112 points over 70 miles of track.

On 3 October, a new £2½ million depot built at Wimbledon for the maintenance of electric trains was officially opened. Stock maintained there covered routes from Waterloo to Horsham, Guildford, Aldershot and the Thames Valley and the Shepperton, Hampton Court and Chessington branches. At the new depot trains entered at one end and departed from the other thus avoiding movement problems. Doors opened automatically as a train approached.

At Paddock Wood, one of the finest and best-equipped railway terminals in Europe was opened on 28 October. It handled horticultural and agricultural produce, its main function to discharge trainloads of produce transported daily by Transfesa of Madrid, who financed the project, to the UK from the growing areas of Spain. However, it also dealt with produce from other European countries.

Between 5 August and 6 September 1974, Cannon Street station was closed completely to enable trackwork and signalling to be entirely replaced as part of the London Bridge modernisation scheme. As a 'dummy run' the entire new track layout was assembled at Hither Green, on waste land, before being transported to Cannon Street in 'kit form'.

The diesel multiple-unit image was improved in 1974 when a Metro-Cammell three-car set was modernised to show a different standard of interior styling. Externally, the train carried a striking experimental livery of white bodywork with a Rail Blue waist band. Fluorescent lighting and alternative colour schemes for the seating, walls and floor covering graced the interior. The train performed a three-month tour with viewing arranged at certain major stations. This was the livery of the future!

On 12 June, BR published the 'Railways Bill of 1974'. Within this bill were reprieves for six lines previously seriously considered for closure. These were the Cambrian Coast, the Kyle line, Ashford-Hastings, Bedford-Bletchley, Stockport-Stalybridge and Wimbledon-West Croydon. However, Haltwhistle-Alston was still eventually for the axe.

The good news for steam enthusiasts in 1974 was that British Rail announced, on 18 November, approval of 1,000 route miles for steam running. Earlier in the year, on 27 April, No 35028 *Clan Line* returned to steam on BR metals from Basingstoke to Westbury with a special, and on 26 October it was in steam again when it hauled a special from Didcot to Stratford upon Avon.

On 18 May services on the Severn Valley Railway were extended from Highley to Bewdley, the first passenger train to run the entire length from Bridgnorth to Bewdley being GWR diesel railcar No 22. Earlier in the year, on 3 February, the Tenterden Railway Co operated its first service between Tenterden and Rolvenden. The train comprised an SR 'Terrier' and two coaches.

Above:
The 4-CEP Class 411 units were introduced from 1956-63 for use on the Southern Region's South Eastern Division main lines. They were refurbished from 1979-84. A Class 411/2 unit, No 7129, is seen emerging from Chislehurst Tunnel at Elmstead Woods on 16 May 1974 forming the 13.10 Charing Cross-Margate train.
Brian Morrison

Right:
On a wintry 6 February 1974, Class 415/1 4-EPB electric unit No 5359 nears New Eltham, on the Dartford Loop, with the 11.43 Charing Cross-Dartford working. These units were the first of a new generation electric multiple-unit, the first of which emerged from Eastleigh Works in 1951, being direct descendants of the 4-SUB fleet but with many modern innovations included.
Brian Morrison

Above:
Construction of Class 25 locomotives carried on from the Class 24s, resulting in, externally, the early Class 25s looking similar to the final 24s. The second Class 25 locomotive built, originally numbered D5152, seen here as No 25002, rounds Nigg Bay out of Aberdeen, on 28 March 1974, hauling a southbound unfitted freight which includes fish vans from Fraserburgh.
Brian Morrison

Left:
Aberdeen Ferryhill shed on 21 March 1974, and Barclay Class 06 0-4-0 diesel-mechanical shunter No 2423 prepares to work with steam crane No RS1074/30. This locomotive had a lifespan of over 21 years, being withdrawn in June 1980. One of the class was eventually preserved.
Brian Morrison

Top right:
The Chislehurst-St Mary Cray loop is pictured on 28 August 1974 showing a Class 71 electric, No 71006, with a transfer freight from the Eastern Region to Dover. These locomotives were fitted for both third-rail electric current and for overhead current in yards where a third-rail electric system would prove dangerous.
Brian Morrison

Right:
The 'AL2' (later Class 82) electric locomotives were sub-contracted by AEI/Metro-Vickers to Beyer Peacock for mechanical construction and this small class of 10 locomotives was introduced in 1960. The fleet spent most of its life allocated to Longsight depot and, on 12 June 1974, No 82006 commences the climb to Shap Summit from Tebay, on the WCML, with the 1S55 Motorail service from Kensington Olympia to Scotland. *Brian Morrison*

'Rail 150': Shildon

The big event of the year, and for many a year, was the 'Rail 150 Cavalcade' at Shildon, celebrating the 150th anniversary of the opening of the Stockton & Darlington Railway. A collection of some 60 locomotives and items of rolling stock representing all periods of railway history was on display at Shildon from 24 August 1975 and the celebrations culminated with the 'Grand Steam Cavalcade' from Shildon to Heighington along the line of the original Stockton & Darlington track. The Grand Cavalcade was led by a replica of *Locomotion* and the last locomotive in the cavalcade was BR's High Speed Train. The locomotives in the cavalcade ranged from No 4472 *Flying Scotsman* to Wantage Tramway 0-4-0ST *Shannon* and from SR 'Merchant Navy' No 35028 *Clan Line* to No 790 *Hardwicke*. Prior to the Grand Parade, the atmosphere of the busy steam locomotive depot was created as the vast variety of motive power simmered away in the yard outside Shildon Works to the delight of the many railway enthusiasts who had travelled from far and wide. To the disappointment of many photographers, the seating situated on the lineside for the purpose of viewing the cavalcade faced the sun, but it was an event not to be repeated in an enthusiast's lifetime — and not to be missed. The parade was made up of 35 locomotives but four locomotive types were sadly missed — a Stanier 'Duchess' Pacific, a Stanier rebuild of a Fowler 'Royal Scot' and, from the GWR, a 'King' and a 'Castle'. However, it was a day to remember!

On 27 September, the National Railway Museum at York was officially opened by HRH Prince Philip, Duke of Edinburgh. The Duke of Edinburgh arrived in appropriate style — in 1906-built L&NWR Royal Saloon No 798. The new museum, built around the two ex-York engine shed turntables, placed on view Stirling Single No 1, NER Bo-Bo electric No 26500, SE&CR 'D' class 4-4-0 No 737 and a sectional view of 'Merchant Navy' Pacific No 35029 *Ellerman Lines* together with many other locomotives and items of rolling stock, and with many items of rail ephemera. From those early days many new exhibits have graced this 'hall of fame' of Britain's railway heritage.

A 'U' class 2-6-0, No 31806, was purchased for the Mid-Hants Railway from Woodham Bros at Barry in 1975. This locomotive was originally an ex-SR 'River' class 2-6-4T *River Torridge* and had been subsequently rebuilt as a tender locomotive.

More and more schemes were being set up each year to help save other locomotives lying in Barry scrapyard.

Horwich Works was involved in steam preservation early in 1975 when it overhauled LNER 'B1' No 1306 *Mayflower*. The locomotive left the works in April in good time to be available for the Shildon cavalcade.

On the Festiniog Railway, volunteer work on the 'deviation' line, necessary due to the flooding of the original trackbed beyond Ddaullt, was well underway in preparation for blasting of a new tunnel later in the year by professional tunnellers. The new tunnel would be 310.6yd-long with a bore 3.8yd wide and with a height of 4.9yd on the centre line.

At the other end of the scale the British Speed Record was again broken, in August, this time by the APT-E. In July, the 4-car train moved from Derby to the Western Region for extensive trials reaching speeds of 151.3mph near Goring & Streatley on 3 August.

From 5 May, the prototype HST commenced services on the Western Region between Paddington, Bristol and Weston-super-Mare. The train included the prototype Mark 3 kitchen and buffet vehicles — the first new catering vehicles (apart from 'specials') to be built for 20 years. Now known as the 'InterCity 125', on 3 November the High Speed Train commenced passenger evaluation trials between Paddington and Swansea. Speeds of up to 100mph were attained. Prior to this a 24-mile stretch of the line, between Westerleigh Junction and Wootton Bassett, was closed for five months from 5 May to enable engineering works to be carried out in preparation for the new high-speed services. This resulted in trains to and from South Wales being diverted via Bath adding up to 20min to a journey. During these engineering works, signalling was also improved.

In the northeast, tests were carried out at Backworth, near Newcastle upon Tyne, with a prototype articulated vehicle developed by Metro-Cammell for the forthcoming Tyne & Wear light transit system. The test track of 1½ miles in length followed the course of the former Duke of Northumberland's mineral railway, and a 110yd tunnel using various forms of track was also included. Traction supply was at 1,000 volts dc.

During the year, Swindon Works was involved in the refurbishing programme on the Southern Region's BEP and CEP electric units. This was necessary as these units, introduced in 1959 and 1963, were based on Mk I stock and had become 'dated'. Refurbishment included double glazing, public address system, fluorescent lighting, new seating and inside panelling.

On the locomotive front Class 47 diesel No 47046 was rebuilt, after recent collision damage, with a Ruston Paxman 2,500hp engine and renumbered 47601, for use as a test bed for the forthcoming Class 56 locomotives.

Early in April the experimental Class 87/1 electric locomotive appeared from Crewe incorporating thyristor control equipment and was numbered 87101.

The Class 35 diesel-hydraulic 'Hymeks' became extinct in 1975, the last four survivors, Nos 7011/17/18/22, being withdrawn in March. These locomotives never carried five digit TOPS numbers.

On London Transport new trains were under construction for the Piccadilly Line. This order included 87 six-car trains and one three-car train, the latter for the Aldwych branch. The existing 'silver' trains on the Piccadilly Line were eventually passed to the Northern Line, the remaining 'red' trains on the Piccadilly being scrapped. On 19 July, London Transport's Heathrow extension opened from Hounslow West to Heathrow Airport (Hatton Cross).

On 27 October, British Rail's 'Total Operations Processing System' (TOPS) was completed. Computers based at Marylebone were linked to 155 centres providing information as to the whereabouts and operational status of every wagon on British Rail, estimated at around 313,500, together with 2,700 locomotives. Four-digit headcodes on locomotives were now fast disappearing during the year and were being replaced with two white lights placed horizontally.

Line closures in 1975 included the Western Region's Hemyock branch in October due to the closure of the Unigate Factory at the end of the line. Milk traffic had ceased in the August. Passenger traffic had ceased in September 1963 — a victim of the Beeching axe.

Three significant accidents occurred in 1975 at Watford Junction, Nuneaton and at Moorgate on the London Underground. The Watford Junction accident, on 23 January, involved electric locomotives Nos 83003 and 86204, derailed by an obstruction when double-heading a Manchester to Euston train. The 22.15 Euston to Glasgow sleeper was in turn derailed by the wreckage, the train's locomotive, No 86209, plunging down the 50ft embankment. The driver of No 83003 was killed and 11 people were taken to hospital. At Moorgate, on the London Underground, 42 people were killed and 70 injured, on 28 February, as a Northern Line train on the Highbury branch overran the platform at speed and collided with the end of a short extension tunnel, creating terrible carnage. On 6 June, at Nuneaton, the 'Night Caledonian' sleeper, double-headed by electric locomotives Nos 86006 and 86242 became derailed on approaching Nuneaton station. The second locomotive mounted the platform and there was extensive damage to the first eight coaches. Class 25 diesel No 25286, which was hauling a coal train through Nuneaton at the time, also suffered extensive damage.

Below:
On 4 June 1975, the Class 445 4-PEP unit No 4002 arrives at Clapham Junction with the 15.26 Waterloo-Hampton Court service whilst in the near platform, Class 423 4-VEP No 7771 prepares to continue its journey with the 15.28 Victoria-Brighton working. The PEP units were the prototype for a new generation of electric multiple-unit stock with sliding passenger-operated doors to facilitate quicker loading and unloading of trains during peak periods. Those prototypes paved the way for Classes 313, 314, 315, 317, 455, 507 and 508 and many more to come. *Brian Morrison*

Above:
Soon after leaving Teesport Oil Refinery on
7 October 1975 Class 37 No 37216 roars through
Grangetown with a train of bogie tank wagons
bound for Jarrow. This locomotive carries the
four-character centrally-placed single indicator
panel, a feature fitted to the Class 37 locomotives
after 119 had been built with split headcode
boxes and front communicating doors.
Ken Fleming

Left:
On 5 May 1975, the prototype High Speed Train
unit, No 252001, commenced revenue-earning
service on the Western Region between
Paddington and Bristol/Weston-super-Mare,
covering around 750 miles each day. This entry
into service also signified a step forward in the
development of on-train catering, automatic
doors helping kitchen staff with trolleys and
passengers with their luggage. This view of
No 252001 shows the handsome-liveried train
after emerging from Twerton Tunnel with the
16.45 Paddington-Bristol Temple Meads train,
during the first week of service on 8 May 1975.
Philip D. Hawkins

Right:
The Midland Railway opened St Pancras station in 1868 and for nearly 100 years the train shed had the largest station roof in the world. In the days when 'Peaks' were 'King' at St Pancras, Class 45 No 45067 pulls out from this impressive terminus with the 13.05 service to Sheffield, on 25 March 1975. *Brian Morrison*

Below:
At the other end of the line, an aerial view of Leeds City station on 15 March 1975 shows another 'Peak' hauling the 10-coach 09.16 working from St Pancras, with Class 45 No 45130 in charge. A fine view of the city can be seen from this point. *Brian Morrison*

Above:
On 25 June 1975, Class 31/1 diesel No 31122 enters Norwich Yard with a Fakenham to Norwich freight working. Sadly, the Fakenham line is now no more, closing to passengers on 5 October 1964 and to freight some 20 years later. Note the line of diesel refuelling points in the background. *Brian Morrison*

Left:
'Rail 150' at Shildon was the steam event of the year where a fine array of steam locomotives lined up and paraded in front of thousands of delighted enthusiasts. In this view preparations are taking place for the cavalcade and unusual bedfellows on view are GWR 0-6-0PT No 7757, ex-L&YR Aspinall 0-4-0ST 'Pug', No 51218, Great Western 'Modified Hall' No 6960 *Raveningham Hall* (complete with bell) and LMS 'Black Five' No 4767 together with many, many more. Will they all be around to celebrate the 200th anniversary in 2025? (I probably won't!) *Mike Esau*

Romanian Imports

The first two Romanian-built Class 56 diesel-electric locomotives arrived at Harwich from Zeebrugge on 4 August 1976 having been assembled at the Craiova Works of Electroputere. Brush Electrical of Loughborough supplied the traction motors, ac generators, control equipment and certain electronics. This class totalling 120 in all, with 30 coming from Romania and the remainder of the class from BREL at Doncaster and Crewe, were built specifically for freight operation after an original plan to build 25kV ac locomotives entirely for freight work had been dropped. The Class 56 English Electric 16RK3CT power unit was a direct lineal descendant of the engines used in the prototype main line diesels Nos 10000 and 10001 of 1947/48, but now developed twice the power of the prototypes. However, faults were found in the machining of the centre axle of each bogie on the first 11 imported Class 56 locomotives, as a result of having been machined to incorrect tolerances. This resulted in the removal of the axles at Doncaster and Derby for rectification. The locomotives eventually entered service early in 1977, their initial allocations being Tinsley and Toton.

On the passenger front, new electric multiple-unit stock (designated Class 312) entered service on the London Midland Region. These units were built specifically to provide fast, comfortable travel on long-distance commuter services. The design was based on the earlier Class 310 units of 1967 but with maximum speed being increased to 90mph as against the Class 310's 75mph. A corridor connection on the Class 312s was also an improvement over the Class 310 units. More Class 312 units were under construction at BREL's York Works for use on the Eastern Region's Liverpool Street to Shenfield, Chelmsford, Colchester and Clacton lines and Class 312-operated services commenced to Chelmsford and Shenfield from 12 July.

New units for the Great Northern suburban services (Class 313) from Moorgate commenced trials in May 1976 with scheduled services using these units to Welwyn Garden City and Hertford North starting on 8 November. These Class 313 electric multiple units were the first ac/dc units to be built by BR and comprised two driving motor coaches and a central trailer carrying the rectifier equipment. Accommodation consisted of 232 open-plan second-class only seats. The route from Moorgate to Drayton Park being 750V dc resulted in the change-over at this station to overhead ac by a push-button mechanism within the cab, with indicator lights showing which 'system' had been selected. An audible warning was given if a train ran on to a live conductor rail with the equipment connected for overhead contact. These trains also incorporated power-operated doors.

On 8 November, the commencement date of the Welwyn and Hertford North electrified services, the Secretary of State for Transport announced in the House of Commons that he had given consent for the electrification of the St Pancras-Bedford line at a cost of £80 million.

On 14 January, the first Class 87 electric locomotive to carry a name, No 87001 was ceremonially named *Stephenson* at Euston station prior to its departure for Glasgow. The two stainless steel nameplates it carried were presented by the Stephenson Locomotive Society. Named on this occasion to commemorate the 150th anniversary of the Stockton & Darlington Railway (held in 1975) No 87001 carried the name *Stephenson* only until July 1977 — the name eventually (on 12 October 1977) being transferred to the unique Class 87/1 thyristor control-fitted No 87101, at the consent of the Stephenson Locomotive Society, to commemorate the 118th anniversary of the death of Robert Stephenson.

As a 'Western' class diesel-hydraulic, No 1062 *Western Courier*, was purchased for preservation in 1976, its proposed new home being the Torbay Steam Railway, the prototype Brush Type 4 Co-Co locomotive No D1200 *Falcon* came face to face with the cutter's torch in March.

The production HST's first proving run, involving No 253001, took place on 7 January between Crewe and Shrewsbury. On the Western Region, from 4 October, InterCity 125 trains were operating 32 services each day — 22 between Paddington and South Wales (11 in each direction) and five each way between Paddington and Bristol. The Cardiff service using the HST units was accelerated by 23min and the Bristol service by 15min. The new accelerated services increased passenger traffic in the first two months of operation by 15%.

As the Class 24 diesels were being withdrawn from Crewe to be replaced by boilered Class 25s during the year, large numbers of Class 24s could be seen stored in Crewe South Yard.

Extra 'cheap-day' trains from Derby, Nottingham and Leicester to Skegness operated on Mondays to Thursdays, often hauled by two Class 20 locomotives, and were known as the 'Jolly Fisherman' (from the 'Skegness is so bracing' poster).

There were cut-backs, in May 1976, resulting in the diversion of London to Glasgow services from the Settle & Carlisle route (previously named the 'Thames-Clyde Express') and the 'Tees-Tyne Pullman's' life was also terminated. However, the 'Hull Pullman' and the 'Yorkshire Pullman' were retained. In fact, the Settle & Carlisle celebrated its centenary in 1976, the centenary train from Carnforth being double-headed by *Hardwicke* and *Flying Scotsman*.

On 3 May, passenger services were withdrawn from the Haltwhistle-Alston branch — a line which once saw 'J39's, LMS 2-6-4Ts and finally diesel multiple-units.

A brand new station opened without a ceremony in January 1976 — Birmingham International — but it was not formally inaugurated until September.

In Scotland, the ex-Highland Railway's Muir of Ord station reopened to passenger traffic having being closed since June 1960.

The freight news for 1976 was the clinching of a contract with the British Steel Corporation on 23 June, totalling £19 million, to move up to 59 million tons of iron-ore over 12 years from Port Talbot to Llanwern, following a successful three months of the heaviest freight trains in Britain conveying 2,000 tons of iron-ore hauled by three Class 37 locomotives over this route.

New air-braked freight services were introduced in October 1976 from Dover to Dundee, via Warrington, from Birmingham to Newcastle and from Humberside to Glasgow and in the week ending 23 October, Freightliners Ltd carried more containers than in any week since their inception — 17,276.

Gale-force winds hit the London Midland Region on 2 January blowing down catenary wires between Euston and Rugby, but the worst affected area was the Cambrian coast where high winds combined with exceptionally high tides. Barmouth Bridge sustained damage, facilities at Gogath Halt were blown into a neighbouring field and the sea wall blocked the line at Llanaber. The River Conwy burst its banks and half a mile of track was submerged under water. Near Bettws-y-Coed, a Park Royal two-car set (M56155/50408) collided with a fallen tree shattering the cab windows.

Numerous steam-hauled railtours were approved by the BR Board during 1976, involving such locomotives as *King George V*, *Princess Elizabeth*, *Flying Scotsman*, No 1000, *Clan Line*, *Hinderton Hall*, *Hardwicke* and *Burton Agnes Hall*, much to the delight of all steam enthusiasts.

On the Bluebell Railway, a new acquisition was SE&CR 'H' class 0-4-4T No 31263, and *Blackmore Vale* returned to steam on 15 May. At York, *Duchess of Hamilton*, the LMS Pacific, was placed on view on 27 May to commemorate the birth of its designer, Sir William A. Stanier FRS. On the narrow-gauge Talyllyn Railway, on 22 May, the extension to Nant Gwernol was formally opened.

The former Great Western CME, Frederick Hawksworth, passed away in July 1976 at the grand old age of 92. He will be remembered for his fine locomotives, such as the 4-6-0 'Counties', his 'Modified Halls' and the unusual '15xx' class 0-6-0 tank locomotives.

Right:
On 22 September 1976, the 12.00 (SX) Bury train departs from Manchester Victoria. The two-car Class 504 electric unit is made up of cars M65452 and M77173. This route was energised at 1,200V dc and these Wolverton-built units were constructed specifically for the line, which is now part of the Manchester Metrolink system. *Brian Morrison*

Below right:
The unusual sight of a locomotive-hauled passenger train leaving Bury (Lancs), on 3 July 1976. Class 40 No 40130 is pictured with a holiday special to Llandudno, this being the first day of the town's annual holiday. *David A. Flitcroft*

Below:
A fitted 'Speedlink' freight from Corpach to Mossend heads round the curve between Roy Bridge and Tulloch on 27 May 1976 with Birmingham RC&W Class 27/0 No 27008 providing the power. *Brian Morrison*

Above:
With Ford Motor Co containers for Dagenham, Class 85 electric No 85012 powers through Bushey on the West Coast main line on 30 June 1976. In June 1989, this locomotive was renumbered to 85104, after having its ETH equipment isolated, and was restricted to 75mph for freight-only duties. *Brian Morrison*

Left:
Three pairs of master-and-slave shunters (Class 13) were introduced in 1965 for hump shunting at Tinsley Yard. Originally numbered D4500-D4502 they were formed from Class 08 diesel shunters Nos D4188/D3698 (D4500), D4190/D4189 (D4501) and D4187/D3697 (D4502) — the first named of the pair being the 'master'. On 6 October 1976 No 13003 (ex-D4502) returns from the Tinsley 'hump'. *G. W. Morrison*

Top right:
The scene is Sowerby Bridge in the industrial West Riding of Yorkshire and, on 26 June 1976, a six-car train forming the 15.15 Manchester Victoria-Bradford and Leeds service pauses briefly. The train comprises a three-car Metro-Cammell Class 111 unit leading, coupled to a Birmingham RC&W three-car Class 110 set. *L. A. Nixon*

Right:
A two-car Class 502 electric unit, with car No M28311M leading, leaves Liverpool Exchange on 23 September 1976 with the 11.44 service to Ormskirk. These units were introduced in 1939 as three and five-car sets for Liverpool-Southport services and were fitted with air-operated sliding doors. By now part of Liverpool Exchange had been taken over by a different kind of transport. *Brian Morrison*

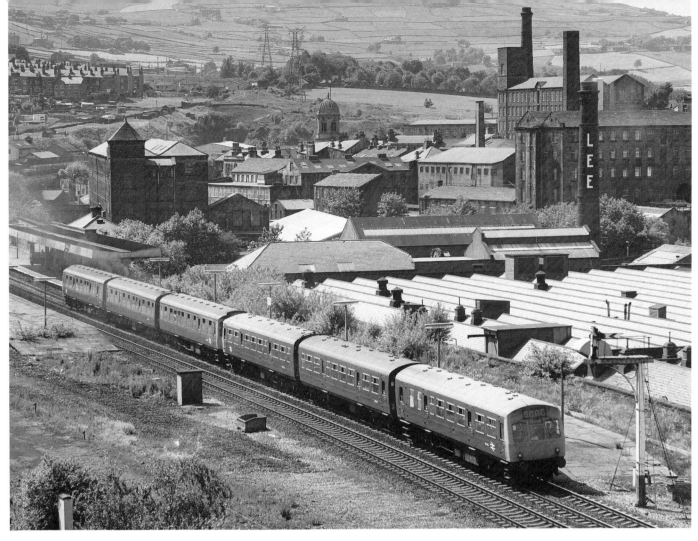

Hydraulic Demise

By February 1977 the last diesel-hydraulic locomotive was taken out of BR service when the last five Class 52 'Westerns' were withdrawn. The last to go were Nos 1010, 1013, 1023, 1041 and 1048 (all of which are now preserved). This was a sad end for the diesel-hydraulic transmission locomotives of the Western Region which incorporated the 'Warships', the North British 'D63xx' class and the 'D95xx' class Paxman central-cab shunters. Gone now were the unique 'Westerns' loved by all diesel enthusiasts, remembered over the years for their liveries of Desert Sand, Brunswick Green, Maroon and Blue as they hauled West of England expresses. For the first time in diesel history we saw enthusiasts' specials carrying headboards with names such as 'Western Requiem', 'Western Lament', Western Talisman' and Western Finale'. Enthusiasts clamoured to be involved in the preservation of a 'Western' and by the end of 1977 No D1062 *Western Courier* was fully restored and operating in preservation on the Torbay & Dartmouth line. The final withdrawal of the 'Westerns', in February 1977, coincided with the withdrawal of the prototype HST No 252001, the forerunner of the HSTs which eventually took over the fast West of England services.

It was also farewell to the GWR 'Castle' No 4079 *Pendennis Castle* which left Avonmouth Docks for Australia, bound for its new residence with the Hammersley Iron Co. Its final passenger run was on 29 May with 11 coaches and saloon GE No 1 from Saltley to Didcot and steam-enthusiasts lined the route to bid a sad farewell to this beautiful locomotive.

To delight the steam enthusiasts, more steam runs were granted for 1977 including York-Carnforth, Guide Bridge-Sheffield, Shrewsbury-Newport, Leeds-York, Barrow-Skipton, Saltley-Didcot and Newcastle-Stockton. Locomotives operating these services included many of those used in 1976 plus *Mayflower, Clun Castle, Evening Star, Sir Nigel Gresley* and various 'Black Fives'.

On the Keighley & Worth Valley Railway, Standard Class 4 4-6-0 No 75078 was steamed for the first time since its withdrawal in 1966 and it was the first of this class to be returned to service after being rescued from Barry scrapyard. On the Nene Valley Railway, 'Battle of Britain' Pacific No 34081 *92 Squadron* was undergoing restoration and on this 'new' railway, public passenger services through Nene Park, Peterborough, over a five mile stretch of track were inaugurated on 4 June as a result of a successful partnership between volunteers and a new Town Development Corporation. Further south, on the Mid-Hants Railway, the Alresford-Ropley section opened to passengers again, on 30 April, after a trial run on 3 April. Throughout the Mid-Hants Railway's first season all services were operated by 'N' class Mogul No 31874 (which operated the first train) or former Longmoor Military Railway 0-6-0ST No 196 and from 30 April to 23 October a total of 51,898 fare-paying passengers were carried — a remarkable achievement. On 22 October the West Somerset Railway reopened the line from Bishop's Lydeard to Williton with GWR 0-6-0PT No 6412 *Flockton Flyer* working the first train. Also, Dunster signalbox on this line was removed, by rail, to Minehead for reuse at the terminus.

The Vale of Rheidol Railway celebrated 75 years of service in 1977 and 1924-built No 9 *Prince of Wales*, fresh from Swindon Works, appeared in a startling lined blue livery with a polished metal BR emblem on its cab-sides. Services for the year commenced on 6 April. On 7 July, the tunnel on the Festiniog Railway extension to Llyn Ystradau was approved for regular services and trains from Portmadoc carrying passengers passed through the tunnel from then on.

On 29 April, the first of the Doncaster-built Class 56 diesel locomotives emerged. These were the first new locomotives to be built at Doncaster for 11 years. Certain Class 56 locomotive parts were manufactured at other BREL Works establishments such as roofs, fuel tanks and cab frames (Ashford), cab desks (Eastleigh) and radiator housings (Swindon). This was necessary due to insufficient staff being employed at Doncaster.

As it was Her Majesty the Queen's Silver Jubilee year, a 'new' named train appeared from 8 June — 'Silver Jubilee'. This was the 07.45 King's Cross-Edinburgh (1S12) and the 15.00 return journey (1E20), both of which carried a headboard incorporating the jubilee motif. These trains ceased to be named 'Silver Jubilee' after 30 December 1977.

Two new Royal Saloons were introduced on 16 May when the Royal Train was hauled from Euston to Glasgow by Class 87 No 87004 for the Silver Jubilee tour of Scotland. The old Royal Train coaches were limited to a speed of 70mph and had no modern air-conditioning. The new saloons were built as prototypes of Mk 3 passenger stock in 1972 — No 2903 was the Queen's Saloon and No 2904, the Duke of Edinburgh's Saloon. The Royal Train of 16 May comprised 10 coaches. Prior to the Royal Tour, trial runs with the new Royal vehicles took place on 3/4 March following a previous visit by the Queen to Wolverton to inspect the progress of the new coaches. The new Royal Train was used prolifically throughout the Silver Jubilee year.

A list was published in 1977 of names which were to be affixed to both Class 87 electric locomotives and Class 50 diesels. On 11 July, No 87001 was officially named *Royal Scot* at Euston to coincide with the 50th anniversary of the named train which ran from Euston to Glasgow. Other members of the class received their names later in the year. Class 50 diesels, it was decided, would be named after Warships, regenerating the diesel-hydraulic 'Warship' class theme. Nameplates were fitted gradually over a period when locomotives required maintenance.

On 22 June 1977, the first of three pre-production Advance Passenger Trains (APT-P) were delivered to RTC Derby for BREL Derby Works and as preparations were being made for HSTs to operate over the East Coast main line in 1978 (Class 254), train formations were finalised — nine-car trains for the Western Region (Class 253) and 10-car trains for the Eastern (Class 254). On 7 November, the new Heaton depot to take the new Class 254 High Speed Trains was officially opened by Peter Parker. The first HST delivered for the Eastern Region, No 254001, was handed over by BREL at York on 7 September 1977.

King's Cross remodelling plans commenced in 1977 providing a simplified track layout, new crossovers between Holloway and Gasworks tunnels and increased headroom at the southern end of Gasworks Tunnel under Regents Canal. Suburban electric services to Royston and Hitchin, operated by the new Class 312 units, commenced on 3 October.

On Merseyside, Liverpool Exchange station closed on 29 April after 127 years of service and a new underground link joining the Mersey/Wirral and Southport/Ormskirk lines under the city opened on 2 May 1977 when electrification to Kirkby was also inaugurated. Class 502 and 503 units were used on the new link and loop services initially pending delivery of the new three-car Class 507 stock.

On the Glasgow Underground system, services were suspended from the end of May pending 18 months work on modernisation, incorporating new workshops at Govan.

On London Transport, 'Silver Trains' of '72' Mk 2 stock were transferred from the Northern Line to the Bakerloo Line. These trains were eventually destined for the first stage of the new Fleet (later Jubilee) Line and, on 16 December, the extension of the Piccadilly Line through to Heathrow Central was officially opened by Her Majesty the Queen.

Above:
Double-headed Class 20 diesels Nos 20136 and 20134 pass Rufford Colliery sidings, near Mansfield with a loaded coal train from Clipstone on 14 April 1977. No 20134 was one of eight Class 20s renumbered into the 203xx series in April 1986 when they were dedicated to construction traffic for ICI trains from Tunstead. They all reverted to their old numbers in November/December of the same year when this duty was taken over by Class 37s. *L. A. Nixon*

Right:
The remote Georgemas Junction is where the Wick and Thurso trains to and from Inverness join up and split. On 30 May 1977, Class 26/1 diesel No 26034 shunts the BG off the 06.15 Inverness-Wick train. The Class 26/1 locomotives were all fitted with vacuum brakes and steam heating. *Brian Morrison*

Top left:
English Electric Class 37 diesels regularly worked London-East Anglia trains in 1977 and, on 10 September of that year, No 37038 is seen leaving Liverpool Street with the 14.05 Cambridge train. These locomotives were built both at the Vulcan Foundry and at Robert Stephenson-Hawthorn; the one in this view being a Vulcan Foundry version. *Brian Morrison*

Left:
Charing Cross station on 14 September 1977 and Class 411/2 4-CEP electric unit No 7193 departs with the 12.04 service to Ashford (Kent). Other platforms are taken up by EPB units and a lone Hastings DEMU. The station fascia bears the letters SR and, before Southern Railway days, Charing Cross was a South East & Chatham Railway station. *Brian Morrison*

Top right:
The attractive 'Trans-Pennine' diesel units were introduced in 1960 and comprised three-car sets usually working in pairs. On 31 July 1977 one of these units emerges from Standedge Tunnel, past the site of Diggle station, with the 16.00 Leeds-Liverpool service. The original 1849 Standedge Tunnel bore is seen on the right. *Larry Goddard*

Right:
The only BR passenger working which starts and ends in Surrey is the Staines-Weybridge service. A 2-SAP unit No 5938 calls at Chertsey on this service in September 1977. The 2-SAP units were downgraded 2-HAP units (second-class only). *John G. Glover*

Above:
The Grand Union Canal is crossed by the Metropolitan Line between Watford and Croxley and an 'A60' train to Baker Street crosses this fine viaduct on 20 April 1977 — an unusual LT view. *John G. Glover*

Left:
On 8 October 1977, the scene is the Keighley & Worth Valley Railway but the train is the 'Fife Coast Express', a through working from Falkirk to Oxenhope. The SRPS Special is pictured at Oakworth with the motive power being ex-GNR 4-4-2 No 990 (built 1898) piloting the more modern Standard 4-6-0 No 75079. No 990 was the first British Atlantic tender engine ever built and acquired the nickname 'Klondyke', a name which continued to be associated with all these 'C2' class locomotives. *Brian Stephenson*

HST:
London-Edinburgh

From the new summer 1978 timetable, six Class 254 IC125 units went into traffic on the East Coast main line. These new high-speed trains cut journey times from London to Edinburgh to 4hr 50min, reducing the travelling time by 38min, and between London and Newcastle to 3hr 4min, 31min faster. During the year Class 254 units continued to be loaned to the Western Region due to shortages. Although scheduled services operated by Class 254 units did not commence until May, the first revenue-earning HST on the ECML appeared in March.

The last semaphore signal arm on the East Coast main line disappeared on 27 September with the lowering of the signal arm from Decoy No 2 SBNo48 up main home signal, south of Doncaster. This followed the passage of the northbound 'Flying Scotsman' — the signal can now be seen in the National Railway Museum, York. The ECML was now colour-light signalled throughout, as earlier in the year, on 11/12 March, colour-lights were brought into use between Edinburgh and Berwick.

On 5 May, the Eastern Region discontinued Pullman operations with the last 'Yorkshire Pullman' and 'Hull Pullman' services. On that day, both up Pullmans were 'Deltic'-hauled.

A 'full' electric service between King's Cross and Royston commenced on 6 February 1978 using new Class 312 units and brought the end of the through King's Cross-Cambridge 'buffet' services, thus ending a through service to Cambridge which dated from 1866. Permission was refused to extend electrification to Cambridge.

On the London Midland Region, the 'new' Bedford Midland station was officially opened by Sir Peter Parker on 9 October. The new station was situated just north of the original 1857 Bedford station and was in preparation for the forthcoming St Pancras to Bedford electrification scheme.

On Merseyside, the Wirral celebrated a centenary as, on 1 April 1878, the line between Hoylake and West Kirby had been opened to traffic. In 1978, the first stage of the new Merseyrail project reached completion with the opening of the former Cheshire Lines Committee route to Garston on 3 January and the completion of the Moorfields Interchange between the Northern and Wirral lines in July. The first Class 507 three-car electric units for Merseyrail were delivered in October 1978 and Her Majesty the Queen inspected the new system, on 25 October, which now formed an integral rapid transit system through Merseyside and beneath Liverpool.

West Midland PTE's new cross-city line in Birmingham was instantly successful as trains were introduced between Four Oaks and Longbridge Cross. Twenty-one extra Class 116 diesel multiple-units were allocated to this busy new project.

In Scotland, the Falkirk Tunnel on the Glasgow-Edinburgh route closed for 11 weeks until 18 December whilst engineers carried out improvements including the lowering of the tunnel floor in preparation for the introduction of the Class 47/7-hauled fast push-pull service using adapted Mark 3 coaching stock. Gradually, the speed limit over the line would be increased from 60mph to 90mph.

Scotland was also in the news on the preservation scene as the Strathspey Railway opened for traffic on 22 July from Boat of Garten. At this early stage the railway's station at Aviemore was not ready for use, but over the 30 operating days, from 22 July to 1 October, 16,053 fare-paying passengers took advantage of this new service, predominantly worked by Ivatt Mogul No 46464 occasionally assisted by LMS 'Black Five' No 5025.

On 24 March unrebuilt 'West Country' Pacific No 34105 *Swanage* arrived at the Mid-Hants Railway and later in the year they received one of the Ruston & Hornsby Class 07 Southampton Docks shunters, for restoration. At the Bluebell Railway, on 12 October, the SR 'S15' 4-6-0 No 30847 was offloaded after a long road journey from Barry scrapyard.

Class 76 dc electric locomotive No 26020 was delivered to the National Railway Museum, York on 31 August following a repaint in black livery at Doncaster and No D1041 *Western Prince* joined the ranks of preserved diesels having been stored at Newton Abbot since withdrawal in February 1977.

No 70000 *Britannia* was steamed again at Bridgnorth on 18 May. Restoration had taken seven years to complete. Another mass of weekend steam-hauled specials made it a glorious year for enthusiasts. Locomotives involved included *Scots Guardsman*, 'K1' No 2005, *Mallard* and some of the old favourites from previous years.

The dearly-loved Bishop of Wakefield, The Right Revd Eric Treacy MBE, famous for his brilliant railway photography, sadly died at Appleby station on the Settle & Carlisle line whilst doing one of the things he loved to do best of all — waiting to photograph a steam special — on this occasion *Evening Star*. A plaque to commemorate this fine gentleman can now be seen on Appleby station. A steam special was organised on 30 September as a memorial, hauled by *Flying Scotsman* and *Evening Star*, whose whistle sounded at his memorial service on that day.

Naming, both officially and unofficially, took place during 1978. Unofficial names included No 47460 *Great Eastern* at Stratford and Class 08 shunter No 08725 started carrying the headboard *Perth Station Pilot*. Officially, No 86101 was named *Sir W. A. Stanier FRS* (the first Class 86 to be named) and the first Class 50 diesel to carry a nameplate was No 50035 *Ark Royal*, officially named on 17 January.

In preparation for the new High Speed Train services scheduled for the West Country route, and to speed up the flow of stone traffic, work started on the remodelling of the junction at Westbury on 17 September. Multiple aspect signalling was also installed. In October, crew training on IC125 units commenced between Plymouth and Penzance.

A 10-year contract between BR and Foster Yeoman was signed in April 1978 to convey 3 million tons of limestone from Merehead Quarry to Acton in 1,400-ton payload stone trains hauled by double-headed Class 37 locomotives. Also, the London Brick Co renewed their contract for containerised bricks from Stewartby, in Bedfordshire, to London, Liverpool and Manchester. New Speedlink services from Hull and Teesside/Tyneside, and from Parkeston Quay and Thamesside were introduced in 1978 and Freightliners Ltd returned to BR Board total ownership from 4 August.

In London the rebuilt London Bridge station was officially opened by the Bishop of Southwark on 15 December 1978 and on the London Underground, the last seven-car train of 1938 tube stock ran on the Northern Line on 14 April. Three days later the first train of 'C77' stock on the District Line went into service between Edgware Road, Putney Bridge and Wimbledon.

On the Southern Region, Class 423 4-VEP units intended for conversion to 4-VEG units for Gatwick Airport services started appearing with a fluorescent marking strip at cantrail height over second-class sections bearing the words 'Rapid City Link Gatwick-London'.

In the northeast, the first production Tyne & Wear Metro cars were delivered in August, being hauled to South Gosforth depot by Class 47 No 47514.

On the weather front, 1978 proved to be as bad as 1947 and 1963 in certain areas. On 19 January, snowstorms brought down power cables in the Leicester area and high winds troubled contractors rebuilding Leicester station. On 28 January an Inverness-Wick train was stranded in deep snow-drifts resulting in passengers having to be airlifted to safety by helicopter the next day after being transferred to one coach as others became derailed as the train tried to break through the snowdrift. The line was closed until 6 February. On the Southern Region there was heavy snow in mid-Sussex on 9 February causing delays and points were frozen up in Kent. Conditions in the west of England deteriorated following snowstorms on 18/19 February resulting in deep snow covering Devon and Dorset. All this brought the usual chaos to Britain's railways — would we ever find a solution?

Below:
An aerial view of Exeter St David's station on 21 July 1978, showing the yard where Class 47/0 diesel No 47136 passes through with a down freight consisting mainly of China Clay empties. This view clearly shows the route taken by freight trains not passing through the station and also, in the top left of the picture, the remains of the old steam shed. *Brian Morrison*

Right:
The Class 33 Birmingham RC&W Type 3 Bo-Bo diesels were, and remain, very reliable locomotives and were all initially allocated to Southern Region duties. Every locomotive in the class was first allocated to Hither Green. This view shows the fine signal gantry at Southampton, on 13 May 1978, with a Class 33/0 version, No 33002, passing through on an Eastleigh-Fawley oil tanker train. *Brian Morrison*

Bottom right:
A King's Cross departure on 11 September 1978 and in charge of the 17.12 to Grantham is Class 40 No 40164. The locomotive has had its multiple control equipment removed as can be seen by the two large holes in the buffer beam. *Brian Morrison*

Left:
Certain Class 47 locomotives, without train heating facilities, were classified 47/3 and renumbered in the 473xx series. Some were fitted with slow speed control for working merry-go-round trains at power stations. Two of these locomotives, including No 47308, lie snow-covered at Knottingly shed on 12 January 1978. *Rex Kennedy*

Below left:
Radlett station on the former Midland main line from St Pancras to the north and on 6 April 1978 two Class 127 BR Derby/Rolls-Royce four-car diesel multiple-units stop *en route*. This scene changed with the onset of suburban electrification to Bedford. *L. A. Nixon*

Right:
On 6 May 1978, this Broad Street station scene shows empty electric multiple-unit stock formed of a six-car Class 501 train (2 sets) in the foreground and, in the distance, a three-car Class 501 unit awaits departure with the 12.14 service to Richmond. These units were introduced in 1957 for this line and Euston-Watford services. *L. A. Nixon*

Below:
Two 'younger' enthusiasts admire the Kerr Stewart 0-4-0ST No 4 *Edward Thomas* as it waits at Abergynolwyn station on 2 June 1978 with a Talyllyn Railway service to Tywyn. *Edward Thomas* was one of the two Corris Railway saddle tanks sold to the Talyllyn Railway in 1948. *Brian Morrison*

Southern EMU Facelift

Swindon's famous 'A' Shop was the chosen location for the Southern Region's major refurbishment programme on their CEP fleet. These express units were built for the Kent Coast Electrification scheme from 1956 onwards and, in an endeavour to extend their life by 20 years, units were virtually gutted to provide improved ventilation, new second-class seating in open saloons and a new interior decor. All that was to remain from the vehicles brought in for refurbishment were underfames, bodyshell, external doors and motor bogies. Blue asbestos was also removed. Refurbishment followed the lines of the prototype modernised 4-CEP, No 7153. This was to be a 5-year project for Swindon and up to £3 million would be spent to equip the shops to handle this work. The 4-CEPs were in good company in 'A' Shop, rubbing shoulders with *King George V* and the last 'Westerns', in for dismantling!

On 1 March, fire substantially destroyed 4-CEP units Nos 7130 and 7210 at Victoria, an incident which closed the station for a while as firemen fought the blaze which left only one of the eight coaches undamaged.

On 9 August, the first new Class 508 unit arrived at Strawberry Hill depot (only to be blacked by BR staff). This problem created a delay in the driver-training schedule due to commence in August. Test runs eventually commenced on 25 October between Strawberry Hill and Shepperton — a route often used for trying out new electric units. The Class 508 units, built at York, were scheduled for South Western inner suburban services from Waterloo.

On 23 February 1979, at Hampton Court Junction, a 4-SUB unit working a Hampton Court-Waterloo service collided with a Basingstoke-Waterloo train made up of a 4-VEP and a 4-CIG unit, pushing two cars of the Hampton Court train down an embankment, injuring seven people.

In Scotland, the first push-pull-fitted Class 47/7 locomotive, No 47701 *Saint Andrew*, arrived at Haymarket early in the year but this locomotive, and others that followed during 1979, was employed on more 'general' duties pending the start of the new fast services from Glasgow Queen Street to Edinburgh Waverley. The first of the push-pull driving trailers worked test trips from RTC Derby in June and crew

training over the designated Scottish route commenced with No 47704 *Dunedin* early in August. On 22 October, the first new push-pull trains entered service. The train comprised five Mk 3 coaches and a DBSO headed by No 47709 *The Lord Provost*.

The new 25kV ac overhead 'Argyle Line' from Rutherglen was energised from the rebuilt Glasgow Central Low Level station on 4 June. The 'Argyle Line' scheme incorporated the modernisation of five stations — Dalmarnock, Bridgeton, Anderston, Finnieston, (formerly Stobcross) and Glasgow Central Low Level. Rutherglen and Partick stations were relocated and a brand new station appeared at Argyle Street. Services commenced on 5 November with the use of units of Classes 303 and 311, with additional destination display giving more precise routeing information.

On the East Coast main line, on 17 March, during improvement work on Penmanshiel Tunnel, 35yd of roof collapsed bringing down 2,500 tons of rock on to the track, killing two men. This naturally created havoc with ECML services with rerouteing necessary via Carlisle with connecting services to the WCML from Newcastle to Carlisle. There was also concern registered over the safety of the rest of the bore after the clearance of the rubble. It was decided to divert the ECML around Penmanshiel Tunnel at a cost of £2 million. The diversion opened on 20 August but it was estimated that £3 million in revenue was lost due to this disaster.

The Class 370 APT test runs between Glasgow and Carlisle commenced during midsummer and speed signs *en route* bore the legend 'APT 125'. In fact, on 20 December, the prototype recorded a speed of 160mph between Quintinshill and Beattock. Also in Scotland, the 40-mile freight-only line from Dyce Junction to Fraserburgh (ex-GNSR) closed to traffic on 6 October, 14 years after withdrawal of passenger services.

On the Western Region, in October 1979, a record-breaking MGR service came into being from Newport and Cardiff Docks to Didcot when coal imported from Australia and America was conveyed in trains of 45 MGR wagons, with a total payload of 1,350 tonnes, hauled by Class 56 locomotives. This beat the previous South Wales coal train record of 35 wagons.

Class 56 locomotives were also successfully tested on the Port Talbot-Llanwern iron-ore trains in 1979 resulting in further Class 56s being transferred to Cardiff Canton depot.

The Class 47/6 locomotive, No 47601, fitted with the Ruston-Paxman 16-cylinder engine, later used in Class 56 locomotives, was re-engined at BREL Crewe in 1979 with a prototype 12-cylinder engine to be fitted in later Class 58s, and renumbered 47901. Class 50 locomotives commenced crew training over the Waterloo-Exeter route in November in preparation for revised services commencing the following May.

In October, four IC125-operated services commenced between Paddington, Plymouth and Penzance but the units were not permitted to work over the South Devon banks with only one power car operational. Assistance was always required in these circumstances. By now, work was well under way on the new depot and servicing facilities at Laira in preparation for the new HST units.

On the Eastern Region, on 20/21 January, the Shenfield-Southend line was converted from 6.25kV to 25kV ac power supply. Work continued on the conversion to Liverpool Street throughout the year resulting in the lowering of tracks and platforms 11-13 at Liverpool Street in preparation for the new 25kV overhead wires.

'Paddington 125', on 1 March, saw the return of steam to this terminus as No 6000 *King George V* together with No 5900 *Hinderton Hall* graced the station with their presence, and again in September for the 75th anniversary of Old Oak Common depot, with No 5051 *Dryslwyn Castle* and No 92220 *Evening Star*.

Preservation news in 1979 was the arrival of 'Battle of Britain' Pacific No 34059 *Sir Archibald Sinclair* and No 73082 *Camelot* on the Bluebell Railway, ex-LB&SCR 'Terrier' No 46 *Newington* on the Isle of Wight Steam Railway from the 'Hayling Billy' pub car park on Hayling Island and even Lyme Regis station building was acquired by the Mid-Hants Railway for use in extending facilities at Alresford.

On 19 July, at the Festiniog Railway, the new Fairlie locomotive *Earl of Merioneth* hauled its first passenger train, the former *Earl of Merioneth* reverting to its original

1885 name, *Livingston Thompson*, and becoming a museum piece.

On a final note, as winter came upon us, weather conditions reminded the Scottish Region of the previous winter's problems when trains were stranded in snowdrifts and (in anticipation) trains carried emergency food hampers on certain 'remote' routes. These hampers contained emergency rations for around 50 passengers for 24 hours — there is nothing like being prepared!

Right:
Gloucester RC&W parcels car No TDB975023 (ex-W55001) approaches Paddington with a parcels service from Slough in August 1979. These Class 122 units were introduced in 1958 and prior to conversion for parcels use were fitted with 65 second-class seats. *Brian Morrison*

Below:
A scene from the past at Roxton Sidings between Harbrough and Stallingbrough, near Immingham. A fine example of a Great Northern somersault signal, a GNR signalbox and a manually-operated level-crossing gate, as ex-works Class 55 'Deltic', No 55007 *Pinza*, passes by with the 13.05 King's Cross-Cleethorpes express on 13 September 1979. *L. A. Nixon*

Above:
The fleet of Swindon-constructed InterCity units were originally used on outer suburban and main-line duties from Paddington but were transferred to Hull Botanic Gardens in the mid-1970s where they later operated with the Class 124 'Trans-Pennine' units. On 15 September 1979, a four-car rake passes Chinley North Junction forming a Manchester-Sheffield Trans-Pennine service. In the background, awaiting a favourable signal, Class 45/0 'Peak' No 45001 heads a Tunstead to Margam mineral train. *L. A. Nixon*

Left:
Trains pass at Grindleford on a wet 28 May 1979. On the left is a new-liveried Class 101 two-car unit with the 16.33 Sheffield-New Mills train, whilst on the right a Class 108 two-car set arrives with the 16.15 New Mills-Sheffield working. Looking at the scene it looks,by now, as if all the waiting passengers want to do is to go home and sit by a nice warm fire. *L. A. Nixon*

Top right:
A double-headed northbound train of chemical tanks leaves Beattock loop on 2 August 1979. Long gone are the days when steam bankers would lie in wait here to offer assistance to heavy trains. On this occasion the two electric locomotives in charge are Class 83 No 83013 leading and Class 86 No 86024. *Peter J. Robinson*

Right:
The Advance Passenger Train carried out tests during 1979 over the West Coast main line. This view, showing the train at speed in September 1979, is near Lockerbie. During this time the Class 370 APTs were housed at Shields Road depot in Glasgow. *D. Haviland*

Above:
On 22 July 1979 South Gosforth shed housed new Tyne & Wear Metro sets and this view shows two of these yellow & white units, together with a Tyne & Wear 0-6-0 diesel shunter No WL1, sat outside the depot building. These diesel shunters were eventually sold to TML for construction work on the Channel Tunnel. *Rex Kennedy*

Left:
LNER 'A4' Pacific No 60009 *Union of South Africa* approaches Arbroath with an Edinburgh–Aberdeen excursion on Easter Saturday, 14 April 1979. This locomotive is owned by John Cameron and, prior to its main line sojourn, was based on the Lochty Railway in Fife. The locomotive is currently stored at Markinch station for use on main line railtours. *L. A. Nixon*

Rainhill

The event of the year was the 'Rocket 150' celebrations at Rainhill to commemorate 150 years of the Liverpool & Manchester Railway. For the occasion, the historic locomotive *Lion*, built in 1838, having spent its later life as a static exhibit in the transport gallery of Liverpool Museum, was restored to full working order by Ruston Diesels Ltd, the company occupying the historic Vulcan Foundry site. *Lion* worked for seven years on the Liverpool & Manchester Railway as No 57 and for 14 years on the Grand Junction Railway & L&NWR as No 116. By 1980 *Lion* was 142 years old and claimed to be the oldest original operating locomotive in the world.

The Liverpool & Manchester Railway opened on 15 September 1830 and much to the surprise of critics who thought the line would sink without trace, was constructed across Chat Moss, a spongy peat bog.

To commemorate this historic occasion, a series of events and exhibitions were held from 1 May to 31 December 1980 — the highlight being the Rainhill Trials re-enactment and Cavalcade at Rainhill from 24-26 May. Naturally, some originally proposed participants fell by the wayside but there was still a glorious array of motive power on view. However, it was not a sell-out with only 100,000 of the 145,000 grandstand seats sold. In the cavalcade one could see such locomotives as GWR 'Castle' No 5051, SR 'Schools' *Cheltenham*, LMS Class 5 No 5000, *Sans Pareil*, *Lord Nelson*, *Duchess of Hamilton*, *Leander*, and of course, *Lion*. Modern traction was represented by 'Deltic' No 55015 *Tulyar* , Class 47 *Great Eastern*, and representatives of Classes 25, 45 and 56 as well as APT-P unit No 370004.

Also in 1980, Liverpool Road station, Manchester, celebrated its 150th anniversary with an exhibition being held in the original station building. This station was the world's first passenger railway station and was the terminus of the Liverpool & Manchester Railway.

As mentioned, one of the Rainhill exhibits was the new APT-P unit and throughout 1980 the proposed revenue-earning service using these new trains was postponed as trials did not go exactly to plan. On 18 April a fault occurred on one of the bogie's wheelsets and associated braking system. On 3 October, the press were allowed access on a Euston-Crewe proving run. An eight per cent 'tilt' was recorded at Bushey at 125mph and a change of angle of 26% at Wolverton at 120mph — quite an

experience. However, the noise factor was disappointingly high, it was thought.

In May 1980, full IC125 services were introduced between Paddington and the West Country and InterCity, as a whole, recorded business worth £460 million during the year.

On the East Coast main line work commenced on the building of the 14.7-mile diversion around Selby in Yorkshire between Temple Hirst and Colton as the original route was being undermined by workings in the new Selby Coalfield.

Passenger services continued to be diverted over the Woodhead route during 1980 using diesel multiple-units but the DMU service from Inverness to Aberdeen ceased on 10 March changing to Class 27/1-hauled six-coach trains including a buffet car.

The new Class 47/7-hauled Glasgow-Edinburgh expresses commenced full operation and were affectionately known as 'discos' because of the frequency with which the carriage lighting dimmed and brightened due to surges in power as, initially, the wiring for these new trains was controlled through the existing lighting circuit. However, there were teething troubles with these new trains and problems *en route* in Falkirk High Tunnel.

On 16 April 1980, the new modern Glasgow Underground system opened to the public. The new orange-liveried Metro-Cammell units gave the system the popular name 'The Clockwork Orange'. Track gauge was 4ft and vehicles were 7ft 8in wide. The system had a 'flat fare' and included 15 stations and running time for the 6½ mile circuit was 22min, with a maximum speed of 33mph.

The first stage of the new Tyne & Wear Metro system from Haymarket to Tynemouth officially opened on 7 August. This route was termed 'Metroline 3' and was one of four Metrolines under construction. The system covers 26 miles of former BR track north and south of the River Tyne in addition to newly-constructed trackwork. A fleet of 90 twin-articulated 50mph Metro cars were built by Metro-Cammell and carried the attractive yellow & white Tyne & Wear livery.

On 2 June, the Leyland Experimental Vehicle (LEV1) arrived at Ipswich for 10 days of trials between Ipswich, Saxmundham and Lowestoft.

A further section of the GE suburban lines was energised to 25kV on 3 March between Gidea Park and Forest Gate Junc-

tion and Class 315 units appeared on Liverpool Street inner services.

On the Southern, the 'Night Ferry' sleeper service was withdrawn on 31 October ending a service between Victoria and Brussels/Paris which had been in operation since 1936. A variety of Southern motive power had been used on this service but it will be best remembered for the Bulleid Light Pacifics, with their circular headboards, later to be replaced by Class 71 Bo-Bo electric locomotives.

From Reading, with effect from 12 May, commenced a new DMU fast hourly service to Gatwick Airport, with a journey time of 1hr 20min.

Class 50 locomotives replaced Class 33s on the Waterloo-Exeter trains, also from 12 May, clipping around 15min off the overall timing, but their performance was inclined to be a little erratic and there were regular failures.

Refurbished Class 411 sets started returning to the Southern Region at Strawberry Hill from Swindon Works and the first facelifted set entered service between Ramsgate and Victoria on 14 February. The new SR numbers scheduled for display on all Southern electric units were already applied to these refurbished sets and, in theory, all Southern unit numbers were to bear the class prefix numbers.

In Wales, on inspecting the bridge over the Mawddach Estuary which carried the Cambrian Coast line at Barmouth, it was found that the Teredo shipworm had been at work and the bridge was closed to all traffic from 12 October. The parasite had bored holes in the timberwork weakening the bridge in many places.

Steam was in the news again, this time in an unusual manner, when on 21 August a Carlisle-Severn Tunnel Junction freight, hauled by Class 40 No 40179, failed south of Garsdale and LMS 'Jubilee' *Leander*, following with a 'Cumbrian Mountain Express' came to the rescue hauling the freight into Garsdale.

Various purchases were made from Woodham's scrapyard at Barry Docks in 1980 including 'West Country' Pacifics *Taw Valley* and *Sidmouth*, Urie 'S15' No 30499, '9F's Nos 92214 and 92134 and No 31638. Also No 928 *Stowe* arrived at the Bluebell Railway from Cranmore.

Sadly it was the end for the Class 44 'Peaks' and even the Class 84 electric locomotives became extinct. The last three Class 44s — loved by all diesel enthusiasts — were withdrawn in November 1980.

Left:
Crianlarich on the West Highland line as Class 27 No 27032, complete with snowploughs, arrives with the 21.50 Euston-Glasgow-Fort William train on 11 April 1980. Crianlarich was also the junction for the Callander & Oban line eastwards which, along with the associated Killin branch, closed in 1965. *L. A. Nixon*

Left:
A Class 119 BUT-engined Gloucester RC&W unit, with car No W51074 leading, crosses the River Wye at Chepstow on 12 April 1980 whilst forming the 13.00 Newport-Gloucester service. This bridge was built by Brunel in 1852 and originally carried double track (broad gauge). In 1962 the bridge lost its original 300ft wrought-iron spans being replaced by deck-type mild steel trusses bolted to the underside of the existing spans. *Brian Morrison*

Right:
This rural Cornish scene, located between Lostwithiel and Par, shows Class 50 No 50020 *Revenge* with the 11.10 Sunday working from Plymouth to Penzance on 29 June 1980. The Class 50s first moved south to the West Country in late 1972 as they became redundant on the WCML due to electrification. This enabled the diesel-hydraulic 'Westerns' to be withdrawn as the Class 50s took over their duties. *Brian Morrison*

Last Days of the Woodhead route

Despite strong opposition, the ex-Great Central Trans-Pennine 1,500V dc Woodhead route finally closed to traffic on 20 July due to annual losses of £2½ million. Early in 1981, there were a series of derailments and mishaps which could have brought on earlier closure. One derailment, on 8 April, involved a Barton-Immingham train carrying anhydrous ammonia at a crossover near Hadfield. This resulted in 13 loaded tank wagons leaving the track. Thirty nearby houses were evacuated as a precaution. A third mishap in four months occurred on 9 July when a torrential downpour of rain washed out the line west of Crowden and a landslip blocked the railway. The Woodhead route was first considered for electrification in the 1920s but this idea was shelved until 1950.

As the electrified Woodhead route closed, a 4½ mile electrified section of line from Coatbridge to Mossend was formally opened on 11 August. This small stretch of line cost £930,000 to electrify but it linked Coatbridge Freightliner terminal with the WCML.

On the Edinburgh Waverley-Glasgow Queen Street route, the Class 47/7 push-pull trains were now proving to be extremely reliable, and in January 1981, despite bad weather conditions, 50% of trains arrived early at their destination.

On 6 October, the first four Class 37 diesels allocated to the West Highland line were named. They were Nos 37043 *Loch Lomond*, 37081 *Loch Long*, 37026 *Loch Awe* and 37027 *Loch Eil*. Significant reductions in journey time were apparent on the West Highland line following the introduction of the Class 37s.

The first use of a new type of 'Open Station' system on BR occurred on 2 November. This new scheme involving passengers buying a ticket before boarding trains started in the north of Scotland and covered 51 stations from Aberdeen to Inverness, Dunkeld-Inverness and the lines to Kyle and Wick/Thurso. Failure to purchase a ticket prior to boarding resulted in 'full fare' plus £1 being paid.

Scotland was graced with the twin-car Class 140 Leyland-engined prototype in September, which was a development of the LEV1 railbus, when it arrived at Aberdeen from Strathclyde where it operated selected local services. Initially, the new two-car unit travelled from Derby to Leeds on 22 May where it made a debut trip on the Ilkley line. The 47-ton set fitted with 'Leyland National'-style bus seats then carried out demonstration runs to Newcastle, Carlisle, Cardiff, Carmarthen, Bristol, Plymouth, Derby and Cambridge. Trials were carried out between Birmingham and Stratford upon Avon, in Lancashire and in Yorkshire before going to Scotland. Each car had a 218hp underfloor horizontally-mounted turbocharged Leyland TL80 six-cylinder engine.

During the latter part of 1981, prototype Class 210 units came on the scene. Each power car had a single diesel-engine mounted in the body (similar to the Southern Region's DEMUs) with orthodox electric transmission. In October, commissioning runs were held with Class 210 units on the Derby-Leicester line.

On 22 November 1981, the last Class 306 Shenfield unit was withdrawn but several units were reinstated for mail-train use during the Christmas period with 'Mails Only' stickers on their doors. The class will long be remembered for its 32 years of service between Liverpool Street and Shenfield. It comprised 92 three-car units (formed of DMBS, TS and DTS). There were eight units built for the Manchester-Glossop/Hadfield route which were mechanically identical but the latter included first-class seating and their electrical equipment came from a different manufacturer to the Shenfield sets. The Shenfield sets were converted from 1,500 volt dc to 25kV ac in 1960.

Also in November, four-car Class 508 electric units were taken out of service from the South Western Division of the Southern Region due to problems arising from wheelslip on autumn leaves. The problem was created by the disc brakes which did not clear the rims of leaf debris. Before the end of the year, two Class 508 units were transferred to Merseyside to operate as three-car sets. The spare trailers were used on later Class 455 units.

In the northeast, another section of the Tyne & Wear Metro system was opened when the first metrocar travelled across the new Metro Tyne bridge on the Haymarket-Heworth route. Regular services over this route commenced in November 1981.

On 12 January 1981, the first stage of the Bedford-St Pancras electrification was completed over the 23-mile section between Luton Hoo and Bedford and the first Class 317 units scheduled for the new electrified Bedford line arrived at Cricklewood by October.

The first revenue-earning APT service operated on 7 December 1981 between Glasgow and London. On the return journey a 'tilt' problem occurred on one coach and the train arrived in Glasgow 30min late. On the next scheduled run, 9 December, moisture in the brake pipes froze and the train only got as far a Carstairs. On the third run weather conditions caused the train to arrive at Crewe 2½hr late.

New depots opened at Plymouth (Laira) on 30 September for the purpose of maintaining IC125 units and at Clacton in mid-July to cater for the day to day maintenance of some 66 electric units of Classes 308, 309, 312 and 313. On 1 July 1981, Finsbury Park depot lost its allocation of main-line diesels although locomotives continued to be stabled there. Class 31 No 31191 was allocated to Finsbury Park for 21 years (from 1960) — the longest serving locomotive at the depot.

In Wales, work was in progress on the Barmouth Bridge, closed since 12 October 1980 due to damage to the timber piles. Glass reinforced cement was used in the repair work to deter the Teredo shipworm from attacking again. The first train traversed the repaired bridge on 22 May 1981.

Severe weather conditions again hit Britain late in December 1981 resulting in snow blocking the Ormskirk line, but the West Country suffered the most when blizzards swept across the area and the following thaw caused flooding. Services in Wales were also badly affected by heavy falls of snow and in Scotland temperatures fell to minus 13° centigrade at Glasgow.

On 6 October the first four VSOE fully restored Pullman cars — *Cygnus*, *Perseus*, *Ibis* and *Phoenix* were given a test run behind a Class 40 diesel from Carnforth to Carlisle via the Settle & Carlisle route.

On 10 October two new Mk 3 sleeper

cars, manufactured at BREL Derby, were handed over to BR. These were the first of 210 of two types to be built — some 13 compartment, and others 12 compartment plus an attendant's compartment. The bodyshell closely followed the IC125 Mk 3 stock. With the introduction of new fire prevention measures together with extra noise insulation, the sleeping cars cost £250,000 each to build and were the first overnight sleepers to be built since 1964.

We had now experienced three summers of the 'Cumbrian Coast Express' which, in 1978, was a major breakthrough in steam-hauled railtours. When introduced, trains were hauled by *Flying Scotsman* and *Sir Nigel Gresley*, but since then, a variety of

steam power had been used. A new venture for 1981 was the 'Welsh Marches Express' which first ran on 7 February from Crewe to Newport — steam-hauled from Shrewsbury to Newport. Locomotives involved during the year on the 'Welsh Marches Express' were *Hagley Hall*, *Princess Elizabeth*, *King George V* and 'Black Five' No 5000, and 23 May saw the first run of the 'Scarborough Spa Express' with Stanier Pacific *Duchess of Hamilton* in command.

The Welshpool & Llanfair Railway opened their new station at Welshpool (Raven Square) on 18 July. It was 50 years since passenger trains travelled this route into Welshpool and 25 years since any train had operated into the town.

Woodham's scrapyard on Barry Docks was now selling locomotives at such a rate that it was becoming like a used-car lot but cutting up also commenced there in 1981 including 'Warship' No D601 *Ark Royal*, a North British Bo-Bo, and two steam locomotives, including '9F' No 92085.

Below:
The Leicester-Carnforth 'Wyvern Express' runs steam-hauled through Edale on 31 October 1981 with Fowler ex-S&D 2-8-0 No 13809 in command, carrying its 22C Bath Green Park shedplate. This was one of the many locomotives saved from the cutter's torch at Barry.
L. A. Nixon

Left:
On 30 July 1981, two Class 25 diesels propel an ore train for Northwich from Tunstead Sidings at Great Rocks Junction. The view clearly shows No 25236 hauling the train whilst No 25141 offers assistance at the rear. *L. A. Nixon*

Above:
The 10.43 Grangemouth-Bishopbriggs oil terminal train of oil tanks passes through Greenhill Junction on 17 June 1981 with double-headed Class 37 locomotives, Nos 37028 and 37196, in charge. Greenhill Junction is situated near Falkirk and this location also sees fast expresses to Stirling and the north. *Rex Kennedy*

Below:
A fascinating view of a Class 56 locomotive with MGR empties, as it passes through Wellingborough on the down slow line on 13 October 1981. No 56054, pictured here, was one of the Doncster-built versions of the class. *Michael Ricks*

205

Above left:
The fine architecture of Stirling station creates an impressive sight as three-car Class 101 diesel unit No 101338, comprising cars Nos SC51466, SC59689 and SC51516, forms the (2G55) 12.58 Dunblane-Edinburgh service on 20 June 1981. The cleanliness of this station at the time was a credit to the staff. *Rex Kennedy*

Centre left:
On a rough 15 June 1981, as can be seen from the choppy sea, Trans-Clyde three-car Class 126 diesel unit No 126410 passes through Falkland Yard after leaving Ayr station with the 12.45 Ayr-Glasgow Central service. These units, in their later years of service, had their gangway connections removed and the end was 'plated over', as can be seen in this view. *Rex Kennedy*

Bottom left:
The prototype Class 140 two-car railbus, No 140001, is pictured at Thornliebank on a Glasgow Central-East Kilbride service on 27 August 1981, bearing its blue and grey livery with yellow ends. As can be seen, air horns were roof-mounted and jumper cables were fitted below the cab windows. *Tom Noble*

Above:
Merseyrail's West Kirby station on 16 September 1981, and 1938-built Class 503 electric unit, with car No M28375 leading, pulls out of the station with the 10.08 service to Liverpool Central. This interesting scene shows other stabled Class 503 stock waiting to be put back to work from this Wirral terminus. *Brian Morrison*

Right:
On 12 December 1981, a Metropolitan line train of two 4-car A60/A62 units masters the snow-covered track and leaves Harrow-on-the-Hill on a midday stopping service to Baker Street. We never picture London Transport scenes of this nature when travelling by tube. *R. G. Bradford*

'Deltic' Farewell

The beloved 'Deltics' finally went out of service on 31 January 1982, the last to be withdrawn being Nos 55002 *The King's Own Yorkshire Light Infantry*, 55009 *Alycidon*, 55015 *Tulyar* and 55022 *Royal Scots Grey*. Naturally, they did not disappear without their fair share of 'farewell tours', most significantly the 'Deltic Scotsman Farewell' tour on 2 January hauled by *Tulyar* from King's Cross, although green-liveried No 55002 had been scheduled for the northbound run. Mk 1 stock was used on this train and *Tulyar* sported its white cab window surrounds. The return journey from Edinburgh to King's Cross was under the command of *Royal Scots Grey*. The withdrawal of the 'Deltics' coincided with the conversion of the King's Cross to York semi-fast services to IC125 with accelerated timings.

Other ECML news was the introduction, on 17 May 1982, of the 'Nightrider' service between King's Cross and Aberdeen/Glasgow in an endeavour to compete with cut-price coach operators. Fares of £12-£16 offered a new deal for overnight seated passengers in first-class air-conditioned coaches. The launch of the inaugural run included attractive girls in nightshirts, a Highland piper, *Wee Willie Winkie* and *Skimbleshanks*, the railway cat. From October, extra stops were incorporated at Dundee, Kirkaldy and Falkirk Grahamstown, the Aberdeen and Glasgow portions being split/joined at Edinburgh. The train became so popular that loadings often reached 90%. Also in Scotland the new brand-name 'Scotrail' was introduced from 17 May.

On 8/9 January, heavy snow storms again hit Britain and a two-car diesel multiple-unit was stranded for 20hr at Tonfanau on the Cambrian Coast line. A 'rescue' train also became stranded 1½ miles away from the train it was trying to rescue. Marooned passengers were eventually taken off by helicopter.

On the East Coast main line a 30ft hole appeared during late January just north of York due to a burst 21in domestic water main resulting in all traffic being diverted via the goods yard and, during the same month, an embankment slip north of Grantham created a cavity 60ft long, 12ft deep and 9ft wide, closing the ECML and resulting in diversions via Spalding and Lincoln. On 9 December, near Fleet, Hampshire, on the Southern Region, a Waterloo-Bournemouth train ran into two trees which had been brought down by high winds and had fallen across the track.

Although the first Class 491 (4-TC) unit was completely derailed no one was seriously hurt.

At St Pancras station work was carried out on track remodelling and resignalling and, by early summer, the Bedford to Moorgate line was energised in connection with the Bedford-St Pancras electrification scheme. The final section from Kentish Town to St Pancras was switched on from 27 September. From 4 October, IC125 trains were introduced on the Midland line from St Pancras but, in the early days, late starts from St Pancras were the result of trains arriving late from Bounds Green depot. IC125s were also introduced to northeast-southwest services from January 1982. Their introduction reduced the Plymouth-Edinburgh journey time by two hours and on Bristol/Cardiff to Newcastle services by half an hour.

On 9 December the first Class 58 locomotive, No 58001, in a new striking livery, was handed over to Railfreight at Doncaster. The locomotive carried the name *Railfreight* on the cabsides but this was only in the form of a transfer. These powerful 3,300bhp freight locomotives were destined chiefly for merry-go-round workings and they weighed 130 tons and had a maximum speed of 80mph. Eight of these locomotives, Nos 58001-08, entered traffic the following year and were initially allocated to Toton depot.

On the night of 5/6 December 1982, the Western Region carried out tests with a single trainload of 66 PGA 51-tonne hopper wagons representing a trailing load of 3,336 tonnes. The train, which left Merehead Quarry for Southall, comprised two rakes of 33 wagons and was hauled by two Class 56 locomotives. The train split at Southall, the front portion going to Acton Yard, the second to Brentford. From Westbury to Reading, two Class 37 locomotives followed 'light' to provide assistance if required.

On 30 July, a loaded Worksop to Immingham MGR train, hauled by No 56004, collided with a loaded double-headed petrol train leaving the Lindsey Oil Refinery at Killingholme. The crews of the Class 56 and the two Class 31s hauling the petrol train jumped clear but all locomotives received extensive damage, petrol tankers were punctured and petrol spilled into nearby dykes.

On the Southern Region in January 1982, Class 508 units were still on test, and No 508002 was still to see revenue-earning service, having been delivered two years previous. It eventually entered passenger

service in November 1982. Work was still being carried out on these units to solve the problem of wheel-slip on wet leaves which caused their withdrawal during the previous winter. On 21 April, Nos 508019/31 overran Shepperton station and demolished the stop blocks and a brick wall, the front bogie of the leading vehicle overhanging the street.

On 22 March, the first Mark 2E air conditioned vehicles for the forthcoming 'Gatwick Express' services were delivered to the Southern Region. These vehicles were for six-coach Class 73-hauled push-pull trains and the driving trailers were to be converted Class 414 vehicles. The new trains did not enter service until 1984.

The first Class 455 electric units (originally to be classed 510) arrived on 10/11 November. This marked the return to an all-steel constructed unit rather than the aluminium bodies of PEP-derived stock.

In November, work commenced on a five-year renovation programme on the west side train shed roof covering platforms 1-10 at Liverpool Street station and, at the other end of the line, at Norwich, Crown Point depot opened. All this was in preparation for electrification of the East Anglian line to Liverpool Street.

From 1982, Motorail services which previously started from Kensington Olympia station, were transferred to Euston, avoiding the change from diesel to electric power at Mitre Bridge Junction.

Following the completion of the restoration of the Pullman coaches in 1981, the inaugural run of the Venice-Simplon Orient Express took place on 28 May from Victoria to Folkestone, connecting by ferry with a Boulogne-Venice train of 'Wagons-Lits' sleepers. The train was the brainchild of the Group President of Sea Containers, James Sherwood. During the year, the VSOE worked numerous excursions over the Southern Region.

The preservation scene gave us Bulleid Pacific *City of Wells* on the Settle & Carlisle line, *Sir Lamiel* in steam on the main line, *Blue Peter* and *Butler Henderson* in steam again, and steam returned to the Kyle of Lochalsh line after a period of 20 years, using LMS Class 5 No 5025. The Vale of Rheidol Railway celebrated its 80th birthday by restoring No 9 *Prince of Wales* to the yellow ochre livery which it carried between 1902 and 1913 and, on 25 May, the Festiniog Railway ran the first passenger train since September 1939 through to Blaenau Festiniog from Portmadoc.

Above:
Class 206 'Tadpole' unit No 1206 leaves
Appledore in Kent on 27 July 1982 with the
16.45 Ashford-Hastings service. These three-car
DEMUs were originally formed for the Reading-
Guildford-Redhill-Tonbridge route to avoid
closure of the line, a policy which proved to be
successful. *Brian Morrison*

Right:
In March 1967, ex-London Transport tube stock
was introduced to the Isle of Wight. Although
closure of the Isle of Wight railways seemed
inevitable, it was regarded as 'socially necessary'
to keep the line open from Ryde Pier Head to
Shanklin. It was decided to electrify the line but
no suitable units were available apart from
'vintage' LT stock. A seven-car train with
Class 486 (3-TIS) unit No 486036 leading nears
Smallbrook with the 17.21 Shanklin-Ryde Pier
Head service on 13 June 1982. *Brian Morrison*

Top left:
On the evening of 21 February 1982, Class 50 No 50019 *Ramillies* awaits departure from Plymouth with the 18.15 Cardiff train. By the end of 1991, *Ramillies* was one of the 11 Class 50s which had been saved for preservation. *Brian Morrison*

Left:
This interesting view of the Southern Region network of lines between London Bridge station and Waterloo East in September 1982 shows Class 415/1 4-EPB electric unit No 5176 with the 12.44 Hayes-Charing Cross service. Imagine this view in steam days before the skyscrapers emerged. *Brian Morrison*

Above:
The Class 508 units followed the new concept of Southern electrics demonstrated by the prototype 4-PEP, with passenger-operated sliding doors. At a snow-clad Clapham Junction, on 10 January 1982, Class 508s Nos 508027 and 508015 form the 11.38 Waterloo-Epsom-Effingham Junction working. The Class 508s were later transferred to Merseyside *Brian Morrison*

Right:
Although it did not have 'Town Centre' on the blind, that is nearly where it almost ended up! On 21 April 1982, Class 508 unit No 508031 having 'just arrived' from Waterloo with the 06.34 service continued on through the buffer stops at Shepperton (but it did stop at the lights) creating a great deal of local interest and concern. *Colin J. Marsden*

Left:
Class 03 204hp diesel shunters required cut-down cabs to pass through restricted areas over the Burry Port & Gwendraeth Valley line in South Wales. A regular occurrence was the operation of these diesel shunters in trio with coal trains for Burry Port. Nos 03120, 03151, and 03152 are seen carrying out this duty on 18 August 1982. *L. A. Nixon*

Below:
Steam locomotive preservation has resulted in engines appearing in territory foreign to that in which they were accustomed. But whatever the motive power, what a wonderful sight to see steam in action once again on Britain's main lines. 'West Country' Bulleid Pacific No 34092 *City of Wells*, rescued from Barry many years before, is pictured near Armathwaite on the Settle & Carlisle route, on 13 February 1982, with a southbound 'Cumbrian Mountain Pullman'. *R. Lumley*

'Diamond Scotsman'

On 24 February 1983, Sir Nigel Gresley's 'A3' Pacific No 4472 *Flying Scotsman* celebrated its Diamond Jubilee, having been built in 1923. Through its life the 'Scotsman' had carried the number 1472 (when built), 4472 when named in February 1924, 103 in the 1946 LNER renumbering scheme (and reclassified 'A10'), 60103 under British Railways after 1948 and back to 4472 whilst in preservation. Appearing in green and wartime black it carried the letters NE, L&NER, LNER and British Railways with various BR emblems over the years. A series of railtours to commemorate the Diamond Jubilee of *Flying Scotsman* were organised in February and March 1983 over the East Coast main line and these trips, it is reported, could have been sold out '10 times over'. On 27 February it hauled the SLOA Pullman train from Grantham to York and hundreds of enthusiasts swarmed over the track during a service stop at Newark causing serious delays to InterCity services.

The 'Compound', No 1000 and the 'J72' *Joem* were again steamed in 1983 and the Severn Valley Railway took over ownership of two LMS 'Jubilees', No 5690 *Leander* and No 45699 *Galatea*. In June, a new 'steam special' ran every Sunday from Paddington to Stratford upon Avon — the 'Shakespeare Express'. This was the first regular through train to operate between these two locations for many years.

A plethora of namings were bestowed upon the Eastern Region's Class 254 IC125 power cars during 1983 — 10 in all — including such names as *Yorkshire Post*, *City of Bradford*, *University of Durham* and *The Light Infantry*. Eight Class 47s were also named during the year together with three Class 56 locomotives.

On the East Coast main line, the 'Selby diversion' opened to traffic, the first train to run over the northern section being the Eastern Region General Manager's saloon, a converted two-car DMU, on 21 March. Full use of the new diversion took place from 3 October but a speed restriction of 60mph was placed on the 'bypass' until 1984 to enable the track formation to settle in.

Following torrential rain, early in May, a section of cliff face collapsed near Lamberton, on a stretch of the ECML north of Berwick, resulting in partial closure of the line and the rerouteing of main line services, yet again, via Carlisle and Carstairs.

The main Scottish Region news was that although union representatives had been informed of a rundown in repair work on locomotives and rolling stock, there would be a gradual increase in refurbishing work on Scottish EMUs. By the autumn work had started there on a £17 million programme to refurbish 50 of the original Class 303 'Blue Trains' which first entered service in 1960.

From August 1983 a new colour scheme was introduced by the Scottish Region for their Strathclyde units, known as 'Govan Orange'. This was the new Strathclyde PTE livery and each unit carried the legend 'Strathclyde Transport'. This new livery was the precursor of many new PTE liveries which were to appear on multiple-units throughout Britain in the next decade.

An experimental Sunday service from Inverness to the Kyle of Lochalsh and return was introduced which proved to be a great success, 200 passengers being carried each Sunday until 11 September.

The long-awaited formal notice by BR of the intention to withdraw passenger services over the Settle & Carlisle route and to close Settle and Appleby stations was finally issued on 15 December.

On Merseyside, the Merseyrail Northern line route was extended from Garston to Hunt's Cross on 16 May. Platforms were also being extended at Wirral line stations in preparation for the coming of the Class 508 units. During the year, Class 508 units were being moved north to Birkenhead from the Southern Region pending entering service.

The introduction of Class 317 'Midland Electrics' resulted in the demise of the Rolls-Royce-engined Class 127 diesel units on the 'Bed-Pan' line. Unfortunately, there were 'teething problems' on the Class 317s resulting in units being returned to BREL Wolverton Works for modifications to the transformer mountings. Others were being worked on at Cricklewood depot. These problems resulted in DMUs and locomotive-hauled trains again being used on Luton-St Pancras services. By late summer Class 313 electric units were drafted in from the Eastern Region to assist and they lasted for some months on the 'Bed-Pan' line.

From St Pancras the 1983/84 timetable for the Midland main line showed only two locomotive-hauled services in each direction, all other services being operated by IC125 sets.

From October, 58 trains to and from London were designated 'Executive' — a service for first-class business travellers where passengers could elect to pay a premium to cover seat reservation, and could obtain meal vouchers to the value of £7, free parking and a 10% discount on car hire at their destination. On the Western Region, train names were revived on certain 'Executive' services such as the 'Red Dragon', 'Merchant Venturer', 'Mayflower' and 'St David'. Mark 3 sleeping cars were introduced on the Paddington-West of England services from 11 July. The overnight London, Plymouth and Penzance service was now named the 'Night Riviera'.

On 16 July, a special high-speed run from London Bridge to Brighton took place resulting in a 41min 38sec timing — an average speed of 73.6mph. The event was to celebrate the 50th anniversary of the Brighton main line electrification and the run by the Class 421 (4-CIG) units, Nos 7363/64, was almost nine minutes quicker than the normal non-stop scheduled time.

London Bridge, Cannon Street and Charing Cross stations were brought to a standstill in August, when an electrical fault in a power-supply cable near London Bridge resulted in 20 48-core and seven microcore cables, each with over 200 wires which controlled points and signals, being burnt through. Where possible, services were diverted to and from Victoria.

In 1983 it was farewell to the Class 4-SUB units, a development of the prototype units Nos 4101-10 which first appeared in 1941. However, the basic design was established during 1946/47 (Nos 4111-30). Almost a month after the 'last appearance' of a 4-SUB in service, units Nos 4279 and 4291 worked a Waterloo-Windsor & Eton train. No 4732 was painted green and appeared at open days and on a railtour from London Bridge on 22 February; the unit was eventually preserved.

The first Class 455 units entered service on the Southern Region's South Western Division in March, initially on the branches to Hampton Court, Shepperton and Chessington. Earlier in the month one of these units was involved in push-pull test working on the Shepperton branch which involved Class 33 locomotive No 33109. The second and third batches of Class 455 units received a modified front-end design.

On 22 September, the first of the Class 141 two-car railbus sets was handed over to Provincial Services at Litchurch Lane Carriage Works, Derby. It resembled a 'Leyland National' bus body more than the Class 140 prototype body. Each two-car set seated 94 passengers and the first 20 ordered were scheduled for Yorkshire routes. The delivery of the Class 141 diesel units, in addition to 'blue asbestos' problems, resulted in the withdrawal of considerable numbers of older DMUs, such as the 'Trans-Pennine' sets. Withdrawal of most of the Scottish Region Class 126s was already well underway. But the 'blue asbestos' problem was to haunt us for a while as much of the older BR unit and coaching stock contained this, and new regulations regarding its use were a serious problem for BR.

Right:
Roller coasters are not only to be found at fairgrounds as can be seen from this view at Moira Colliery on 1 July 1983. 'Speeding' along the undulated track, Class 56 No 56083 conveys empty MGR wagons from Drakelow power station. No 56083 has the revised front-end layout fitted to all Class 56s from No 56056 onwards. *Brian Morrison*

Below:
Class 46 'Peak' No 46025 leaves the yard to the east of Taunton with the up 09.05 St Blazey-Severn Tunnel Undy Yard 'Speedlink' working on 2 September 1983. Semaphore signals are still apparent in the background. *John S. Whiteley*

215

Left:
From May 1980, as sufficient Class 50s became available from Paddington-Bristol services they took over Waterloo-Exeter St David's trains, replacing the less powerful Class 33s, which had previously taken over from the 'Warships'. On 16 April 1983, No 50009 *Conquerer* is seen passing Vauxhall, in London, with the 09.10 working to Exeter. Vauxhall displays an impressive array of platforms for a comparitively 'minor' station. This was necessary in the railway's early days as all up and down trains stopped at Vauxhall station to take on 'ticket checkers'. *John S. Whiteley*

Bottom left:
At Penmaenmawr, on the North Wales coast, when Class 40s ruled supreme in the area, No 40143 shunts ballast wagons at the quarry terminal, on 9 August 1983, prior to departure for St Helens, as No 40172 approaches the station with an eastbound freight for Llandudno Junction. *L. A. Nixon*

Right:
An idyllic rural setting in Devon as preserved Great Western 0-4-2T No 1450 potters across the River Dart, on 3 April 1983, near Buckfastleigh on the Dart Valley Railway, hauling its chocolate & cream-liveried coaches, creating the Great Western branch line reborn. *Mike Esau*

Below:
Sunlight and thundery clouds create this unusual scene as the ex-LNER 'K1' Mogul, No 2005, hauls Pullman stock on the Newcastle-Leeds-Settle & Carlisle-Newcastle special on 20 March 1983. It is pictured near Selside. *L. A. Nixon*

'Gatwick Express'

The new Victoria-Gatwick Airport express service commenced on 14 May 1984 with trains every 15min from 05.30 to 23.30. The smart outfit of locomotives and rolling stock was painted in the new express livery. For the inaugural occasion No 73123 was named *Gatwick Express* on 10 May and carried a headboard which cleverly adapted the BR double arrow crest so that the top half of the motif indicated an aircraft in flight. The headboard also said 'Victoria to Gatwick in 30 minutes'. The driving guard's luggage vans for these trains were converted from Class 414 (2-HAP) driving motor coaches. The first press run of a 'Gatwick Express' was carried out on 6 February with No 73105 at the helm. Prior to this, crew familiarisation was undertaken between Victoria, Brighton, Newhaven and Worthing. A promotional 'Gatwick Express' toured the north of England for four days in March hauled by Class 33 No 33113. On 6 August, services temporarily reverted to being operated by Class 411 (4-CEP) units due to pick-up problems on the Class 73/1 locomotives caused by a short break in the conductor rail outside Victoria. A modification was quickly fitted to the locomotives to cope with the problem.

The first length of conductor rail for electrification of the Tonbridge-Hastings line was laid on 19 July 1984 at Robertsbridge. On 30 November the line was branded the '1066 Route' and appropriate stickers were applied to Hastings units.

Further new Class 455 units started to arrive in early summer at Hornsey depot, where modifications were carried out before transfer to the Southern Region. Earlier, Class 508 trailers, which had been removed from units allocated for Merseyrail services, went to BREL York for overhaul and incorporation into the Class 455 sets. Units from the second batch of Class 455 units (Nos 5701-43) entered service in July on the South Western Division before all members of the first batch had been commissioned.

Ex-Southern Region Class 508 units were introduced on Wirral line services on 18 June 1984 and by July these new trains were to be found on services from Liverpool to West Kirby, New Brighton and Rock Ferry resulting in the withdrawal of a number of Class 503 units. By the end of September, Class 503s were working only on Monday-Friday services — Saturday services being in the hands of units of Classes 507 and 508. Another 'transfer' of

units occurred in 1984 when 2-EPB sets took over from Class 501 units on the North London line prior to Class 313s being released from Great Northern trains. The 30-year reign of the Class 306 'Shenfield' units also ended in 1984.

Class 150 'Sprinter' prototype proving trials were carried out in the summer of 1984 between Derby and St Pancras. Earlier in the year BREL won a £22 million order to construct 50 two-car Class 150 Sprinters for Provincial Services and in November, the prototype entered revenue-earning service on the Derby to Matlock line.

In April, the first Class 141 railcar appeared in the West Yorkshire PTE livery of Verona Green & Buttermilk, when these two-car sets entered revenue-earning service. Its debut in service was made between Leeds and Goole on 19 April. However, reliability was poor and, by May, 10 sets had failed due either to brake failure or transmission problems. As the new railcars appeared on the scene in Yorkshire, the much-loved 'Trans-Pennine' sets disappeared from the scene. These attractively designed units are sadly missed by enthusiasts.

At Ayr depot, in January, fire damaged buildings and rolling stock resulting in seven diesel units being withdrawn. It was believed to be an act of vandalism.

In the northeast, the last section of the Tyne & Wear Metro (from Heworth to South Shields) finally opened on 23 March after a delay due to union negotiations over flexible rostering.

On 27 July, plans to invest £305 million to electrify the East Coast main line from Hitchin to Leeds and Edinburgh were announced — a project scheduled to be phased over a seven-year period.

Speed was the order of the day in 1984, when an IC125 train, formed of five trailers and two power cars, completed a record-breaking run between Paddington and Bristol on 30 August. The train reached 130mph and completed the journey in 62min 33sec — an average speed of 112.8mph — 5min 2sec faster than the previous record-breaking run in 1977. From Euston the 'Royal Scot', and its return run, was timed for 110mph running from 14 May as were the up and down 'Executive' services bringing Glasgow within just over five hours from London. This was made possible as the Class 87 locomotives were now fitted with new lightweight pantographs as fitted to the APT. These trains

were painted in APT-style livery as applied to the 'Gatwick Express'.

On 1 October, Inter City's new overnight London-Glasgow train — the 'Starlight Express' — was launched. For the occasion Class 86 No 86231 was named *Starlight Express* by Andrew Lloyd Webber, creator of the show of this name, and was newly painted in InterCity livery.

Deliveries of Class 56 freight locomotives were completed by November 1984, and this month also saw the end of the Class 46 Sulzers, introduced in 1961. Prior to withdrawal, stored members of the class could be seen beside the main line opposite Swindon locomotive works. The last to go were Nos 46010/11/25/27/35/45 and the only named member of the class, No 46026 *Leicestershire and Derbyshire Yeomanry*. However, No 46009 met its fate in an experiment at Old Dalby on 17 July when it hit a CEGB nuclear flask at 100mph in an effort to prove to the public that, in an incident as severe as this, there was no danger of leakage from the flask. The flask was placed on display at the National Railway Museum.

In Scotland, on 26 March, mixed-train working returned, when a new daily container service came into operation between Aberdeen and Wick. The containers were conveyed on freight wagons attached to passenger workings. At Thornton a new depot appeared and stations reopened at Dyce, Auchinleck and Kilmaur.

Steam returned to the West Highland extension to Mallaig in May 1984 but dry weather, which was causing lineside fires on steam runs, was creating problems elsewhere, especially in the case of 'A4' Pacific No 60009 *Union of South Africa*, over the Easter weekend. In September, *Clan Line* returned to main line running when it hauled a 'Welsh Marches Express'. On the preserved line scene, the Severn Valley Railway opened its extension to Kidderminster.

Due to criticism in the wording of the closure notice relating to the Settle & Carlisle line, amended versions were published in April and May 1984. New notices included the Blackburn to Hellifield line and 'listed' the stations for closure.

On London Transport, tunnelling work on the Piccadilly Line's extension to Heathrow's terminal 4 proceeded at record pace and was completed by April. The first 1983 tube stock entered public service on the Jubilee Line on 2 May and 1938 tube stock was repainted in November and used on the Bakerloo Line.

As the year ended, Class 86 electric locomotives were introduced to the ex-Great Eastern main line out of Liverpool Street to allow for crew training from Ilford depot which commenced in October. The first Class 86-hauled passenger services were due to take over on the Liverpool Street-Ipswich section in May; from Ipswich on to Norwich a diesel-electric would be used with a locomotive change at Ipswich.

Right:
The 'Gatwick Express' trains were formed of Class 73/1 locomotives fitted for push-pull working with adapted MK 2f stock with 1983/84 Class 414/3 2-HAP DMBSOs in use as a GLV. These non-stop trains ran at 15-min intervals and, in this view, in Clapham Cutting, on the first day of operation, 14 May 1984, No 73123 *Gatwick Express* is seen with the 14.15 service from Victoria. *Brian Morrison*

Below:
A minor task for a total of 3,250bhp as Class 40 locomotive No 40195 and Class 25/1 No 25182 haul a BOC Ditton-Broughton Lane train of five long-wheelbase tanks through Winnick Junction on 16 June 1984. *L. A. Nixon*

Left:
Great Rocks Junction and double-headed Class 20 diesels Nos 20141 and 20185 leave the tunnel with loaded Tunstead-Northwich hoppers on 26 June 1984. This fine view captures the atmosphere of Great Rocks with its industry and winding dry stone wall framing the train. *L. A. Nixon*

Bottom left:
On 21 July 1984, Vale of Rheidol 2-6-2T No 7 *Owain Glyndwr* approaches Devil's Bridge with a train from Aberystwyth. The last steam-hauled Vale of Rheidol service in BR ownership was also performed by this locomotive, on 4 November 1988 prior to the railway's transfer of ownership to the Brecon Mountain Railway. *John Chalcraft*

Right:
Southern 'N15' 'King Arthur' No 777 *Sir Lamiel* heads a 'Santa Steam Special' northbound through Horton-in-Ribblesdale on 27 December 1984 — an appropriate setting for a 'Santa Special'. *L. A. Nixon*

Below:
On 1 April 1984, Brush Class 31/1 locomotive No 31170 hauls a 'dead' Class 86 electric, No 86209 *City of Coventry*, out of Euston, up Camden Bank, with the 12.55 service to Liverpool Lime Street. This was due to the electrical power being switched off to allow engineering works to take place in Primrose Hill Tunnel. *Brian Morrison*

The Livery Explosion

Exciting new liveries started to appear in 1985 following the green & buttermilk that appeared on West Yorkshire Class 141 units in the previous year. This was the start of a new 'colourful' British Rail which, perhaps, would attract more business. As Passenger Transport Executives throughout Britain were becoming involved in the running of local railways, they wanted to put their own stamp on their trains. Strathclyde units were painted in orange & black, Greater Manchester PTE sets carried an orange & brown livery and even British Rail painted some West of England units in the old Great Western chocolate & cream livery. Soon to follow were Tyne & Wear-liveried units in yellow & white and West Yorkshire PTE livery was later to change to red &white. As new Class 142 and 143 units were built they were painted in the livery relating to the area they were to work — in later years creating slight confusion as units were moved around Britain. As the Class 150 'Sprinters' appeared, they carried the attractive two-tone blue & white 'Provincial' livery.

BR stock was now receiving an interesting face-lift. On 6 February even British Telecom provided what was termed as the 'World's first colourtrain' with interior advertising display panels. In this year of 'GWR 150', certain diesel locomotives were painted 'Brunswick Green' such as Class 47s Nos 47070 *G. J. Churchward* and 47484 *Isambard Kingdom Brunel*. This new 'Colour of British Rail' policy was to continue in locomotives, multiple-units and rolling stock.

The first Class 142 two-car railbuses built by BREL and Leyland Bus were delivered for Provincial services on 17 May. Each two-car set accommodated 122 seated passengers. The electro-pneumatic brakes, a redesigned cab layout and a modified suspension system were an improvement on the earlier Class 141 railcars, and they were compatible to work with other multiple-unit stock. The first Class 142s delivered were painted in Greater Manchester PTE livery and others were in chocolate & cream and called 'Skippers' (for services in the southwest), or in Provincial blue & white.

The first Class 143 railbus was delivered to the Derby Research Centre early in August 1985 — the second '143' unit went direct to Heaton for Tyne & Wear operation. Class 143 seating was as the Class 142 railcars but construction was of aluminium only. A press run with the new Class 143 'Pacer' took place on 2 October between Hexham and Newcastle.

On 21 January, Class 150 diesel unit No 150001 performed a demonstration run between Birmingham New Street and Aberystwyth and then went on to Cardiff to be demonstrated in the valleys. In May, No 150001 moved to Scotland whilst the other prototype of the class, No 150002, worked services from Derby to Lincoln and Crewe. From August, Metro-Cammell Class 151 experimental units worked the Derby-Matlock branch.

Electrified services from London to Ipswich 'officially' commenced on 13 May 1985 but the first electric-worked train to Ipswich actually ran on 6 May. Nine Class 86/2 electric locomotives were allocated to operate these new services and Class 47/4s were used for the onward journey to Norwich. Electrification work was progressing at Norwich and also *en route*. There was also intense activity on the ECML regarding catenary mast erection north of Hitchin by midsummer and necessary bridge works were progressing. By mid-August, masts had reached Peterborough.

Many new electrification schemes had now been authorised for completion by May 1991 including the South Croydon to East Grinstead line, the Paisley to Ayr/Ardrossan/Largs line, and the Bishops Stortford to Cambridge line, in addition to the Norwich route and the ECML to Edinburgh.

On 2 June, there was virtually a seven-week shutdown of Crewe station as track was remodelled and overhead wiring was removed.

The inaugural run of the 'Royal Scotsman' took place on 15 May from Edinburgh for a six-day £1,115 tour of Scotland calling at Oban, Mallaig, Kyle of Lochalsh and Helmsdale. Three and six-day tours were also later available at £930 and £1,650 per person respectively. The eight-coach train, made up of restored CR/West Coast Joint Stock observation car No 41, ex-GNR family saloon No 807, ex-L&NWR dining car No 5159 and four converted Mark 1 sleeping cars with a BSK as as support vehicle, all painted in L&NWR livery (except No 807 and the BSK) was steam-hauled between Fort William and Mallaig.

To celebrate 150 years of the Great Western Railway, 'GWR 150' was launched, which incorporated an exhibition train that travelled over former GWR metals from 29 May to 22 September, an excellent variety of steam runs, and appropriate diesel and IC125 namings at various Western Region venues. An 'open day' was also held at Old Oak Common on 15 September. An exhibition due to be held at BREL Swindon Works had to be cancelled due to industrial action relating to the announced forthcoming closure of the works. However, steam-hauled trains ran between Swindon and Gloucester during August and 17,620 passengers took advantage of this unique service. The Great Western Society at Didcot, of course, went to town with special open days, and 'steam specials' were hauled by a variety of Great Western motive power including Nos 7029 *Clun Castle* and 4930 *Hagley Hall*. No 5051 *Drysllwyn Castle* was used on the exhibition train. Sadly, *City of Truro* was not ready to be steamed until later in the year and after being painted in the 1904 GWR livery on the Severn Valley Railway, the 'classic' GWR 4-4-0 worked a press run over the SVR on 4 September and was seen in all her glory at the railway's enthusiasts' weekend of 28/29 September.

Steam returned to Marylebone with appearances by *Sir Nigel Gresley*, *Clan Line* and *Duchess of Hamilton* hauling the extremely popular 'Shakespeare Limited' and 'Thames-Avon Express' regular workings to Stratford-upon-Avon, via Warwick. 'A3' Pacific No 4472 *Flying Scotsman* also worked out of Marylebone during the year.

The Bluebell celebrated 25 years of preservation in 1985 and the Mid-Hants Railway commenced regular workings through to Alton on 25 May — the first passenger train into Alton being worked by 'West Country' Pacific No 34016 *Bodmin*.

From 13 May 1985, a new £5 million fleet of 22 new Mk 3D open-first Pullman coaches were used on Monday-Friday services between Euston and Manchester and between Euston and Liverpool. All cars were named, the Liverpool set including names such as *John Lennon* and *William*

Ewart Gladstone and the Manchester set bearing names like *Emmeline Pankhurst*, *L. S. Lowry* and *Sir Stanley Matthews*.

Authorisation was given by the end of the year for the withdrawal of 29 APT trailer vehicles and three power-cars as it was agreed that it was no longer an economic proposition to use an APT set for regular passenger services. The end of another (short-lived) era, but the research had been invaluable and much of the knowledge gained would be used in future developments.

Top:
On 10 August 1985, Class 47 No 47518 passes beneath the fine restored bridge at Bolton with a Glasgow-Harwich express. The overgrown sidings to the left of the picture still appear to be used. *L. A. Nixon*

Right:
Class 58 No 58010 is seen with the 17.15 Didcot-Kingsbury Colliery empty MGR wagon train (6M28) approaching King's Sutton, south of Banbury, on 12 June 1985. *Brian Morrison*

Top left:
On 15 June 1985, Class 37 No 37111 *Loch Eil Outward Bound*, sporting its 'Scottie Dog', arrives at Bridge of Orchy on the West Highland line with the 22.10 overnight service from Euston to Fort William. No 37111 is coupled to 'Ethel 1' (Electric Train Heating Locomotive No 972501) to provide heating for this winter service which cannot be provided by the Class 37 locomotive. Subsequently the locomotive was renamed *Glengarnock*. *G. W. Morrison*

Left:
Class 33 Birmingham RC&W No 33038 creates an unusual sight as it wends its way out of Ripple Lane Yard on 23 September 1985 with a train of oil tanks for Furzebrook Oil Terminal in Dorset. *Brian Morrison*

Above:
A variety of diesel power graces Bristol Temple Meads on 10 August 1985 as the city awaits a downpour of rain. From left to right Class 33 No 33028 has just arrived from Portsmouth Harbour whilst Class 47 No 47125 prepares to leave with a West Country train. The 'Peak' No 45142 has arrived on a sleeper from Glasgow and Class 119 diesel unit No B586 heads for the depot. *G. W. Morrison*

Right:
A late arrival at Huddersfield (01.15) on 10 February 1985 is the ex-Edinburgh excursion hauled by Class 40 No 40122. This locomotive was originally numbered D200 and was the first English Electric Type 4 Co-Co to be delivered, in March 1958. It is now to be found in the National Railway Museum. *L. A. Nixon*

Network SouthEast

Following Chris Green's success as General Manager of Scotrail, he was appointed Director of the London & South East Sector from 6 January 1986. This sector appeared under the new banner 'Network SouthEast' from 10 June, and a major launch of a new identity brought many improvement schemes including a startling new livery of red, white & blue, refurbished stations, and brighter station signs. The launch of Network SouthEast on 10 June incorporated a press party travelling from Waterloo to a refurbished Richmond station in a new-liveried Class 455 unit, and London termini displayed the new colourful stock of the type worked from the station where it was on view. The new Network SouthEast extended to Whimple (on the Salisbury-Exeter line), Weymouth, Bedwyn, Banbury, Northampton, Bedford, Huntingdon, Cambridge, Harwich, Shoeburyness and Southend and included the entire Southern Region. The days were numbered for the plain blue, uninteresting look of the rolling stock in London and the south.

Also included in Network SouthEast territory was the newly-electrified Tonbridge-Hastings line which received a Royal opening on 6 May when Her Majesty Queen Elizabeth the Queen Mother unveiled two plaques — one at Tunbridge Wells and one at Hastings. On the weekend of 10/11 May, the Southern Electric Group and LCGB ran specials from Charing Cross to Hastings to commemorate the passing of the Hastings DEMUs and the introduction of the new electrified services.

From 3 May, the 'Bournemouth Belle' reappeared in the form of a summer Saturday VSOE all-Pullman service calling at Southampton and Brockenhurst using the restored Pullman cars. The new 'Belle' catered for visitors to Beaulieu and Broadlands and the £99 return fare incorporated visits to these two stately homes, and meals.

Services commenced on the Eastern Region's new-electrified line on the Wickford-Southminster branch from 12 May following the switching on of the current on 17 March, and the Great Northern Class 317 units made their press debut on 3 March on the Royston line. The cascading Great Northern Class 312 units from the line were destined for Great Eastern services after overhaul at Wolverton Works resulting in the demise of Class 302 units on these lines.

East Coast main line electrification was now well underway, catenary masts being in position north of Peterborough by late January and by the end of the year, the £18 million track and resignalling scheme centred on York, replacing 1950 equipment, was in hand. Whereas in the past cold weather and storms had created havoc on British Rail, it was now found that the warm weather of June and July 1986 was creating its own problems to ECML IC125 services. Failures of power cars resulted from breakages of exhaust manifolds created by excessive heat over long distances, which was exacerbated by the warm weather.

As new diesel units were rolling off the production line, the Class 142 'Skippers' were temporarily withdrawn due to track circuiting problems. Consequently, by May, old diesel units were temporarily reinstated to Looe and Gunnislake.

Class 143 'Pacer' units were introduced on Tyneside from 20 January and on 25 September the new Class 142/1 'Pacer' unit was launched between Liverpool, Wigan and Preston, with regular services starting on 29 September. On 11 December 1986, the new Alexander/BREL Class 144 'Pacers' were officially unveiled at Neville Hill depot. This was followed by a trial run to Ilkley and Bradford.

On the new locomotive front, an 'unusual' design for Britain's railways arrived at Southampton Docks on 21 January. These were the four Class 59 locomotives destined for Foster Yeoman Ltd at Merehead Quarry for working stone traffic. These powerful locomotives from General Motors, USA, were powered by GM 645E3C 16-cylinder engines of 3,300hp and, soon after arrival in Britain, trials were carried out from Derby RTC to Dudding Hill. By February, they were in revenue-earning service. On 28 June, all four Class 59 'Yeomans' were named at a 'family day' for Foster Yeoman employees; both the Union Jack and the American Stars & Stripes adorned the event.

On 1 October, the experimental Class 89 locomotive, No 89001, left Crewe Works for Litchurch Lane Works, Derby, hauled by a Class 25 locomotive. Earlier, an old favourite returned to traffic when, on 12 July, Class 44 'Peak' No D4 Great Gable appeared, after extensive rewiring, at Butterley.

Another welcome return was that of BR Pacific No 71000 Duke of Gloucester which made its first trial run in steam since restoration over the Great Central Railway on 25 May. In fact it worked as a 4-4-2-2 as its trailing rods were absent. Another fine steam locomotive, 'A4' Pacific No 4468 Mallard returned to main line steam on 9 July when it headed the first 1986 'Scarborough Spa Express' and an 'undressed' Sir Lamiel appeared (less smoke deflectors) in 1986.

Push-pull running trials commenced on the WCML between Birmingham and Liverpool early in the summer of 1986 with Class 87/1 No 87101 Stephenson and withdrawn GER 'Jazz' lines electric unit No 305439, modified by RTC Derby. The work included the removal of the unit's pantograph.

The Hazel Grove Chord, linking the ex-L&NWR Stockport-Buxton line with the former Midland main line from Manchester Central to New Mills South Junction, was opened on 29 April and was the first new line to be built in South Manchester since 1910. This link enabled Liverpool to receive improved cross-country and Trans-Pennine services.

In Scotland, the first of the Class 318 units to operate Glasgow-Ayr services appeared in June, and electric services between Glasgow and Ardrossan South Beach commenced on 24 November — eight weeks ahead of schedule.

Following a 100mph collision, south of Colwich, on 19 September, involving a Liverpool-Euston train and a Euston-Manchester train (which passed a red signal), Class 86 locomotives Nos 86211 City of Milton Keynes and 86429 The Times were written off. Also for the cutter's torch were 10 coaches of APT stock which were hauled to Booth's scrapyard at Rotherham.

InterCity trains returned to the Cambrian Coast line from 14 April following the strengthening of the Barmouth Bridge after the wood-boring marine termites had been at work and, on the Settle & Carlisle line, regular train services were restored to eight stations, despite the continuing threat of closure, after a lapse of 16 years.

'Coal rustling' took place in the Welsh Valleys in February 1986 as groups of thieves ambushed coal trains. Gangs of up to 50 people were involved and hundreds of tons of coal were loaded into adjacent lorries and vans. Sleepers were placed on lines to stop trains. The thieves' intention was to provide for the old and needy through the cold winter.

Above:
The vast expanse of Rannoch Moor on the West Highland line is the scene for this aluminium train, bound for Fort William, on 28 May 1986, behind Class 37 No 37408, proudly displaying its 'Scottie Dog' emblem. The aluminium traffic for Fort William (and Kinlochleven) together with the Wiggins Teape paper mill traffic has helped secure the future of this picturesque line.
L. A. Nixon

Right:
The Highland line from Perth to Inverness passes over some mountainous terrain via Druimuachdar and Slochd summits. This view shows double-headed Class 26s No 26028 and 26031 having descended from Druimuachdar Summit as they pass through Dalnaspidal with the 15.10 Inverness to Millerhill freight on 29 May 1986. The final wagon in the train seems to be an afterthought! *L. A. Nixon*

Above:
The Class 143 'Pacers' carried two different liveries. Nos 143001-019 were in the Provincial Sector's blue & white and Nos 143020-025 sported the Tyne & Wear yellow & white colours. No 143006 heads the two-car 13.35 Carlisle-Newcastle train on 20 July 1986 and is seen arriving at Haltwhistle where the branch line to Alston, which closed to passengers on 3 May 1976, joined. *W. A. Sharman*

Left:
The 10.10 service from Barnstaple to Exmouth pulls into Umbersleigh station on 9 July 1986. The service is operated by a pair of Class 142 'Skipper' railbuses, Nos 142019 and 142024. Passengers for the train appear to be restricted to 'one man and his dog'! *Brian Morrison*

Top right:
An unusual aerial view of Plymouth station area on 27 August 1986, showing a variety of motive power on duty. Class 37 No 37196 *Tre Pol and Pen* approaches with a down train of empty china clay wagons whilst Class 50 No 50043 *Eagle* awaits departure with the 10.30 Penzance to Liverpool Lime Street service. An IC125, and a Class 08 shunter performing station pilot duties, complete the scene. A picture which calls for endless scrutiny as it provides so much interest. *John S. Whiteley*

Right:
'Yeoman' Class 59/0 3,300hp diesel locomotives were built at Chicago in the USA by General Motors. These are maintained at the Foster Yeoman premises at Merehead by BR staff. On 20 February 1986, No 59004 passes the Ford Motor Co works, near Dagenham Dock station, over ex-LT&SR metals, with the Merehead to Purfleet stone train. In June 1986, the locomotive was named *Yeoman Challenger*. *Brian Morrison*

Railfreight

Railfreight displayed its new image at Ripple Lane depot on 17 October 1987. New two-tone grey-liveried locomotives could be seen bearing the new sub-sector body markings and their cast diamond-shaped cab-side depot plates. Cast plates, bearing the Ripple Lane 'Torch' logo, were affixed to Class 37 No 37892 prior to its naming (*Ripple Lane*) at the event. Also on display were locomotives bearing Stratford's 'Cockney Sparrow' and Crewe's 'Cheshire Cat'. Chevron style markings denoted Railfreight sub-sectors; Construction, Coal, Metals, Petroleum and Distribution.

Prior to this, on 6 April, Freightliner announced its intention to close eight of its 22 terminals (at Aberdeen, Dundee, Edinburgh, Newcastle, Hull, Manchester Longsight, Nottingham and Swansea). After an absence of 25 years, a trainload of fish returned to the West Highland line when Speedlink conveyed 200 tons (plus ice) in 11 insulated wagons to Grimsby early in the year.

On 9 May the recently delivered last member of the Class 58 was named *Toton Traction Depot*. This locomotive was fitted with special SEPEX control equipment which was tested at the depot and the long line of withdrawn Class 45s at the depot were useful in providing a 'dead-weight' load for adhesion tests.

The formal separation of British Rail Engineering Ltd took place on 1 April creating two groups — BREL and BRML (BR Maintenance Ltd). BRML became a further subsidiary of the BR Board and was responsible for all major traction and rolling stock maintenance performed at Eastleigh, Wolverton, Doncaster and Glasgow (Springburn), and at BR's upgraded Level 5 major depots at Chart Leacon, Slade Green, Selhurst, Stratford, Bristol (Bath Road), Laira, Birkenhead North and Neville Hill. Later in the year BREL's Doncaster Wagon Works was sold to RFS Industries — the first to be sold as a going concern to the private sector. It was run by a team of ex-BR management staff.

On the passenger front, 1987 saw the abolition of the term 'second-class' to be replaced by 'standard-class' and, with the start of the new BR summer timetable, new Pullman services were introduced to link London with Birmingham. We were introduced to 'The Cornishman' (Newcastle-Penzance), 'The Devonian' (Leeds-Paignton) and 'The Cornish Scot' (Edinburgh/Glasgow-Penzance).

An 'observation saloon' (a refurbished DMU trailer) entered service on 21 May on the Inverness-Kyle of Lochalsh route. The conversion cost £6,000 and incorporated loose seating, and a public address system to enable a hostess to provide a commentary *en route*.

On 2 October, Birmingham Snow Hill station reopened and, two days later, special services ran to the Birmingham Railway Museum at Tyseley and the BR Open Day. Full passenger services commenced the following day. This 'classic' Great Western station, which closed in 1967, was now back in business. The new station, provided with four platforms, was much less ambitious than before!

The new Cardiff City line opened on 5 October. This linked West Cardiff with the city centre and the Valley lines and Provincial's new Class 150/2 units provided 131 extra train services a day over the Valley lines.

By 1987, station 'revivals' since the Beeching closures had reached 150 with the opening of the Chiltern Line's Haddenham & Thame station. Other revivals were Kettering-Corby services on 13 April and the Coventry-Nuneaton line on 11 May, the latter after a closure of 22 years. A passenger link to Heysham was reopened also on 11 May to provide connections for the Isle of Man ferry services.

In London, the rebuilt Fenchurch Street station opened on 21 September but the big news was the opening of the Docklands Light Railway which formally took place on 30 July and was launched by Her Majesty the Queen. The first public train ran on 31 August departing from Poplar station. A 'Train Captain' was on board each train. On opening, the railway comprised two lines from Island Gardens, one to West India Quay (near Poplar) and the other, via Bow, to Stratford.

Electrification continued apace on the ECML in 1987 and a construction depot at Millerhill was opened on 13 April. The section from Hitchin to Peterborough was also energised. The new electrified service over the GE lines to Cambridge which commenced on 19 January was hampered by a shortage of EMUs resulting from the previous week's bad weather. The fully refurbished station at Cambridge was officially reopened on 23 March. Electrified services to Norwich commenced on 11 May powered by Class 86/2 locomotives. Other electrified lines in Britain energised in 1987 were the Sanderstead-East Grinstead line in September (normal services commencing on 5 October) and the extension of the Ayrshire electrification scheme to Ardrossan Harbour and Largs.

The first Class 319 ThamesLink unit arrived at Strawberry Hill for test running from BREL York in September and the first of the impressive Class 442 'Wessex Electrics' was handed over to Network SouthEast by BREL Derby on 18 December. These units were heralded as the new flagship of NSE and contained many revolutionary features such as new-design aircraft-style seating in an endeavour to bring in new standards of comfort for passengers.

During May, trial running over the West Coast main line took place with the prototype Class 89 locomotive, reaching speeds of up to 124mph and, on 6 August, No 89001 hauled a Holyhead-Euston train from Crewe, being detached at Willesden. On 31 October the first of the new Class 90 locomotives left Crewe Works for Derby RTC, towed by a Class 31/1 diesel, for research tests.

On 1 November 1987, a new world speed record for a diesel train was set up over the ECML when an IC125 train, powered by Nos 43102 *City of Wakefield* and 43159, achieved 148mph during high-speed test runs for the new Swiss-built SIG bogies.

Western Region Class 142 'Skippers' were modified at Laira with flange lubrication equipment in the spring which, at first, seemed to solve the problem of running over Cornish branches but by September the units were withdrawn from services and sent to Newton Heath as they were found still to be unsuitable. On 16 March new Class 150/2 'Sprinters' were introduced to Yorkshire and from October they worked services from Cardiff. Also by October six Class 155 units were delivered to Cardiff for Birmingham services and the first of the Class 156 'Super Sprinters' was handed over by the end of the year.

In January the weather created havoc on Britain's railways when the lowest temperatures for over 40 years, together with huge snowdrifts, brought services to a standstill. Freezing points, and trains frozen to the track or overhead wires, created so many problems. For example, on 14 January Waterloo station had to be closed, and the 09.43 Newcastle-Penzance did not reach its destination until 09.00 the following day after five changes of locomotive *en route*. There was an unprecedented appearance of the Inverness snowblower in Kent as the heaviest snowfalls for 20 years hit the southeast. In October, gale force winds hit

Britain, bringing down thousands of trees and paralysing the Network SouthEast system. More extreme weather created flooding in Wales resulting in the collapse of the Glanrhyd Bridge over the River Towy on the Central Wales line, on 19 October, whilst a Class 108 unit was about to cross, the leading car going into the river. However, the tragedy of the year occurred at King's Cross Underground station when fire broke out behind an escalator resulting in many fatalities both to passengers and rescuers.

On the preservation scene, the East Lancashire Railway opened on 25 July when its inaugural train ran from Bury to Ramsbottom. On the same day public services commenced on the Yorkshire Dales Railway extension to Holywell. In the south, the Mid-Hants Railway replaced rails on the Medstead-Alton section in time for the summer season and in Wales, steam returned to the Cambrian in the summer when *Hinton Manor* and BR Standard No 75069 were in steam.

Below:
China clay hoods in abundance at Lostwithiel on 24 August 1987. Locomotives on view are Class 37s Nos 37675 and 37671 (now carrying the nameplates *Tre Pol and Pen*), on the Carne Point-Marsh Mills (Plymouth) empty clay hood train, seen passing a packed yard. Trains from various china clay dries are assembled at Lostwithiel prior to being hauled to Carne Point where the china clay is exported. *Brian Morrison*

Above:
A powerful restart from Bodmin Parkway on 14 August 1987 as the sunlight catches IC125 No 253043 (led by Class 43 powercar 43168) with the 07.45 Paddington to Penzance express. The HSTs replaced the Class 50s on these West of England services. *Brian Morrison*

Centre left:
Work on the L&SWR's underground line from Waterloo to Bank station, in the heart of the City of London, commenced in 1894, was completed in 1898, and was a very successful alternative to the fleet of two-horse buses which had previously carried commuters from Waterloo to Bank. Known to nearly everyone as 'The Drain', the Waterloo & City Railway runs beneath the River Thames on double track and the journey of 1 mile 1,012yd is scheduled to take six minutes. On 11 May 1987, Class 487 W&C stock, DMBS No 54 leading, is seen sporting Network SouthEast livery at Bank station. *Brian Morrison*

Bottom left:
Adverse weather conditions in January 1987 created havoc on GE main-line services and by 14 January services were reduced to an 'all stations' shuttle between Ipswich and Liverpool Street, handled by 'older' EMUs on a makeshift timetable. In this view Class 302 No 302266 enters Colchester with an up shuttle service. *Michael J. Collins*

Top right:
BREL York-constructed Class 150/2 diesel unit No 150211 approaches Walsden, south of Todmorden, on 21 August 1987, forming a local service from Leeds to Manchester Victoria. The train is seen crossing the Rochdale Canal. *L. A. Nixon*

Right:
On 4 June 1987, Class 45/0 'Peak' No 45037 emerges from Manton Tunnel at Manton Junction with empty ZHV wagons bound for the Corby line. The line seen to the right of the ex-MR signalbox is from Stamford. *Brian Morrison*

Left:
A preserved Johnson Midland Railway design, dating from 1878, and rebuilt with a Belpaire boiler, Class 1F 0-6-0T No 41708, sporting an 18D (Staveley Midland) shedplate, hauls a train near Butterley at the Midland Railway Centre, near Ripley on 6 June 1987.
J. H. Cooper-Smith

Below:
A new departure point, since preservation, for ex-LNER Gresley 'V2' No 4771 *Green Arrow* was Marylebone, on 2 August 1987, when this fine preserved 2-6-2 was employed on the 10.55 'Shakespeare Limited' during a series of steam specials to Stratford upon Avon. *Green Arrow* created an impressive sight as it stormed away from the London terminus. *Brian Morrison*

Wessex Electrics

The Waterloo-Weymouth Class 442 five-car 'Wessex Electrics' — NSE's new flagship — entered revenue-earning service on 16 May 1988. This followed the energising of the line from Branksome to Weymouth on 11 January and the run of the first electric train to Weymouth on 1 February — a test train of Class 411 (4-CEP) units Nos 1621 and 1611 led by Class 33 No 33106, in case problems arose. Proving runs for the Class 442 units commenced on 11 February. However, delays in delivery of the new 'Wessex Electrics' for the new summer 1988 timetable resulted in only four units being available for the introduction of the fast comfortable trains to Weymouth and constant problems occurred with the power doors, which often created long delays when they refused to close or open or blew open in tunnels. Also, on the early services, the splitting of the 10-car train at Southampton caused additional delays. By mid-March only two Class 442s had been delivered to Bournemouth — one with test equipment fitted and the other with seating missing. A special non-stop express run from Waterloo to Weymouth took place on 14 April and reached a speed on 109mph — a world 750v third-rail traction record.

On the East Coast main line, 140mph speed indicator boards started to appear as the 25kV line from Bretton, near Peterborough, to Grantham was energised on 7 March and on 4 July the line was energised into Leeds. Class 89 locomotive, No 89001 became the first electric locomotive to haul a passenger train to Leeds, on 12 August. At Edinburgh Waverley, in March, work was carried out on the eastern end of the station in preparation for electrification, resulting in the closure of platform 10. Also in 1988, the ECML was linked to the WCML by overhead electric wires (25kV) over the North London line. This was initially for inter-regional freight services.

On 3 July, the first Class 89 passenger solo duty was a special over the ECML from London to Doncaster to commemorate the *Mallard* speed record of 3 July 1938. At Doncaster, No 4468 *Mallard* took over to York, via the new Selby diversion and continued on to Scarborough. The Class 89, No 89001, took over again at Doncaster, after the return run by *Mallard*, and returned the train to King's Cross. In May, *Mallard* had been hired by the Post Office to celebrate the 150th anniversary of the TPO service hauling the 'Postal Pullman' and 'Pennine Postal Pullman'. The first Travelling Post Office ran on 11 January 1838 and, on 20 January 1988, a train left Euston for Carlisle — 'The North Western Travelling Post Office Night Down' — traversing the very route which between Birmingham and Warrington saw the operation of that very first train, 150 years before. Also to commemorate the event, the new Dover-Manchester TPO was introduced on 16 May 1988 following the naming of Class 73 locomotive No 73138 *Post Haste* at Tonbridge, five days earlier, although it was never used on the service.

Test runs took place involving Class 90 electric locomotives from February and, within a few days of its release from BREL Crewe Works, No 90005 worked its first passenger-carrying train, on 30 March, after being named *Financial Times* at Euston. Problems occurred during tests involving computer equipment and braking. It was not until September that BR accepted the first nine members of the class and in addition to working WCML services, they commenced crew training duties on the GE lines in preparation for through Railfreight operation. The first test runs of a Class 90 with the new Mk 3 DVT (No 82101) over the WCML were carried out by Nos 90006 and 90009.

On 12 February, the GEC Class 91 made its public debut at BREL Crewe Works. On Easter Monday, No 91002 made its first test run with 'eight-up' to Peterborough and No 91004 carried out trials at Crewe, but teething troubles were hitting the Class 91s as well. The Class 91's Doncaster debut was on 17 June with a DVT and, on 2 October, history was made when No 91002 achieved 145mph on the GN main line.

On 25 April, at Blackfriars station, Her Royal Highness The Princess Royal officially launched the new 'Thameslink' service. This new service passed through the reopened Holborn Snow Hill Tunnel and was operated by the Class 319 units. However, later in the year modifications to 10 of the mechanical and electrical components within the Class 319 units commenced to improve reliability.

The first Class 321 electric unit left BREL York on 15 September. These new units were destined for suburban services from Liverpool Street increasing the carrying ability of trains over BR's newest region; 'Anglia'. The new region's future projects to improve services would include the completion of the Liverpool Street/Broadgate redevelopment. The Class 321s were also for use on services out of Euston.

The Watford Junction-St Albans Abbey line became 'live' on 4 July and electrified services commenced on 11 July with the introduction of the Class 313s on the 'Abbey Flyer'. The Royston-Cambridge line was also electrified.

After withdrawal, reinstatement and withdrawal of the last Class 45 'Peaks', life finally came to an end for these 'old favourites' in August 1988, apart from No 45106 which was withdrawn the following year. In August, No 45106 emerged in green livery and appeared on East Midlands services from St Pancras and on railtours. No D200 (40122), the first Class 40 diesel to be constructed in March 1958, hauled its final train on 16 April between Liverpool Street and Norwich, the route of the 'inaugural run', and then hauled its special train of Mark 1 coaches to York via the Ely avoiding line to Peterborough and York over the ECML. No D200 can now be seen in the National Railway Museum.

The end came for others on BR in 1988. For instance, freight lines closed to Oakamoor and Blodwell, Redbridge Foundry closed in October, Lickey banking ceased, Cornish Clay hoods were replaced by modern CDAs, the last newspaper trains ran in July and Woodham's scrapyard at Barry docks gave up its last locomotive, GWR 2-8-0 No 2873 — the 213th to be sold from this site.

But many new stations appeared, six of them on the new Cynon Valley Line to Aberdare which reopened on 27 September from Abercynon; it formed a new 'Sprinter'-operated route. Class 33-hauled trains on Portsmouth-Bristol-Cardiff services were replaced by Class 155 'Super Sprinters' in 1988 but these units hit problems in December with faulty doors and the fleet was temporarily taken out of service being replaced by a variety of motive power including Class 156s. Norwich had received its first Class 156 'Super Sprinters' in January and units for the new northwest-Anglia services later went to Manchester.

On the preservation scene, the Swanage Railway opened its extension to Harman's Cross and work commenced on the Bluebell Railway's extension. Steam returned to Birmingham Snow Hill less than a year after the station reopened when, on 14 September, *Clun Castle* hauled a train conveying HRH The Prince of Wales to the

Birmingham Railway Museum at Tyseley. Bulleid Pacific No 35027 *Port Line* was also steamed.

At Staples Corner, Cricklewood, on 28 October 1988, two Class 31 diesels Nos 31202 and 31226 almost ended up on the road below, No 31202 breaking its back. But more seriously, following a series of bad accidents during the year at Hyndland, St Helens and Newcastle upon Tyne, the most tragic disaster for 20 years occurred on 12 December approaching Clapham Junction when a Bournemouth-Waterloo express ran into the rear of a Basingstoke-Waterloo train. This was followed by a Waterloo-Haslemere empty stock working hitting the wreckage causing devastation, and numerous injuries and fatalities.

Below:
The first revenue-earning service for a Class 90 locomotive was on 12 July 1988 when No 90003 hauled the 13.40 InterCity service train from Blackpool North, seen here arriving at Euston. Class 86/4 No 86413 *County of Lancashire*, with pantograph down, is coupled to the Class 90 and was acting as emergency standby which was not necessary on this occassion. *Brian Morrison*

Right:
The Class 442 'Wessex Electrics', introduced on Waterloo-Bournemouth-Weymouth electrified services in 1988, are capable of achieving 100mph. These five-car sets run regularly as 10-car trains, especially at peak periods, but early problems with doors and uncoupling created delays. A 10-car train comprising Class 442 units Nos 2403 and 2409 is pictured near Woking with a Waterloo-bound train on 28 May 1988, soon after entering service. *Alex Dasi-Sutton*

Bottom right:
A Blackfriars-Sevenoaks service in the hands of an eight-car Class 413 4-CAP unit with Class 413/2 No 3209 leading, proceeds to negotiate the junction at Lewisham after leaving the viaduct on 8 February 1988. The line seen on the approaching incline emanates from Charing Cross. *Brian Morrison*

Above:
The Class 141 was a development of the Class 140 unit and had a modified Leyland bus body mounted on a four-wheel rail chassis. Introduced in 1983 they were all initially allocated to Neville Hill, Leeds and painted in the green & white 'Metro' livery. No 141004 arrives at York, after passing under Holgate Bridge, forming the 09.50 ex-Selby service on 14 May 1988. *W. A. Sharman*

Left:
Class 207 diesel-electric multiple-unit No 207011 makes the scheduled Rye stop on 26 July 1988 forming the 15.05 Hastings-Ashford train and is passed by Class 205/1 unit No 205101 heading for Hastings with the 15.04 from Ashford — the platforms at Rye station are staggered. Both types of these DEMUs were constructed at Eastleigh with the Class 205s being introduced from 1958 and the Class 207s from 1962. The black triangle on the units indicate to the railway staff the luggage van end of the train. *Brian Morrison*

Above:
On a remote line in Kent, Class 33/0 No 33031 pauses at the remains of the old Lydd Town station, on 4 August 1988, for the rickety crossing gates to be opened by the 'second man' prior to conveying its nuclear flask load from Dungeness. Eventually bound for Sellafield, it will now continue up the branch towards the junction where it will join the main line at Appledore. Tests by using a Class 46 'Peak' colliding with a nuclear flask at 100mph proved these flasks to be leak-proof. *Brian Morrison*

Centre left:
Disaster struck two Class 31 locomotives, Nos 31202 and 31226, high above the North Circular Road near Cricklewood in October 1988, when the locomotives ran away down the embankment and almost on to the road. This scene was captured after the incident, on 28 October 1988. Both locomotives were withdrawn as a result of the damage sustained. *Brian Morrison*

Below left:
On 10 November 1988, Class 419 motor luggage van No 9004 stands at a 'deserted' London Bridge station with parcels for Ashford. The MLV is sporting its new but short-lived red 'Royal Mail' livery. These single-car units were introduced to carry excess passenger luggage for the Southern Region's Eastern Section boat trains. *Brian Morrison*

Settle & Carlisle Reprieve

On 9 March 1989, the Minister for Public Transport announced a 'stay of execution' for the Settle & Carlisle route at least until October and existing services would change very little. The line would join the Cumbrian Coast, Tyne Valley and Esk Valley lines and be included in the BR Provincial 'leisure lines' promotions for 1989 and brochures to promote the route were prepared. This reprieve also applied to the Blackburn-Hellifield line. This was wonderful news for the Friends of the Settle & Carlisle Line Association who had been campaigning hard to keep the line open. However, a temporary closure did take place between Settle and Appleby, in October, to allow work to be carried out on the 24-arch Ribblehead Viaduct. The repair work had recently been estimated to be not as expensive as was first thought; originally the cost involved in repairing the viaduct was one of the reasons cited by British Rail in their efforts to close the route.

Throughout the summer of 1989, steam specials continued over the line and steam trains also returned to the North Wales coast route from 14 February — the first for over 20 years. The inaugural run was made by Bulleid Pacific *Clan Line* from Crewe to Llandudno and Holyhead. Other trains during the summer were worked by No 6201 *Princess Elizabeth*, 'West Country' Pacific *Taw Valley* (making its main line steam debut) and 'Black Five' No 5407.

Steam also returned to Lincoln in 1989 for the first time in many years when the Flying Scotsman Enterprise's 'Lincolnshire Poacher' arrived there behind 'Black Five' No 44932. Another 'Black Five' steamed in 1989 was No 44871 — back after 11 years (but not on the main line). Great Western 'King' No 6024 *King Edward I* was steamed for the first time in nearly 27 years on 2 February. Restoration on this locomotive started in 1973 after rescue from Barry scrapyard where it had been rotting away for 10½ years. Also back on the main line was LMS 'Jubilee' *Bahamas* and, in August, Standard 4MT Mogul No 76079 successfully passed steam trials on the East Lancashire Railway. On the Isle of Wight Steam Railway, 0-6-0 'Terrier' tank No 11 was successfully returned to traffic 26 years

after its last outing. This was an excellent year for the steam railway enthusiast.

Apart from the two Class 03 204hp diesel shunters which had been transferred to the Isle of Wight following the withdrawal of the Class 05, all the remaining members of the class were withdrawn following their removal from Birkenhead Docks duties. Also withdrawn was the last Class 83 electric locomotive. On 14 May, the final scheduled Class 50 working out of Paddington took place, their only regular services now being Waterloo-Exeter trains.

Privatisation took place in two very different branches of British Rail in 1989 when, firstly, the Vale of Rheidol steam railway was sold to the Brecon Mountain Railway Ltd (services under new ownership starting in May 1989), and then BREL was sold to a consortium of Trafalgar House plc, Asea Brown Boveri Ltd and BREL's management and employees. The Redbridge Permanent Way Depot near Southampton closed on 3 March 1989 following its foundry closure the previous year.

On the freight side the 'Railfreight 89' exhibition held at Cricklewood in April was a great success. Primarily a business event, the public were invited in for one of the three days. There were around 100 different freight wagons on display for prospective new clients to view and Railfreight's forward looking approach and hard marketing had turned a £281 million loss in 1984/85 into a £44 million profit in 1987/88. A new self-discharge train was launched by Redland Aggregates on 21 March. New wagons had built-in diesel-powered conveyor belts enabling them to be unloaded without the need for special facilities. In Middlesbrough, on 16 June, a new £2.25 million Railfreight Distribution rail/road freight terminal opened.

Network SouthEast were having to wait to show off their new 'toy' — a £500,000 snow blower. Bought to counter severe snows in the south, the heavy snow either failed to turn up or it was the 'wrong kind'. NSE's Class 483 units for Isle of Wight services (refurbished ex-LT 1938 stock) were formally commissioned at Ryde Pierhead on 13 July. They replaced former Isle

of Wight ex-LT 1923 stock. The refurbishment cost £1 million whereas new construction would have involved an expenditure of £3 million. The new trains looked very smart in their full NSE livery.

Other 'new liveries' were unveiled in February by British Rail for the locomotive fleet. These were 'InterCity' (to be used on InterCity-dedicated locomotives involving Classes 87, 89, 91, IC125 power-cars and certain Class 73 and Class 90 engines); 'BR Mainline' (for locomotives used by more than one business, involving Classes 90, 81-86, 73/1, and some 47/4s and 37/4s); 'Railfreight' (a two-tone grey livery with one of six sub-sector identification markings, involving Classes 60, 58, 56, some 47/0s, and some 37/5-37/9 locomotives); and 'BR General' (based on the original 'Railfreight Grey' to reflect the 'workhorse roll' of certain locomotives in Classes 08, 09, 20, 26, 31, 33, 37/0, 47/0 and 47/3).

By September, the East Coast main line electrification scheme was energised from King's Cross to just north of York and Class 89 No 89001 continued to deputise for IC125 power cars on Leeds services, having since Christmas been painted in the InterCity 'Swallow' livery.

July saw the first Class 90 test runs in East Anglia but these locomotives were still suffering from teething troubles. Class 91s were now operating revenue-earning services on push-pull London-Leeds trains, using TDM-fitted IC125 power cars.

On 20 September, BR unveiled its new-generation InterCity Mark 4 coaching stock (to include Mark 4 DVTs) which, in October, took over on Leeds services and later on the Edinburgh trains when electrification was completed to Scotland over the ECML. Improved seating, exterior 'plug' doors worked by push buttons, on-board telephones and a pleasant decor were features incorporated in the new coaching stock.

After temporary withdrawal, the Class 155 'Super Sprinters' were now back to full strength and Class 156 'Super Sprinters' had now taken Scotland by storm. The first Class 158 'Express Sprinter' commenced trials in October between Derby and Leicester. The first of these new units were also destined for Scotland. In February, Bletchley-based Class 321 units commenced crew training and on 25 May a Class 321 unit appeared at King's Cross for the first time. In July, they entered traffic on Northampton line services. On 6 December a mock-up of the Class 471 'Networker' was unveiled at Victoria station.

On 30 June, Brush Electrical Machines handed over the first Class 60 locomotive No 60001 *Steadfast* at Loughborough. It underwent tests on the Mickleover test track.

Due to the collapse of the River Ness bridge, on the north side of Inverness, locomotives and stock required for north of

Scotland services were moved by road on low loaders to Invergordon via the Kessock Bridge and others returned. Temporary servicing facilities were set up at Muir of Ord.

To end the year on an amusing note, a Brighton-London Bridge mail train was held up by masked gunmen at Merstham. The thieves got away with only a sack of Polish newspapers — was this the 'Great Train Robbery (Part 2)'?

Below:
On 25 May 1989, the 18.13 'extra' working from King's Cross to Doncaster was rostered for two Class 321 EMUs — the only recorded occasion that any of these units had appeared at King's Cross. In this view the empty train to form the service, headed by No 321324, enters King's Cross from Gasworks Tunnel, in preparation to carry out this duty and passes Class 91 electric No 91007 lying stabled at the buffer stops. This also gives an excellent view of the Class 91's 'blunt end'. *Brian Morrison*

Bottom:
Sporting the 'Strathclyde' orange & black livery, Class 303 EMU No 303016 departs from Glasgow Central, on 2 September 1989, with the 10.05 Cathcart Circle service, returning to Glasgow Central, via Maxwell Park.
Brian Morrison

Above:
A Class 90 in action as the 08.35 Euston-Inverness 'Clansman', hauled by No 90011 *The Chartered Institute of Transport*, passes through Rugby station on 25 February 1989. The 'Clansman' was first introduced as a named train in 1974. *Brian Morrison*

Left:
A Class 91 at speed as No 91003 emerges from Wood Green Tunnel whilst powering the InterCity 'Charter' set on 23 September 1989 with a BR 'Staff Special' forming the 09.31 from York to King's Cross. Unusually, the locomotive is facing towards London. *Brian Morrison*

Right:
Following the naming ceremony at King's Cross on 16 January 1989, the one and only Class 89 electric locomotive, No 89001 *Avocet* built by BREL Crewe for Brush in 1986, leaves the station with the 12.05 special train to the Royal Society for the Protection of Birds' headquarters at Sandy, Bedfordshire. *Brian Morrison*

Below:
The beautifully restored chocolate & cream Pullman carriages are now regularly seen on VSOE trains to locations such as Bournemouth, Stratford upon Avon and on Christmas Lunch Specials. In addition, they provide sheer opulence on the English part of exotic journeys to Europe such as Venice and beyond for fare-paying passengers. On 12 November 1989, Class 73/1 No 73212 *Airtour Suisse* is pictured in full flight at Bickley Junction with the 11.00 VSOE Victoria-Folkestone Harbour service.
Brian Morrison

'Chunnel' Segments Galore!

By 8 November 1990, 1,000 trains of Channel Tunnel segments had completed the journey from the Transmanche-Link premises on the Isle of Grain to Shakespeare Cliff, Folkestone, generally hauled by double-headed Construction Sector Class 33 locomotives. The segments were used for the lining of the tunnel and the 1,000th train was hauled by Nos 33021 and 33051. These trains had been in operation since 16 May 1988 when the first one was hauled by Nos 33050 and 33051 after being named *Isle of Grain* and *Shakespeare Cliff* at the Isle of Grain site. At first, one train ran each day, but, at the peak, six trains covered the journey daily. In 1991 a single Class 60 locomotive took over the duty and the last segment train ran on 5 May 1991 hauled by the two locomotives which made the first journey. On 30 October 1990 tunnel boring machines approached each other from the English and French sides in the service tunnel and broke through — accurate to 20in after tunnelling 14 miles from England and 10 miles from France, and on 1 December the breakthrough of the marine service tunnel was achieved leaving only a wall of chalk to be dug out by hand. This being done, British and French workers, management and politicians passed through, and history was made.

Amalgamated Roadstone Corporation's quartet of Class 59/1 locomotives arrived at Newport Docks from Halifax, Nova Scotia, in October. British buffers were fitted and the new locomotives were moved to Whatley Quarry and then on to the Derby Research Centre to carry out speed trials on the Midland main line.

The first Class 60 locomotive in revenue-earning service was No 60005 *Skiddaw*, hauling Mountsorrel-Redland aggregates trains. This followed a successful test run on 10 January 1990 with 60 PGAs from Mountsorrel to Clay Cross. Crew training followed from Old Oak Common depot. No 60024 was the first of the class to include all the modifications resulting from the test running and it left the Brush Works, Loughborough, for tests at Old Dalby on 2 August. By the end of the year the Class 60s were working Corby and Workington trains and to Scunthorpe and Ravenscraig.

On the weather front, extreme climatic conditions in January and February produced winds gusting to over 130mph causing structural damage to railway installations over a vast area resulting in the temporary closure of many lines. South Wales and the West of England were the first to feel the brunt of it and later several miles of catenary were brought down on the ECML near Sandy, Bedfordshire. Scotland was hit in early February and serious flooding followed torrential rain washing away railway embankments near the River Tay.

Two 'Parcels' locomotives were named on 1 May to mark the 150th anniversary of the introduction of the 'Penny Post'. They were No 90019 *Penny Black* (at Euston) and No 47474 *Sir Rowland Hill* (at Kidderminster) — the Class 47 being the first locomotive to be painted in the new Parcels red & grey livery. The painting of No 47489 in the Parcels livery followed in June. On 30 July, 'Track 29' was launched — a new service guaranteeing parcel delivery anywhere in the United Kingdom by 17.00 the next day.

Scottish bridges were in the news in 1990, work being completed on the new Ness Viaduct, north of Inverness, following the collapse of the previous structure. The official opening train was made up of Class 156 'Super Sprinter' No 156458. Further south the Forth railway bridge reached its 100th birthday and on the centenary day, 4 March, 'A4' Pacific No 60009, now carrying the name *Osprey*, hauled a special train, named 'The Forth Centennial' over the bridge from Edinburgh to Perth. 'For political reasons' (it was quoted), the locomotive's name was changed from *Union of South Africa* to *Osprey* strictly for the centenary celebrations. The name *Osprey* was originally carried by 'A4' Pacific No 4494.

LNER Pacific No 4472 *Flying Scotsman* returned to main line running on 2 May, following its welcome return from Australia the previous autumn, when it hauled the Cumbrian coast's 'Sellafield Sightseer' to the BNFL establishment. Other 'returns to steam' were 'Schools' class *Repton*, the 'Q7' on the North York Moors Railway and 'Battle of Britain' Pacific No 34072 *257 Squadron* for the Battle of Britain celebrations at Folkestone on 8 September 1990. But the most welcome sight of all was the return to the main line of Standard Class 8 Pacific No 71000 *Duke of Gloucester*. Following a loaded test run on 14 March with '14-up', this impressive locomotive performed well between Marylebone and Nottingham in April and later over the Settle & Carlisle route — a wonderful sight! Standard '9F' 2-10-0 No 92240 also returned to steam on the Bluebell Railway in 1990 after a 12-year restoration programme. Another welcome return to steam in 1990 (after 28 years) was Stanier 'Princess Royal' Pacific No 46203 *Princess Margaret Rose* resplendent in her maroon livery as she performed on the Derby-Sheffield circuit.

In London, Holborn Viaduct terminus closed on 26 January 1990 as part of a redevelopment scheme taking place there, both above and below ground, in relation to the new 'Thameslink' services. At Waterloo, Windsor line platforms (16-21) were demolished to make way for the new 'Waterloo International' station. In January, on the Docklands Light Railway, trials commenced with new articulated trains, introduced to cope with rapidly increasing traffic.

London Transport received five Class 485 cars (ex-LT 1923 stock) from the Isle of Wight for 'active' preservation in December, restoring them in the Morden-Edgware 1923 livery to celebrate the centenary of the Northern line.

By September, the electrified ECML from Edinburgh to Berwick was energised leaving only the stretch from Berwick to Northallerton to complete electrification of the entire route to King's Cross and, during the same month, Class 320 electric units entered service on Scotrail.

A splash of colour was seen at Ilford depot during the summer when they painted three Class 307 units in the red & white livery of West Yorkshire PTE for the Leeds-Doncaster services in lieu of 'Pacer' units, the 307s entering service on 3 July.

On 20 July the first of the five Class 322 electric units specifically designed for the new Stansted Airport link left BREL York and performed a high-speed run to King's Cross, descending Stoke Bank at 112mph. Pending the inaugural run to Stansted Airport, the new units were used on Liverpool Street-Cambridge trains.

The Portsmouth-Southampton/Eastleigh electrification scheme, 'Solent Link', was energised on 14 March 1990, the full service coming into operation on 14 May. The new service was operated by 4-CIG stock and 6-REPs formed from former 4-REP and 4-TC vehicles. This new venture ended Fratton depot's life as a maintenance depot.

The three-year-old Kettering to Corby shuttles came to an end on 28 May and regular services returned to Clitheroe, 28 years after closure to passengers.

Delays in the delivery of new Class 158 units resulted in Scotrail taking delivery of only three of the new trains at the commencement of the summer 1990 timetable instead of the expected 32. This was due to a number of problems, including bogies, found to occur at 80mph during tests. The actual launch of the cross-country 'flagships' did not take place until September and the class entered service on Glasgow-Aberdeen trains during that month. Incidents involving the separation of two sets on a Glasgow to Edinburgh working in December resulted in the eventual reintroduction of certain Class 155 and 156 equipment deleted from Class 158 specifications.

Below:
Easter Monday, 16 April 1990, and the beautifully restored Great Western 'King' No 6024 *King Edward I* emerges from Wood End Tunnel with the 'Shakespeare Express' from Stratford upon Avon to Tyseley. Seeing this picture, it is now difficult to imagine that this locomotive, along with many others now in full working order, were, in the late 1960s, derelict wrecks at Barry scrapyard. All are a credit to the many volunteers who helped save our heritage.
John S. Whiteley

Top:
Until such time as GUV vans were wired through for TDM, it was impossible for DVTs to lead a train which included them. With three such vehicles at the rear, the 14.36 Carlisle to Euston has 'Black' Class 90 No 90031 powering from the front of the train, instead of from the rear, as it approaches Leighton Buzzard on 30 March 1990 whilst hauling Mk 3 DVT No 82122. *Brian Morrison*

Above:
With engineering work taking place south of Watford on Sunday, 18 March 1990, all overnight sleeping-car services into Euston and all down trains until 09.40 were diesel-powered. This created a 'dragging' situation and the 08.00 Euston-Holyhead service is seen approaching Kenton with Class 58 No 58001 piloting Class 87/0 electric No 87013 *John o' Gaunt*. The Class 58 came off the train at Bletchley.
Brian Morrison

Left:
The interior walls of the Channel Tunnel are lined with concrete segments which were transported from the Isle of Grain in Kent to the Shakespeare Cliff site near Folkestone. In this unusual scene, double-headed Class 33/0s, Nos 33021 and 33051 *Shakespeare Cliff*, leave the Transmanche Link manufacturing site on the Isle of Grain with the 1,000th train of concrete segments for the tunnel project, on 8 November 1990. This provided the same motive power as the first train — two Class 33/0 diesels.
Brian Morrison

Above:
Traversing the new concrete and steel bridge over the River Ness at Inverness, which replaced the one previously washed away, two-car Class 156 'Super Sprinter' No 156446, forms the 18.48 train to Wick and Thurso on 31 May 1990. A far cry from the Class 26-hauled trains which previously carried out these duties. *L. A. Nixon*

Right:
The first Class 158 'Express Sprinter' at last entered service between Glasgow and Edinburgh on 17 September 1990. Alongside Class 47/4 diesel No 47461 *Charles Rennie Mackintosh*, heads the late 09.22 train for Aberdeen. No 158708, with Nos 158709 and 158711 attached to form a six-car train, forms the 10.00 working to Edinburgh Waverley as it awaits departure from Glasgow Queen Street station. *Brian Morrison*

Right:
On 29 May 1990, the opening day of St Paul's Thameslink station (which replaced Holborn Viaduct station), the 08.48 Bedford-Brighton train, operated by Class 319 electric unit No 319024, prepares to ascend the 1 in 29 gradient up to Blackfriars station. On 9 November 1991 the name of St Paul's Thameslink station was changed to 'City Thameslink' and this daylight view is no longer possible as trains now surface at Blackfriars. The buildings in the background are part of the old concourse of Holborn Viaduct station. *Brian Morrison*

Below:
Class 37/0 No 37412, previously named *Loch Lomond* by Scotrail, hauls new CDA hopper wagons through Lostwithiel to Carne Point, the ECC depot at Fowey, on 10 September 1990, where the china clay will be shipped abroad. The china clay CDA wagons were manufactured at RDS Doncaster and were introduced in 1988 after some delay. *Brian Morrison*

The Wrong Sort of Snow!

The year started badly when 'the wrong sort of snow' (it was quoted) turned Britain's railway network into chaos, especially on express services operated by Class 317, 319 and 321 units. In fact this was not as silly as it may have sounded as, instead of the usual wet snow which normally falls in Britain, a 'powdery' snow got into the traction motors on diesel and electric multiple-units rendering them unserviceable. Therefore there was nothing that the snow ploughs could do to improve the situation. These weather conditions hit, very severely, the King's Cross-Cambridge services, trains from Liverpool Street, and 'Thameslink' services from Bedford to Sevenoaks and Brighton, in particular. During the autumn that followed, BR was struck by a 'wet leaves' problem, mainly affecting the ill-fated Class 158 'Express Sprinters' as packed leaves on the track caused trains to 'disappear' from track circuit displays. This potentially dangerous situation resulted in the replacement of these units by locomotive-hauled trains or cancellation of services particularly over the Trans-Pennine route, in East Anglia, and on Salisbury-Southampton trains.

The new Class 153 single-car 'Sprinters' were unveiled on 18 July at Hunslet Barclay's Kilmarnock Works. These units were conversions from two-car Class 155 'Super Sprinters'. Conversion entailed the fitting of a new driving end cleverly without changing the position of external doors. The Class 153 units were for use on lightly-used rural lines and could be coupled to other 'Sprinter' and 'Express Sprinter' classes. Each unit seated 74 passengers (or customers as they were now termed by BR). Tests were carried out with the 'pioneer' Class 153 unit, No 153354, between Crewe and Winsford in July and the first revenue-earning service was on 14 August when a Carlisle unit, there for crew training, replaced a failed DMU on the Barrow line. Cab modifications proved necessary after trials and the first Class 153 units were allocated to Heaton and Newton Heath.

Class 158 units entered service on the Newcastle-York-Liverpool/Manchester Trans-Pennine route from 21 January 1991. The new 'Metro' version of these units, incorporating six extra seats (in place of a parcels area and toilet) was launched at Derby on 22 March and was painted in the red & white West Yorkshire PTE livery for use on York-Manchester Victoria/Liverpool Lime Street via Bradford and Halifax services from 8 July.

At Marylebone, on 14 May, the first Class 165 'Networker' was launched with its airline-style plug doors. A new maintenance depot was built at Aylesbury to maintain the new Chiltern Line units. A new depot was also built at Reading for the forthcoming Class 165 'Network Turbo' units soon to be used on the Thames Line from Paddington. The first Chiltern Line 'Turbo passengers' travelled on 9 September between Marylebone and High Wycombe and services with these new units extended to Aylesbury from 2 December.

On the locomotive scene, a new Parcels Sector image, known as 'Rail Express Systems', was launched at Crewe on 11 October in the form of a striking black & red livery with a light blue slatted design, and a naming policy for all Class 47 RES locomotives was adopted with all names starting with 'Res ...' (eg No 47594 *Resourceful*, No 47597 *Resilient* and No 47625 *Resplendent*). Additionally, new-liveried Class 08 shunter No 08633 was named *The Sorter* and No 90020, *Colonel Bill Cockburn CBE TD*, after the Managing Director of Royal Mail.

Another 'change of coat' appeared on Class 73 electro-diesel No 73101 *Brighton Evening Argus* which acquired a 'Pullman' livery for the Brighton line's 150th anniversary on 21/22 September 1991. The locomotive worked 'Brighton Belle' specials with VSOE Pullman stock in addition to No 73128, in Civil Engineers grey & yellow livery, named *O. V. S. Bulleid* especially for the occasion.

July 1991 saw the final withdrawal of the Class 81 electric locomotives followed by the last Class 85 in November. In June, British Rail sold five Class 20 diesel locomotives to preservation groups. The Class 20s were now making way for the new Class 60 freight locomotives being constructed.

On the preservation scene, the Isle of Wight Steam Railway extended their line to Smallbrook Junction, *Blue Peter* returned to steam on the North York Moors Railway, BR Pacific *Britannia* and No 4472 *Flying Scotsman* worked steam specials from Cambridge to King's Lynn, Great Western 'Castle' No 5029 *Nunney Castle* also returned to steam and steam returned to the Folkestone Harbour branch when, on 12/13 September, 'West Country' Pacific No 34027 *Taw Valley* and Standard tank No 80080 operated a push-pull service. In October No 80080 was in action again, this time in the Cardiff Valleys when steam returned from Cardiff to Merthyr, Barry, Treherbert, Aberdare, Rhymney and Penarth — the Penarth trip (at £3) being the only one which offered steam both ways. The last locomotive built at Stratford Works (LNER Class N7 No 69621) was in steam there on 26 March at the Works' formal closing ceremony.

In Scotland, Edinburgh celebrated the launch of ECML electric-hauled services to King's Cross on 8 July although, in fact, the first train had worked through on 11 June. The new 'Flying Scotsman' schedule was 4hr 8min but on a record-breaking run, Class 91 No 91012 completed the journey in 3hr 29 min. The Edinburgh-Carstairs line was energised at 25kV on 4 February and electric services commenced in March.

Scotrail's North Berwick services received ex-LT&S Class 307 units during 1991, the last 'conventional' train ran on the Manchester-Altrincham line on 24 December (making way for Manchester's Metrolink Light Rail system) and the Bury line made way for the same new Metrolink scheme, closing to BR services in August.

In Yorkshire, the first West Yorkshire PTE Class 321/9 unit was handed over at BREL's York Works on 25 July. Entry into service with the winter timetable meant the end for the Class 307 units, acquired in 1990 from Ilford depot.

The two-car Class 456 electric units commenced passenger duties on 30 September on Wimbledon-West Croydon services and, on 19 December, Class 465/0 and 465/2 'Networkers' made their debut at York and Washwood Heath respectively. On 8 April, a new depot at Slade Green was opened in preparation for the forthcoming Class 465 'Networkers'. However, as new depots were being built, the last operational roundhouse-style depot, Staveley Barrow Hill, closed on 10 February 1991. Gone was the 'classic' train spotting location, the roundhouse, which created such a wonderful atmosphere.

In London the new ultra-modern Liverpool Street station was opened in December and the first new station to be opened in the City of London for 90 years, City Thameslink (ex-St Paul's Thameslink), was born in November and The Docklands Light Railway opened its new Bank extension.

The freight news was the axing of 'Speedlink' in September 1991, which had become necessary due to the operation of uneconomical individual loads. From now on, only full train block traffic would be handled. On the night of 25/26 May, Foster Yeoman's 'mega-train' was run. The test train was made up with No 59005 leading, attached to 58 102-tonne wagons, coupled to No 59001 with 57 similar wagons, and No 59003 attached to the back of the 12,017-tonne train.

In November 1991, the public opening of the Newcastle International Airport extension of the Tyne & Wear Metro system took place and also during the same month the system's five diesel locomotives were transported by road to Folkestone, having been sold to TML for Channel Tunnel construction duties.

Left:
In GWR chocolate & cream colours, Tyseley-based Class 117 Pressed Steel set No T305 was used for a shuttle between Bourne End and Marlow (Bucks) on 31 August 1991. Awaiting departure at Bourne End, the 'Marlow Donkey' is made up of DMS No 51410 leading, TC(L) No 59520 and DMBS No 51368. This contrasts well with the new Class 165/0 'Turbo' unit No 165005 which stands in the station on view to the public for the day. *Brian Morrison*

Below:
Amalgamated Roadstone Corporation-owned Class 59/1, No 59104 *Village of Great Elm* hauls the diverted 10.00 ARC train from Allington, and passes through Clapham Junction on 5 October 1991. The Class 59/1 locomotives were constructed at General Motors, London, Ontario (Canada) as locomotive building had ceased at the Chicago factory where the Class 59/0s were built. *Brian Morrison*

Above:
In 1991, Class 73/1 No 73101 *Brighton Evening Argus* was painted in full chocolate & cream Pullman livery. On 6 October 1991, a duty unbefitting a locomotive bearing this fine livery is being performed by *Brighton Evening Argus*. The locomotive is pictured on the 08.30 engineers' train from Clapham Yard to a West London occupation, near Earl's Court. This locomotive has since been named *The Royal Alex*.
Brian Morrison

Right:
The first Class 465/2 'Networker' from GEC Alsthom, No 465201, is unveiled inside their Washwood Heath works on 19 December 1991. During the following year, test runs with the new 'Networker' regularly took place on the Shepperton branch. *Brian Morrison*

Below:
The Docklands Light Railway was the forerunner of many proposed 'light rail' schemes for Britain's cities, virtually bringing a return to the 'trams'. On 5 March 1991, with respective trains for Crossharbour and Tower Gateway, DLR units Nos 21 and 15 cross at Limehouse station.
Brian Morrison

Left:
The inaugural 'Scottish Pullman' from Edinburgh Waverley arrives at King's Cross on 30 October 1991, headed by Mk 4 DVT No 82211 and is propelled from the depths of Gasworks Tunnel by Class 91 No 91030 *Palace of Holyroodhouse. Brian Morrison*

Below:
The first IC125 service train from Euston departs from platform 5 on 30 September 1991, with Class 43 powercar No 43148 leading and No 43151 at the rear, both providing the traction for the 09.03 service for Holyhead. *Brian Morrison*

Right:
On 12 September 1991, BR Standard 2-6-4T No 80080 banks a 'steam special' up the incline from Folkestone Harbour. At the head of the train of Pullman stock is Bulleid 'West Country' Pacific No 34027 *Taw Valley*. The train ran a shuttle service throughout the day between Folkestone West and the Harbour station. *Brian Morrison*

Bottom right:
Back in action on the main line, BR Standard Pacific No 71000 *Duke of Gloucester* powers through Harbury, southbound, with the 'Royal Shakespeare' — a Stratford upon Avon to Didcot excursion — on 6 May 1991. *L. A. Nixon*

'Networkers'

On 19 January 1992 the first Class 465/0 'Networker' was delivered to Strawberry Hill Depot, having had test equipment fitted at RTC Derby. It made its initial test run to Shepperton on 30 January. On the following day, the first Class 465/2 'Networker' left the manufacturers Metro-Cammell for Derby. Although the Class 465 electric units were out of gauge for certain parts of the Kent Link, work was in hand to alter trackbed and work was also being carried out at 16 tunnels, five in the Greenwich-Woolwich area to rectify this problem which BR were fully aware of when ordering the 'Networkers' — despite adverse press comment at the time.

On the diesel multiple unit scene, the new Class 165 'Networker Turbos' were booked to operate all trains between Marylebone and High Wycombe/Banbury from 20 January 1992 and, on 13 April, Class 165/1 units entered service from Paddington on Thames Line trains, units Nos 165029/31 forming the first train into the terminus from Oxford.

Problems continued to arise with the ill-fated Class 158 'Express Sprinters' with faults even being found in the modifications applied to overcome previous faults. In April the first Perkins-engined Class 158 unit was delivered to Norwich for Regional's Central fleet and Rosyth Royal Naval Dockyard was awarded the contract to convert new Class 158 units into 159s for Network SouthEast. On 6 May, a world speed record for an underfloor-powered DMU was claimed by Class 158 'Express Sprinters' Nos 158708 and 158710 between Glasgow Queen Street and Edinburgh, covering the distance in 32min 9sec, averaging 88mph with a top speed of 107mph, despite the wet conditions.

On the Ipswich-Lowestoft line, Class 156 'Super Sprinters' took over duties previously handled by Class 101 units and in January, the new Greater Manchester PTE livery was unveiled on Class 150 'Sprinter' No 150133, providing a larger expanse of white than the previous livery. Also in Manchester, the first section of 'Metrolink' opened from Bury to Manchester Victoria on 6 April after numerous delays, with car No 1012 breaking the tape at Victoria to inaugurate the service.

Over in Yorkshire, the National Railway Museum reopened after a £6 million refurbishment. This incorporated a new 'Great Hall' and now the public would have the opportunity to view the many 'hidden' treasures which previously could not be on view owing to lack of space. New locomotives were now on view, such as Great Western 'Star' No 4003 *Lode Star*, and the Euston gates, not seen by the public since the Doric Arch was destroyed 30 years ago were also on display. There were now to be servicing demonstrations involving the ex-GER 'J17' and a look into the future with a segment of the Channel Tunnel tube; a truly wonderful day out for any railway enthusiast and his family.

On the preservation front, ex-LNER 'A2' No 60532 *Blue Peter* made an impressive return to the main line in February 1992 and in April, BR Pacific No 71000 *Duke of Gloucester* made its first ever visit to Paddington. An unfortunate incident occurred at Westbourne Park, on 22 March, when the safety-valves of Great Western 'King', No 6024 *King Edward I* were sheared off after striking a bridge when returning from a 'William Shakespeare Express' railtour — BR picked up the bill!

In Scotland ex-NBR 'K' class 4-4-0 No 256 *Glen Douglas* left Glasgow Transport Museum after 26 years to be returned to working order at Bo'ness. It is intended to have *Glen Douglas* available for West Highland line service in 1994.

By March 1992, on the Swanage Railway, the railhead had reached the site chosen for Norden Halt, beyond Corfe Castle, and on the Bluebell Railway the first official train passed through Sharpthorne Tunnel, on 6 March, bringing the railway in sight of their next target — West Hoathly. There was a 'first' in the 'Preserved World' on 10 April 1992 when a Royal Train worked on a preserved line for the first time as Prince Philip travelled on the Paignton & Dartmouth Railway to Kingswear. Sadly, 1992 saw the Lochty Railway killed off after 25 years of operation, due to the Health & Safety Act.

Also in Scotland, Class 37s returned to passenger workings to meet the needs of tourists in the Highlands including a new train 'The Young Explorer' from Fort William to Glasgow Queen Street and return. Stagecoach Holdings, the Perth-based international bus conglomerate, attached its own coaches to overnight Inter-City services from Aberdeen to Euston from May 1992, with feeder road coaches operating from Inverness and Perth to Edinburgh.

Ashford marked its 150th anniversary as a railway town in 1992 with a week of celebrations including an open weekend at Chart Leacon depot, incorporating a fine array of steam, diesel and electric power, a steam shuttle involving 'West Country' Pacific No 34027 *Taw Valley* and BR Standard Class 4 No 75069 and a special train from London Bridge station, where Class 33 No 33114 was named *Ashford 150* prior to its run via Redhill and Tonbridge to Ashford. No 33114 was decked out in NSE livery — the first Class 33 to wear these colours.

On 4 January 1992 a record-breaking run to rebuild 17½ miles of railway between Ashford and Folkestone began — lasting 19 weekends — in preparation for Channel Tunnel freight and passenger services, and at the Channel Tunnel site, RFS-modified Class 20 Type 1 diesels arrived to work at both the British and French ends of the tunnel.

On 23 April, Class 86 electric No 86208 was also taken to the Channel Tunnel site for a few days, hauled by Class 47/4 No 47973, for use as an electrification load bank and, in May, Trainload Freight moved its one millionth tonne of Foster Yeoman stone from the Isle of Grain to Shakespeare Cliff for the Channel Tunnel.

On the freight scene, the production run of 100 Class 60 locomotives ended in April after almost three years. Also, two NCB collieries closed, Bickershaw and Sherwood, reulting in the loss of coal MGR trains from these pits to Fiddler's Ferry and Radcliffe power-station respectively.

New speed records were set up by Class 91 No 91029 *Queen Elizabeth II* in 1992 over the WCML between Manchester and Euston and between Euston and Birmingham, whilst InterCity laid down plans to abandon Birmingham New Street station to Regional Railways and build a new 'Heartlands' station, nearer Aston.

New '1990' underground stock was unveiled for London Transport's Central Line but it was the end for the unique testbed diesel locomotive No 47901 and the last Class 114 diesel unit. Class 50s bade farewell to scheduled BR services on 24 May 1992 and it was also the end for the 'Regions', with Class 90 electric No 90007 being named *Lord Stamp* to commemorate the demise of the London Midland Region.

But what will the next 50 years hold for the railway enthusiast and the travelling public? As this period of 50 years ended with its progress and many changes, the Government's White Paper appeared, offering 'New opportunities for the Railways' in its plans to privatise British Rail.

This involves the selling-off of the freight and parcels businesses, the opportunity for the Private Sector to manage and operate passenger services through franchising, the provision of new operators' rights of access over the rail network, and the selling or leasing of stations. The Prime Minister says that this will bring back the 'pride' of the workforce that was there in the days of the pre-Grouping companies and the 'Big Four' — maybe it will. We shall just have to wait and see!

Below:
The Class 60 freight locomotives, built by Brush at Loughborough commenced acceptance trials on BR in 1989. Forming a bogie oil tanks train from Langley to Lindsey on 13 April 1992, No 60026 *William Caxton* leaves Elstree Tunnel on the Midland main line. *Brian Morrison*

Bottom:
The Class 456 units entered service in 1991. On 7 April 1992 units Nos 456023 and 456014 depart from Victoria forming the 10.13 working to Sutton, Surrey. These units are two-car additions to the extensive Class 455 fleet and all were constructed at BREL York. *Brian Morrison*

Below:
A unique occassion at the time was this Class 90/91 combination as, following record-breaking runs from Manchester to Euston and from Euston to Birmingham on 30 April 1992, Class 91 No 91029 *Queen Elizabeth II* leaves Birmingham New Street station returning with empty coaching stock to Bounds Green double-headed with Class 90 No 90007 *Lord Stamp*. The Class 90 had been on standby for the day. This view clearly shows the class differences. *Brian Morrison*

Bottom:
Perhaps the most fitting way to end this book portraying 50 years of railways in Britain is this view with the future in mind. This scene, captured on 5 February 1992, shows engineering works for the new Waterloo International station in an advanced state in preparation for forthcoming Channel Tunnel passenger traffic. Clearly visible are the platforms and station approach. Going about its normal duties is a stalwart of Network SouthEast's commuter transport, a Class 455/8 four-car unit, No 5844. The train is seen passing the site of the new station as it departs from Waterloo with the 12.55 service to Guildford, via Addlestone — the scenic route! *Brian Morrison*